THE
OBSERVATION
OF HUMAN
SYSTEMS

THE
OBSERVATION
OF HUMAN
SYSTEMS

Lessons from
the History
of Anti-
Reductionistic
Empirical
Psychology

Joshua W. Clegg, editor

Transaction Publishers
New Brunswick (U.S.A.) and London (U.K.)

150,9
0141

Library of Congress Catalog Number: 2008027791
ISBN: 978-1-4128-0838-5
Printed in the United States of America

Library of Congress Cataloging-in-Publication Data

The observation of human systems : lessons from the history of anti-reductionistic empirical psychology / [edited by] Joshua W. Clegg.
     p. cm.
  Includes bibliographical references and index.
  ISBN 978-1-4128-0838-5 (alk. paper)
  1. Psychology—Research. 2. Vygotskii, L. S. (Lev Semenovich), 1896-1934. 3. Baldwin, James, 1924-1987. 4. Gibson, James Jerome, 1904-1980. 5. Lewin, Kurt, 1890-1947. I. Clegg, Joshua W.
BF76.5.O27 2008
150.92'2—dc22   2008027791

Contents

1

The Problems of Reductionism
in the Social Sciences

Joshua W. Clegg

Introduction

I imagine many of us of had the experience of conceiving some interesting idea or research question and then thoroughly murdering it with
methodology. We start with curiosity, or perhaps insight, and then try to
reproduce that insight in terms of the dominant methodological requirements of our discipline. Unfortunately, this experience may often leave
us feeling something like guests of the fabled Procrustes. In the Greek
myth, Procrustes was a robber who compelled all of his guests to spend
the night in a special iron bed. According to Procrustes, the bed's most
wondrous property was that it fit any who lay in it. Unfortunately for
Procrustes' guests, the means by which this wonder was accomplished
included either severing whatever appendages remained outside the confines of his bed or stretching the guest's body to match its length. The
more dogmatic method-talk of contemporary institutional psychology
feels much like Procrustes' bed—we are all welcome to lodge under the
broad roof of professional psychology, so long as we are willing to dissect our ideas, interests, and insights such that we discard those aspects
that don't fit instrumental experimentalism. Of course, this requirement
means that we often kill those ideas and replace them with an inanimate
and, worse, uninteresting conglomeration of severed limbs.

I suspect that this experience is not particularly rare among contemporary psychological researchers. As Martin and Dawda argue:

> because many psychological phenomena are complex, multi-dimensional, and context
> dependent, the attempted reduction of these phenomena to a known set of constitutive

1

elements for research purposes seldom is accomplished without injury or alteration to the phenomena in question (Martin and Dawda, 2002, p. 39).

Similar sentiments have been expressed by many important figures in the history of psychology, including those who will be discussed in this book.

This experience is common, at least in part, because a general trend in the history of psychology has been a move towards greater specificity (or narrowness) in the domains, means, processes, and locations of scientific inquiry, a "shrinking in the range of topics for psychological investigation" (Toulmin & Leary, 1985, p. 601). There have, of course, always been particular practitioners or whole traditions that have resisted this move toward method and domain specificity, but the bulk of mainstream psychology has embraced it. Because of this trend, the appropriate domain of scientific psychology has been reduced from subjectivity to a particular kind of sensory subjectivity; the means of conducting and disseminating inquiry have been reduced from language in general to mostly frequentist numerical language; and the processes by which inquiry is carried out have been reduced from observation of all kinds to mostly numeral assignment.

In general, these moves toward specificity have been the result of attempts to fit psychology within the methodological limits of an instrumentalist conception of experimentalism (Danziger 2000); but this institutional reduction of sanctioned methods has not been fully embraced by all psychologists, nor even by all experimental psychologists. Many psychologists have found this trend not only restrictive, but also inherently perilous for the phenomena they studied. This fact is made strikingly clear in the writings of four psychologists whose work is considered in this volume: Lev Vygotsky, Kurt Lewin, James Baldwin, and James Gibson. The authors in this volume have outlined the anti-reductionistic programs of these psychologists in the hope that contemporary psychology can learn from their struggles, and perhaps even develop an approach to observational and experimental methods that is not inherently reductionistic.

The Special Problems of Reductionism in Empirical Psychology

Before outlining the structure of this volume, a word on the problems of reductionism. These problems have been persistent in all sciences at least in part because the will to reduce seems to be an inextinguishable human longing. Indeed, reduction lives in the very heart of the human community. Language is a reduction, as are all the systems of meaning that bind together. Science, then, could hardly be without reduction; science requires that we reduce the complexities of our environment in analytic and explanatory terms. This is why it is important to note at the outset that the problem being addressed in this volume is not "reduction" but "reductionism." Reduction is a necessary analytic and abstractive practice. Reductionism is the notion that any given phenomenon can be reduced to its constituent elements without any loss of meaning. This philosophy is the antithesis of holism—or the notion that there is something about the organization, or relation, of elements that transcends, and cannot be fundamentally reduced to, the elements themselves.

The classic problem with reductionism in psychology is the *reductio ad absurdum*, which flows from reducing human experience to its products—namely, the postulates of science and mathematics. In psychology, this kind of reductionism is manifested primarily in reductions of human experience to "neurophysiological, behavioral, psychometric, or computational terms" (Martin and Dawda, 2002, p. 38). The difficulty with such reductions is that the means of reduction—systems of social meaning like science or philosophy—is also their object.

In philosophy, this is a well-worn issue, perhaps best exemplified by Husserl's devastating critique of psychologism. According to Husserl, psychologism is the notion that "the essential theoretical foundations of logic lie in psychology" (Husserl, 1999/1900, p. 5). What Husserl meant by this formulation was that the processes of consciousness, including logic, mathematics, and science, were considered reducible to and explainable by the principles of scientific psychology. Though this conclusion is the inevitable result of a reductionistic psychology, it is inherently problematic:

> Since science is only a science in virtue of its harmony with logical rules, it presupposes the validity of these rules. It would therefore be circular to try to give logic a first foundation in psychology. (Husserl, 1999/1900, p. 8).

The essential philosophical problem here is not so much the dubious capacity for consciousness to perceive itself, but the absurdity of a reductive fiction that claims that products of consciousness can somehow be more fundamental than, and thus somehow independent of, consciousness itself.

Scientists have also long recognized the limits of pure reductionism—"we know that nineteenth century mechanistic materialism, built so confidently on the foundation of Newton, is inadequate for physics itself, let alone for biological, psychological, and social phenomena" (Sloane, 1945, p. 223)—yet in psychology, material and other forms of reductionism seem to grow rather than diminish in influence (see Orange, 2003 for a review of reductionist philosophy in the social sciences).

The problems with reductionism as an ontological stance seem insurmountable, a fact which has led Barendregt and van Rappard (2004) to argue that "reductionism should be considered distinct from the metaphysical mind-body problem" and considered instead as "a methodology for bridging different theories at different levels" (p. 469). In some ways, this suggestion seems to fit what many contemporary social scientists actually do. Mind-brain reduction seems to be "in the air" for most social scientists but it is rarely explicit and certainly beyond the current state of empirical validation. In contrast, however, the institutionally sanctioned canons of method, particularly experimental method, are overwhelmingly reductionistic.

The practical limits enjoined by this sort of entrenched institutional reductionism are very real, as Wendell Garner illustrated in his description of an attempt to conduct research using a "phenomenological methodology":

> These experiments were very successful in elucidating phenomena not obtainable from reaction times and errors. As a result, I wanted to continue using these methods. However, in the late 1960s I reverted to using a tachistoscope, reaction times, and errors. Why did I do that, if the newer methods were so successful? The reason is that students trained in these techniques could not get jobs when they finished their graduate training (Garner, 1999, p. 21).

For sometimes very pragmatic and political reasons, then, reductionism seems to be most enduring not in its ontological form, but in its methodological one (Martin and Dawda, 2002).

For the purposes of this volume, it is at this methodological level that reductionism is considered. We are concerned not so much with the theoretical implications of particular ontological reductions (though these issues are important and certainly unresolved) as with the methodological implications. Concomitantly, we are also considering the possibility of empirical and experimental methods that are not fundamentally reductionistic.

Non-Reductionistic Experimentation?

At the outset, any attempt to develop theories and methods for non-reductionistic experimentation may seem strange. After all, the most common textbook definition of an experiment is some unwieldy reductionist phrase like "an experiment is the manipulation of one or more independent variables and the measurement of one or more dependent variables, while holding all other variables constant." While admirably specific, this definition encompasses an extremely narrow range of psychological experimentation (what, for example, was the "dependent variable" in the Stanford Prison Study?). Because of the narrowness of such definitions, for the purposes of this volume, experimentation will be defined as "observation with intervention," a definition specific enough to capture the essence of experimentation while still broad enough to include the majority of self-labeled experiments.

Under this broader definition, the notion of non-reductionistic experimentation is at least feasible and the authors in this volume do an admirable job of delineating much of the theoretical and methodological core of that notion. In chapter 2, Alexander Kozulin argues that in their sociocultural approach to development, Lev Vygotsky and Alexander Luria explicitly eschew the reifications of material reductionism and, perhaps more importantly, develop an account of the developing human that demonstrates qualitative, unique, and non-reducible changes both across time and between different levels of organization. Kozulin out lines Vygotsky's arguments that psychological phenomena are not only dependent upon materially irreducible social and cultural frames but also on the constructive qualities of individual consciousness. According to Kozulin, developmental processes that seem easily reducible to maturation can be shown to be dependent on the available socio-cultural tools. He uses Vygotsky's notion of the "zone of proximal development" (ZPD) as a paradigmatic example demonstrating that both development and learning are not meaningfully understood as static capacities, but must be understood in their sociocultural unit.

René van der Veer also discusses Vygotsky's empirical theory in detail. He argues (in chapter 3) that Vygotsky's experimental theory requires an experimenter who transforms, or deforms, what is being investigated, an experimental situation that allows participants to be active, creative participants in their own change, and a methodology that allows experimenters to observe developing processes in vivo. He demonstrates the importance of these principles with a discussion of how ZPD experiments employing the method of double stimulation provided better prediction of academic performance precisely because these examined the process by which a child's cognitive ability can be transformed (i.e., the learning situation) and not static categories such as "intelligence."

In chapter 4, Jaan Valsiner outlines James Baldwin's genetic logic as an instance of anti-reductionism in empirical theory. Baldwin's genetic theory claims that phenomena occur at different levels of organization that are not reducible to one another, and that the unique systems governing different levels cannot be generalized by analogy to other phenomena. According to Valsiner, some implications of Baldwin's genetic view include a focus on "unfolding novel processes, rather than their prediction, or retrospective explanation" (Valsiner, this volume, p. 54). Under this system, all psychic processes are continuous, progressive (developmental), composed in qualitatively distinct events, and can be understood only within their own context and their own mode. Baldwin's genetic theory also implies that the progression of future events is fundamentally indeterminate and genetic logic thus undermines frequentist probability as a foundation for psychological knowledge. Valsiner shows how this system of genetic logic does not permit the static and reductive methodologies of Baldwin's (and our) time and ultimately argues that Baldwin's attempt to formalize psychological concepts in terms other than real numbers is the right direction for the future of psychology.

Next, Eric Charles recounts how J.J. Gibson's work in perception eventually led him (Gibson) to an anti-reductionist empirical program. Charles shows how Gibson's roots in New Realism as well as the practical necessities of perception research led him to reject a reductionistic view of perception in favor of a relational account—i.e., an account of perception in terms of irreducible real relations between percipient and perceived. On Charles' account of Gibson, perception always entails an irreducible unit of active percipient and meaning-laden environment. Thus, the perception researcher, Charles argues, must conceptualize and investigate a percipient whose whole organism is actively employed in exploring an inherently meaningful environment. Such an investigation is only possible in holistic research contexts and not in the highly reduced research paradigms of contemporary perceptual research.

In chapter 6, Aaro Toomela takes up a discussion of Kurt Lewin's anti-reductionist program. Toomela argues strongly that mainstream contemporary psychology's move away from the holistic, idiographic, and theory-driven emphases of pre-WWII Austro-German psychology has produced a less sophisticated approach to theory and method than that of Kurt Lewin. Toomela emphasizes Lewin's commitment to experimentation as a necessary element of empirical psychology and suggests a Lewinian revision of empirical investigation (including experimentation). This revision includes a psychology that is theoretically, rather than methodologically driven, that focuses on whole, integrated systems of relations, rather than isolated phenomena, and whose theories and methods delineate not only empirical relations among constructs but also theoretical relations within constructs. Methodologically, according to Toomela (and Lewin), this means that aggregate data are useless for building psychological theory and should be replaced with formal mathematical models, and that purely phenotypic, or behavioral analyses are misleading and incomplete because they exclude the psychological field of the participant.

Lee Rudolph (in chapter 7) also considers the work of Kurt Lewin, taking up the difficult task of developing a feasible mathematical model for a holistic approach to empirical and experimental psychology, a model that eschews an *a priori* reduction of mathematical modeling in psychology to "number" and "measurement." He follows Kurt Lewin's intuition that qualitative mathematics, and in particular, topology could serve as the basis for such a model and so develops a topological model describing Lewinian life spaces as finite topological spaces. From this effort, Rudolph concludes that the mechanics of topology can be meaningfully and rigorously applied to a Lewinian life space and can, in fact, serve as a basis for rigorous mathematical deductions.

In the penultimate chapter, Jeff Reber and Zachary Beckstead add to this historical account a discussion of more contemporary non-reductionistic empirical methods. They outline contemporary work in two different traditions: systems theory and Lewinian field theory. According to Reber and Beckstead, systems theorists assume that all phenomena are constituted in their relations and so must be investigated within their own complex systems. Reber and Beckstead consider a study in family systems theory as an exemplar of systemic thinking in the social sciences. They discuss the systems-inspired elements of this research, including a theoretical and methodological focus on systems larger than the individual, but they also discuss the limitations of this research—namely, that it employs non-systemic measurement techniques such as the individually completed questionnaire.

Reber and Beckstead also consider some contemporary research in the tradition of Lewinian field theory. They outline the basic tenets of Lewin's field theory, including the assumptions that all of the facts of psychological experience are composed in relations and not static entities and that all the elements in the field of psychological experience, whether represented by an individual or a group, are fundamentally interdependent. They consider one of many possible examples from social psychology that have been influenced by Lewin's holism and conclude that, as in family systems theory, many social psychologists consider dynamic interactions but they undermine this dynamism by reducing it to Likert-style scaling and linear causal modeling. Ultimately, Reber and Beckstead conclude that the philosophical assumptions undergirding contemporary philosophy of science drive otherwise holistically-minded researchers to "separate and isolate variables, infer a pattern of causation, and transform observations into numbers that can be used in statistical analyses," a step that causes them to "lose contact with the relationship among the parts within that whole" (Reber & Beckstead, this volume, p. 161).

These treatments of empirical and experimental psychology are suggestive of many possible themes but, by way of summary, Joshua Clegg considers two of these in the final chapter. The first concerns the holistic imperative that theory, method, and procedure be considered an inseparable and organic whole. The second theme concerns the basic theoretical and methodological implications of an analysis that considers integrated units, systems, or fields of relations rather than collections of isolated characteristics.

In its entirety, this volume offers a strong argument against reductionist methodology in the social sciences. It also draws upon the experience and insight of influential scholars from psychology's past to outline the foundations of a genuinely holistic empirical and experimental social science. It is our hope that through this book, the wisdom and insight from the past of our discipline will lead to more thoughtful and rigorous empirical investigations in that discipline's future.

References

Barendregt & van Rappard (2004). Reductionism revisited. *Theory and Psychology, 14(4)*, 453-474.

Danziger, K. (2000). Making social psychology experimental: a conceptual history, 1920-1970. *Journal of the History of the Behavioral Sciences, 36(4)*, 329-347.

Garner, W. (1999). Reductionism reduced. *PsycCritiques, 44 (1)*, 21-22.

Husserl, E. (1999). *Logical Investigations* (J.N. Findlay, Trans.) In D. Welton (ed.), *The Essential Husserl: Basic writings in transcendental phenomenology*. Bloomington, Indiana: Indiana University Press. (Original work published 1900).

Martin & Dawda (2002). Reductionism in the comments and autobiographical accounts of prominent psychologists. *The Journal of Psychology, 136(1)*, 37-52.

Orange, D.M. (2003). Antidotes and alternatives: perspectival realism and the new reductionisms. *Psychoanalytic Psychology, 20(3)*, 472-486.

Sloane, E.H. (1945). Reductionism. *Psychological Review, 52(4)*, 214-223.

Toulmin, S. & Leary, D.E. (1985). The cult of empiricism in psychology and beyond. In S. Koch and D.E. Leary (eds.), *A Century of Psychology as Science*. Washington, D.C.: American Psychological Association.

2

Sociocultural Paradigm

Alex Kozulin

Scientific psychology usually presents human psychological functions as "objects" that can be identified and studied in more or less the same way as physical or biological objects. For example, a child's reasoning is perceived as an object whose existence is taken for granted and whose properties and natural development can be studied in about the same way as the growth of the child's limbs or changes in the hormonal system. This objectification of psychological functions (or *reification* to use philosophical language) goes hand in hand with the use of objectified, and in this sense reductionist research methodologies. Probably the most explicit of these methodologies is psychometric tests that present intelligence as an object "hidden" in the person's head that can be identified and measured by a battery of standard IQ tests.

The sociocultural approach originating in the work of Vygotsky and Luria (1930/1993) offered a very different perspective by conceptualizing human psychological functions as dynamic sociocultural constructions rather than natural objects. The child's reasoning, for example, is understood as a construction created through the child's involvement in specific sociocultural activities that are mediated by symbolic tools. Thus instead of posing a question regarding the presence of such an "object" as a certain type of reasoning operations in the child's head, the sociocultural theory poses the question regarding the conditions and activities required for the construction of a certain psychological function. From this theoretical perspective psychological function is first positioned as an ideal sociocultural model, and then the constructive process is designed and reflectively analyzed while leading a child or an adult toward this ideal model.

The sociocultural model is based on a number of theoretical assumptions:

1.   Psychological functions are sociocultural rather than natural;
2.   To investigate the function means to uncover its origin, dynamics and modification;
3.   The formation of psychological functions is mediated by the available symbolic tools and sociocultural activities.

From Historical to Cross-Cultural Perspective

Taken as a whole the sociocultural theory (Vygotsky and Luria, 1930/1993) poses three major objectives for a study of human psychology: 1) Reconstruction of the transition from an animal to a human way of thinking and behaving; 2) Investigation of the historical change occurring in human mental functions as a result of the introduction of new cultural tools and sociocultural activities; 3) Investigation of the developmental construction of children's and adults' psychological functions in a given society. The following discussion focuses on the second and the third of these objectives.

The question of the historical development of human mental functions was initially approached by Vygotsky and Luria (see Luria 1976) through a "quasi-historical" field study in Central Asia.

"The research reported here,"—wrote Luria in 1976—"undertaken forty years ago under Vygotsky's initiative and in the context of unprecedented social and cultural change, took the view that higher cognitive activities remain sociocultural in nature, and that the structure of mental activity—not just the specific content but also the general forms basic to all cognitive processes—change in the course of historical development" (p. 8).

The logic of such a "quasi-historical" study was as follows. Since it is impossible to conduct an empirical study of historical changes occurring in the human cognition, the best approximation would be a traditional society with technology, lifestyle, and learning patterns more or less corresponding to the previous historical periods that undergo a rapid sociocultural change. Vygotsky and Luria thought that they had found such a natural historical "experiment" in Soviet Central Asia of the early 1930s. The unique sociocultural situation of this region in the late 1920s and early 1930s was determined by a very rapid invasion of Soviet power into an otherwise very traditional and mostly non-literate agricultural society. As a result, people belonging to the same economic and sociocultural group, often even to the same extended family, found themselves under very different sociocultural circumstances. Some of them, especially those in the remote villages, retained all aspects of a traditional, non-literate culture and way of life. The second group included people involved in new agricultural or industrial enterprises, exposed to the new technology and means of communication, but still without access to systematic formal education. The third group comprised people who attended adult literacy courses and even teachers' colleges.

The research methodology used by Vygotsky and Luria may be defined as a synthesis of anthropological and psychological approaches. On the one hand, the situation of data gathering was closer to an anthropological model with researchers conducting their study in the everyday environment often around the evening campfire. The presentation of tasks was preceded by an unhurried conversation touching on subjects close to the daily concerns of peasants and their opinions on different matters. The tasks themselves were presented as "riddles" quite popular in the local culture. The presentation of "riddles" and the discussion that followed the peasants' responses resembled Piaget's method of dialogical clarification of children's concepts. As far as possible, the "riddles" themselves were cast in a culturally appropriate way and always included several possible solutions. The idea was to let the respondents answer either in a functional way that reflected their immediate everyday experience, or in a verbal-logical way based on more abstractive and hypothetical reasoning.

The underlying nature of the tasks, however, was psychological, rather than ethnographic, and reflected the researchers' concern with such psychological functions as perception, memory, classification, problem solving, and imagination. It is interesting and relevant to our discussion of some other aspects of sociocultural approach, such as the Zone of Proximal Development, that Vygotsky and Luria were not content with just receiving the informants' answers, but also probed into the extent to which they could benefit from learning experiences given in the course of conversation. "We also introduced some learning tasks in the experiment. By offering to help subjects in certain ways, we tried to show them how, and how much, they could use this assistance in solving a given problem and proceeding to solve others" (Luria, 1976, p. 17).

The main conclusions reached by Vygotsky and Luria on the basis of this study were that informants who retained a traditional non-literate culture and way of life tend to solve problems by using functional reasoning reflecting their everyday life practical experience and reject the possibility of looking at classification, generalization, or drawing conclusions from another, e.g., more abstractive point of view. Exposure to modern technology and involvement in jobs based on division of labor tend to increase the subjects' readiness to solve problems both in functional and in verbal-logical ways. It was observed, however, that informants who did not experience formal education rather easily reverted to purely functional reasoning. At the same time, informants who received some form of formal education demonstrated a clear preference for the verbal-logical form of problem solving.

For example, in a study of classification and generalization the informants were asked to group such objects as *hammer, saw, log,* and *hatchet*. One of the informants, a peasant from a remote village who had received no formal education responded in the following way (Luria, 1976, pp. 55-56):

> "They are all alike. I think that all of them have to be here. See, if you are going to saw, you need a saw, and if you have to split something you need a hatchet. So there are all needed here." The researcher then asked: "Which of these things could you call by one word?"

> Peasant: "How is that? If you call all three of them a 'hammer,' that would not be right either."

> Researcher: "But one fellow picked three things—the hammer, the saw, and the hatchet—and said that they were alike."

> Peasant: "A saw, a hammer, and a hatchet all have to work together. But the log has to be here too."

> Researcher: "Why do you think he picked these three things and not the log?"

> Peasant: "Probably he has got a lot of firewood, but if we will be left without firewood, we would not be able to do anything."

> Researcher: "True, but a hammer, a saw, and a hatchet are all tools."

> Peasant: "Yes, but even if we have tools, we still need wood—otherwise, we cannot build anything."

The present author had a somewhat similar encounter with a young immigrant from Ethiopia who had no previous formal education (Kozulin, 1998). First, I showed him pictures of Ethiopian musical instruments and asked him whether he recognized them. The informant confirmed his familiarity with the instruments and provided their Amharic names. Then I asked him to group the pictures. The informant created a number of groups and explained that each group of instruments is played at specific social occasions or during specific festivities. When asked to think of a possibility of grouping the instruments in a different way, the informant reiterated that the instruments can be grouped only in a specified way and there is no other way of doing this. Probably, the most interesting aspect of this episode was the behavior of my Ethiopian assistant and translator, who received some formal education in Ethiopia and later in Israel. He could barely restrain himself from joining the conversation, clearly indicating his awareness that, apart from social-functional grouping, these same items could be arranged into the groups of string, wind, and percussion instruments.

Vygotsky and Luria thus established one of the non-reductionist paradigms that allowed construing psychological functions not as natural objects maturing in the human mind, but as constructs whose emergence depends on specific sociocultural tools and activities. For a variety of social and political reasons, the results of the Vygotsky-Luria study remained unavailable not only to the Western, but even to Russian researchers for a long time (see Kozulin 1990; van der Veer and Valsiner, 1991). With wisdom of hindsight, one can distinguish a number of questions that remained unanswered in this initial research. Vygotsky and Luria seemed to lump together different sociocultural factors such as the acquisition of literacy, formal classroom learning, exposure to modern technology, and participation in labor activities based on the formal division of labor. Each of these factors seems, however, to have a different impact on the construction of cognitive functions and should be investigated separately.

In the 1960s, the Vygotsky-Luria study became known to a young American psychologist, Michael Cole, who decided to replicate it and elaborate some of the sociocultural factors mentioned above. In their widely quoted study, Scribner and Cole (1981) demonstrated that literacy and schooling may have a differential cognitive impact. By conducting their research in an African society where literacy in three different languages was associated with different acquisition and application contexts (school, home, and religious institution) Scribner and Cole showed that literacy does not have an overall impact on problem solving but affects specific cognitive functions corresponding to each one of the contexts. Formal education on the other hand has an impact on problem solving in the tasks that resemble those used in school. In this way the general sociocultural paradigm was reinforced in a sense that the emergence of cognitive functions was linked to more specific sociocultural contexts and activities.

In a more recent study Greenfield, Maynard and Childs (2003) investigated how the overall change in the sociocultural environment affected the problem solving patterns of Maya children in a rural Mexican community. They compared the data collected in the 1970s, when the predominant form of economy in this community was subsistence and agriculture, with data of the early 1990s, when wage economy and commerce became predominant. The tasks given to children included representation of non-verbal patterns derived from traditional textiles produced practically in every Mayan family. Using the structural equation model, the authors were able to identify the transition from subsistence and agriculture to wage economy and commerce as the main factor leading children from more concrete to more abstractive representations. At the same time, in more complex tasks that required selecting a strategy for continuation of the model pattern, schooling proved to have the strongest relationship with the choice of a more abstractive and less imitative strategy, with the involvement in the "new" economy coming second.

In can be concluded that the emergence of abstractive representations is not a natural cognitive process that depends on maturation and can be studied as a "product" of the individual mind, but a constructive process dependent on the overall socio-economic environment. Moreover, not all types of abstract representations have the same underlying sociocultural basis, some of them, such as the progressive extension of a given pattern apparently depend on more specific sociocultural activities that are acquired through formal schooling.

Symbolic Tools in the Sociocultural Paradigm

While in the studies described above the question was posed regarding the constructive role of such macro determinants as changes in the community's socio-economic profile or introduction of such specific sociocultural activity as formal education, one may also inquire regarding the role of specific symbolic tools appropriated (or not appropriated) by a given individual or group. Actually, Vygotsky positioned the notion of psychological tools (Vygotsky, 1930/1979; see also Kozulin, 1998) at the very center of his sociocultural paradigm. Through acquisition and internalization of symbolic tools human beings start regulating and shaping their own cognitive and behavioral processes.

This process includes a number of prerequisites and stages. Each culture or subculture has a definite number of available symbolic artifacts. If a specific tool is unavailable, the members of a given cultural community will solve problems, for example, problems that usually require technical drawing, in an alternative way. Moreover, their cognitive function of representation will depend on these alternative methods and not on such a psychological tool as technical drawing. However, the availability of a certain symbolic artifact in a given culture does not guarantee its appropriation as a tool. For example, for many students such a potential symbolic tool as a table remains just an external artifact without becoming an effective tool of problem solving (Kozulin, 1998, Chapter 5). Appropriation of a symbolic artifact as a tool constitutes, however, just a first step. This tool should be internalized and transformed into the inner psychological tool. In the case of a table, that would mean that individuals who mastered this tool as a psychological one would acquire a "tabular approach" to the organization and representation of data. This turned out to be not such a trivial task, even for educated adults. While quite efficient in using the available tables for problem solving, a group of teachers demonstrated rather low efficiency in coming up with their own tables for the organization of numerical data presented as a disordered sequence (Kozulin 2005).

Below I will show how a cognitive process that appears as a simple product of maturation reveals its sociocultural constructive nature when approached in a non-reductionist way. This particular study was triggered by the research conducted by Marti and Majordomo (2001) on textual and graphic representations made by subjects of different ages when asked to create instructions for using a cellular telephone. The subjects were first tested on their practical ability to use a cellular phone for making a call to a specified number. Then they were confronted with the task of using a sheet of paper and a pencil and to make all the notations necessary to enable their peers to make a call to a specified number from the same cellular phone. The participants were forewarned that this hypothetical peer does not know how to use cellular phones.

The results of the Marti and Majordomo (2001) research indicated that the notations of younger children were not complete, the sequence of the notated actions was not accurate, and the notations constituted continuous text without drawings or other symbolic notations. Older children and adults presented a more accurate sequence of actions, while using a combination of schematic drawings and text, and while using the text presented it as a list with headings 1, 2, 3…. For adults the mean of pertinent actions included in the instruction is 92 percent, while for 8-year-old children—46 percent. Only about 50 percent of 9- and 10-year-old children used a combination of drawings and writing in their notations, while about 80 percent of adults used such a combination. Only adults used the list format in their textual notations, while children preferred to create a continuous text. The authors interpreted their findings as demonstrating an orderly maturational progression of the cognitive function of representation.

The sociocultural approach allows for an alternative interpretation of these results in a different way. Because all subjects in the Marti and Majordomo study belonged to modern urban culture and were exposed to regular formal education, the cognitive changes that the authors associated with maturation might actually reflect the progressive acquisition of specific cognitive tools that were deployed in the task of creating notations. Adult participants of the Marti and Majordomo study were undergraduate psychology students. One could assume that during their high-school and university studies they were exposed to a wide variety of notational systems including schemas, diagrams, etc. To test this alternative hypothesis, I replicated the Marti and Majordomo study with adults belonging to a culturally different group—women educated in ultra-orthodox Jewish religious schools and colleges. In these schools, secular subjects such as mathematics are taught only at a basic level, while science is usually not taught at all, with the bulk of the time devoted to religious subjects. At the same time, these women are exposed to modern technology such as cellular phones.

Nineteen women, teachers or teacher assistants of ultra-religious schools participated in the study. All subjects confirmed that they have cell phones and use them on a daily basis. Then they were told and shown how to switch on a specific cell phone, how to dial numbers, and the location of the "send" button. After that the subjects were asked to note on a sheet of paper instructions to make a call to a specified number for a person who does not know how to use a cell phone. Subjects were asked whether they understood the instructions and their questions (e.g., "does this person know what a regular phone is?") were answered. The cell phone was visible to the participants during their work. The target phone number was written on a whiteboard. All participants finished the task in 30 minutes.

Their notations were analyzed according to the following dimensions:

- *Actions.* The subjects' notations (drawings and text) were analyzed for the presence of a correct sequence of actions.
- *Functionality.* Whether the notation provides unambiguous instructions for performing all three required actions in the correct order;
- *Representation.* Use of drawings, drawings and writing, or text only for conveying the instruction;
- *Notational format.* Instructions presented as a continuous text without any subdivisions. Instructions presented as a list with separate actions listed under each other. Other formats.

Table 1
The analysis of cell phone notations made by ultra-orthodox women.

Actions.	Functionality	Representation	Notational format
Present in 100%	Incorrect number: 31.6%	Drawing and text: 31.6%	List: 68.4% Linear text: 31.6%
	Ambiguous or incomplete instruction 36.8%	Text only: 68.4%	

The results of the notational analysis are shown in Table 1. As expected of educated adults all women referred to three essential actions required for making a cell phone call in their instructions. The sequence of actions was also correct. However, a considerable number of instructions were far from unambiguous. One may consider the predominance of purely textual instructions (68.4 percent) as contributing to a high occurrence of incomplete or ambiguous instructions. In the textual instruction unsupported by pictures it is much more difficult to provide a complete and unambiguous description of the target actions.

The combination of drawings and text (31.6 percent) though effective in conveying the unambiguous instruction were far from accurate in depicting a specific cell phone device. Some subjects seem to use their mental image of a cell phone, rather than a perceptual image of the specific device. Thus in one case, 15 number buttons (5 x 3) were depicted instead of 12 (3 x 4) on the specific device. In another elaborate drawing, a group of four symmetrical operation buttons was depicted, instead of three asymmetrical ones. In another elaborate drawing, one non-existent operation button was added. Three drawings were deliberately schematic demonstrating only those buttons that were essential for performing the required actions.

The results of our study confirmed that facility with certain cultural tools, such as technical drawing or schemas, has a strong influence on the person's notational activity, actually stronger than developmental age. Only 31.6 percent of our subjects used the combination of writing and drawing, which is less than the percent of 9- and 10-year-old children in the Marti and Majordomo research. This reflects the lack of these tools in the sub-culture of ultra-orthodox women. At the same time, a large enough number (68.4 percent) of our subjects used list format in their textual instructions. This corresponds to their previous educational and professional experience, because religious texts typically use all sorts of list notations. Lack of experience with pictorial notations in our subjects may also explain a large number of cases where pictorial image did not correspond to the details of the actually present device.

One may conclude by reitcrating the classical Vygotskian claim that what appears as a natural developmental progression in a given culture often obscures the interaction between maturational processes and sociocultural influences. It is enough to step outside this culture, and the "naturalness" of this progression immediately disappears. Each culture has its own set of symbolic tools appropriated and internalized by its members at different ages and in different contexts. As we have seen even such apparently trivial activity as using notations for giving everyday instructions is deeply influenced by cultural tools available to a person.

A Study of Concept Formation

So far our discussion was conducted on a macro and mezzo level by demonstrating how a given socio-cultural environment or appropriation of certain symbolic tools in the course of education assume a constructive role in the formation of human psychological functions. The Vygotskian approach, however, allows also for a micro-analysis where a certain function is observed in a process of its development during a short experiment-cum-intervention. In this connection, it should be reiterated that in Vygotskian research tradition an experiment is not a means of checking the existent "state of affairs," but rather a means of investigating how a certain psychological function is emerging. In this respect, the study of artificial concept formation initiated by Sakharov (1930/1994) and continued by Vygotsky (1934/1986) and his students is paradigmatic (see Towsey, 2006).

The main theoretical objective of the concept formation study was to investigate how artificial signs become integrated with objective non-verbal properties of the objects, thus creating in the child's mind a new functional system in which signs assume the important role. In the course of the experiment, two initially independent systems—the verbal naming system and the non-verbal reasoning system become integrated. Thought becomes verbal while language becomes a tool of concept formation.

The experiment includes a number of three-dimensional geometric figures of different shape, size and color. To the bottom of each figure a label with a nonsense word—"cev," "bik," "mur," and "lag"—was attached. Each group of figures had its "name," e.g., all small and flat figures irrespective of their shape and color were called "cev." The experimenter explained to children that the figures are toys from some exotic culture and they should guess which figures belong to the same group. After that, the experimenter turned one of the figures, e.g., a small, flat, green parallelepiped and asked the child to read its name—"cev." The child was then asked to place all figures that he or she thought belonged to a "cev" group in a special place on the board. Once the grouping was done, the experimenter asked the child for his/her reasons for selecting the figures. Then the experimenter selected one of the figures that was not picked up by the child and showed that it also had the name "cev." The child's reaction was observed and recorded, after which the turned figure was placed next to the first "cev" figure, while all other selected figures were returned to a general pool and the game of selecting the "cev" figures started again.

Using this methodology Vygotsky (1934/1986) and his colleagues were able to identify a number of patterns of concept formation. Younger children often demonstrate subjective grouping that shows no integration of the "name" with physical properties of the figures. In older children, grouping sometimes looks conceptual and its pre-conceptual nature becomes clear only through the observation of a child's reaction to the demonstration that one of the chosen figures has a different name or one of the non-included figures does have the same name as figures included in the group.

In his analysis, Vygotsky (1934/1986) constantly operates on two planes, one of them is the plane of concept formation experiment, while the other is the plane of observations of children's everyday speech. In this way, Vygotsky connects the child's construction of a collection of objects linked to each other through associative links to the child's everyday verbal thought that also operates by using an associative principle. For example, in the experimental situation, the child may select some objects because they have a common form and then add some that have the same color, and then yet another object that shares the same size with the last one. In everyday speech the child may define a "rich man" as somebody who "is fat and has a good overcoat." In both cases the "concept" is built on the basis of actual, rather then formal-logical properties: figures are added first on the basis of perceptually similar form, and then because a new element has a similar color, etc; the experience of distinguishing a rich person on the basis of being well fed is then connected to a different experience of seeing another rich person in a good overcoat, and so on. From Vygotsky's point of view, the transition to real concepts takes place when the "name" becomes a truly symbolic tool that substitutes for empirically given properties. Once the child advances the hypothesis that the name "cev" signifies small and flat figures, such prominent yet irrelevant similarities as color and shape become suppressed and the child is capable of identifying a virtually unlimited number of empirical objects that would belong to this group. In the same way, once the concept of a "rich man" starts being defined through financial power, such empirically prominent yet irrelevant features as appearance, clothing, car, etc. would cease to dominate the child's thought.

Vygotsky made two observations that seem to remain not fully elaborated in the cognitive theory. One of them is that associative, pre-conceptual reasoning is not confined to child thought and is also widely used by adults in their everyday life. Adult reasoning is multilayered and includes both conceptual as well as pre-conceptual elements. Different forms of sociocultural activity engender and sustain different forms of thought. Thus for an everyday judgment, the association of a person's high economic status with a luxury car might be sufficient, while for economic research such a basis is inadequate. The multilayered structure of thinking of educated adults may explain some of the more recent controversies (see Lave, 1988) regarding so-called "situated cognition." From a Vygotskian point of view, cognition is undoubtedly "situated" in a sense that it is shaped by a specific sociocultural practice. This does not mean, however, that all forms of cognition are "local" and resistant to transfer. Moreover, the acceptance of the sociocultural origins of cognition does not imply that one should not use normative models for investigating it as Lave seems to advocate. Each type of sociocultural practice has its own normative models. Vygotsky made a particular emphasis on the distinction between models engendered by everyday experience and models developed in systematic scholarly practice. Scholarly reasoning is impossible without certain normative models and in this sense it is more generalizable and transferable than local everyday reasoning. Of course the fact that some activities are carried out in the classroom does not make them automatically scholarly or transferable. Russian Vygotskians (e.g., Davydov, 1988) provided a systematic critique of typical school curricula demonstrating that they often fail to develop scholarly concepts, just providing instead a certain enrichment of students' pre-existent everyday concepts. Davydov and his colleagues developed the whole systems of classroom learning based on normative scholarly models leading to highly transferable forms of conceptual reasoning (see Zuckerman, 2004). It would be a mistake, however, to think that conceptual reasoning totally replaces pre-conceptual thought. Efficient reasoning depends not on total suppression of pre-conceptual thought, but rather on skillful identification of the goals of a given problem-solving situation. One manifestation of this multiplicity of situations seems to be captured by Sternberg's (1985) distinction between practical and analytic intelligence.

The second observation made by Vygotsky concerns so-called "pseudo-concepts." The issue of pseudo-concepts is important for the non-reductionist methodology because it demonstrates that orientation toward the product is often misleading. Children who in Vygotsky's concept formation experiment selected almost all small and flat figures might act on the conceptual level and just overlook the remaining figure, but they might also act on a pseudo-conceptual level so that the product of their activity almost coincides with that of truly conceptual reasoning, but the process of reasoning is still pre-conceptual. This underlying process can be determined only through probing the reasons for the children's grouping or questioning them regarding the reason why both one small and flat and another small and tall figure are not included. In the child's everyday speech pseudo-concepts play a double role. Using the "same" words facilitates children's communication with adults and advances their comprehension of certain phenomena. On the other hand adults often overestimate children's understanding exactly because they use the "same" words as adults. Of course, the most extreme situation in which children's pseudo-conceptual thought remains completely unnoticed is the multiple choice tests. It is enough for a child to select the correct answer and it is automatically presumed that his or her understanding of the underlying principle is the same as that of the designers of the test. In reality, however, the so-called "correct" answer may signify only a very partial overlap between the underlying conceptual structures of the student and of the test designers.

Zone of Proximal Development (ZPD)

The notion that links Vygotsky's research on concept formation with more practical concerns of educational psychology is the notion of ZPD. This notion shifts the theoretical emphasis from psychological functions that appear as "naturally" developing in the child's head to the very process of their construction in the dynamic interaction between children and their mentors. When Vygotsky's writings finally became available in translation, the notion of ZPD became one of the most popular non-reductionist approaches in contemporary educational psychology (Chaikin, 2003).

The concept of ZPD first appears in Vygotsky's (1934/1986) discussion of the developmental theory. He drew the attention of his readers to the fact that at any given moment of child development, in addition to psychological functions that are fully mastered by the child there are also a number of emergent functions that are still "invisible" for an ordinary research methodology. Typical assessment methods target only the first type of psychological functions, those that can already be displayed by the child. According to Vygotsky the "invisible" functions, however, can also be identified. What is required for this is the situation of child's cooperative activity with adults or more competent peers (Minick, 1987; Chaiklin, 2003). Such an approach reflects Vygotsky's fundamental belief that social forms of activity form the matrix of children's development (see Kozulin, 1990; 1998). A function that first appears as "shared" by the child and an adult is then appropriated and mastered by the child. Moreover, Vygotsky considered that a normal learning situation for a child is a socially meaningful cooperative activity. New psychological functions of the child originate in this interpersonal plane and only later are internalized and transformed becoming the child's inner psychological processes. Thus the situation of collaborative or assisted problem-solving creates conditions for the development of the new psychological functions. For a certain period of time these functions are not mature enough to be displayed by children in their independent problem-solving. However, in the assessment situation that includes cooperation and help, children are capable of demonstrating the emergent functions that have not yet been internalized. Vygotsky suggested charting individual ZPDs for children by comparing their performance under solitary conditions with performance during the assisted problem solving. For the future discussion it is important to mention that Vygotsky suggested a wide range of interactive interventions to be used during ZPD assessment, such as asking leading questions, modeling, starting to solve the task and asking the child to continue, and so on, but he produced no standardized procedure for the ZPD assessment. Moreover, Vygotsky left open the question about the possible targets of such an assessment; as an illustration of the processes in ZPD he mentioned both general problem solving and school based skills.

Through his notion of ZPD Vygotsky introduced a number of important parameters of what later would become known as a "dynamic assessment" paradigm (Sternberg & Grigorenko, 2002). While such early pioneer of "dynamic assessment" as Andre Rey (1934) suggested allowing the child to learn during the testing procedure, Vygotsky proposed an active intervention on the part of adults as an integral component of the assessment. The child's learning ceases to be a property of the child and, within the ZPD, becomes an expression of his or her ability to function within the sociocultural context. In a sense the entire orientation of mental assessment is changing from that of measuring what the child is capable of doing now, to what kind and what amount of interaction between the child and adults can produce the results that the child is currently incapable of producing him or herself.

Russian followers of Vygotsky developed the concept of ZPD into a system of learning/teaching activities aimed at identification of children's ZPD, realization of the psychological functions situated within this zone, enhancement of children's ability to benefit from assisted learning and in this way further expansion of their ZPD. The following research of Venger (1969) and Holmovskaja (1976) provides us with a rather typical example of developmental study based on the principles of ZPD.

The first stage of such an assessment-cum-intervention is the selection of a particular cognitive ability. In the Venger and Holmovskaja studies the target was the ability of younger children to evaluate the ratio or proportion between different objects or parts of an object. According to Vygotsky's theory, further elaborated by Venger (1969) the development of the child's perception depends not only on maturation and the child's own experiences but also on sociocultural "perceptual standards" (or etalons) conveyed to the child in a given society. For more advanced perceptual functions the impact of sociocultural perceptual standards is stronger.

Though some five-year-old children have an intuitive perceptual grasp of proportions, this intuition is neither conscious nor systematic. To approach any kind of perceptually given ratio problem children need a generalized system of "perceptual standards" that will guide them in solving these problems. In her research Holmovskaja (1976) first established the level of intuitive grasp of proportions in 3- to 6-year-old children. The children were presented with a model—a pair of objects (e.g., toy boats or pencils) that differed in length in the proportion 1 to 2, or 1 to 1.65 or 1 to 1.5. Then children were given a similar object (a boat or a pencil) of a different size and asked to pick up a second (smaller) object so that the lengths of objects in the new pair were proportional to those in the model pair. It turned out that the success rate even in 6-year-old children was only 27 percent.

The second stage of the assessment-cum-intervention was to introduce children to the relevant "perceptual standards" and to see whether the availability of these tools changes children's ability to evaluate proportions. Acquisition of "perceptual standards" and their use is based on the formation of the system of "orienting actions" aimed at identification of the critical properties of the objects under investigation. In the proportion tasks such a critical property is the length of the objects and the main operation is their comparison.

Stage 1. Children are shown how to compare objects along the chosen dimension (i.e., length) and how to label their inequality ("Object A is longer than object B by that much"). Stage 2. Children are taught how to compare the difference between objects ("an extra length") to the longer object. In this way the "extra length" ceased to be absolute and became relative while the longer object became a "measure." Stage 3. Development of actions aimed at comparison of two or several relationships between objects. The objects of these activities were cardboard cutout figures of folktale characters of different sizes. Children were encouraged to use the strips of colored paper as measurement and comparison tools. Gradually the use of these tools became internalized and children started comparing objects in their mind.

The comparison of proportional task performance of children who were introduced to "perceptual standards" and those who were not, demonstrated that for the majority of six-year-olds proportional perception is situated within their ZPD. Children in the experimental group correctly solved 96 percent of the tasks (some by direct estimation, the majority using external tools such as paper strips) while children who were not exposed to "perceptual standards" correctly solved only 30 percent of the tasks. These results indicate that the majority of six-year-old children are capable of appropriating "perceptual standards" and using them successfully for solving proportional perception tasks. Moreover, as demonstrated in another study of Holmovskaja (1976) children who appropriated "perceptual standards" through the activities described above showed considerable advantage in preserving proportions between objects in the drawing task. This indicates that "perceptual standards" had a generalized impact on children's cognition.

In the ZPD-based study, the research situation was transformed from testing whether such a thing as proportional perception exists in the heads of children of a given age into a constructive paradigm that demonstrated what kind of intervention with children of different ages may result in the development of such new ability as proportional reasoning based on perceptual standards.

Learning Potential Assessment as a Non-Reductionist Methodology

While the non-reductionist approaches discussed above originated for the most part in the research settings, the Feuerstein et al. (1979; 2002) concept of dynamic assessment and enrichment of cognitive functions came directly from the field of educational and clinical practice. Though developed without the direct influence of Vygotsky's theory, Feuerstein's approach definitely has a sociocultural orientation. The origin of this approach can be traced to Feuerstein's work with Holocaust survivors and immigrant children from Third World countries. In these children the impact of psychological trauma, bi- and multi-lingualism, and lack of formal education became firmly entangled with more standard signs of low intellectual or learning abilities. After attempting to use standard psychometric as well as Piagetian tests, Feuerstein came to the conclusion that the children's low performance level stems not so much from organic or developmental impairment as from the lack of learning experience mediated by human mediators. This prompted him to postulate two major forms of learning, direct learning and mediated learning. Direct learning occurs in the immediate interaction of children with their environment. It may involve such simple learning processes as recognition of the same face, object, or picture, as well as such complex forms of learning as studying advanced academic texts. In both cases the learning process proceeds directly from the material to the learner without human mediation. According to Feuerstein, the prerequisite for the development of efficient direct learning is the experience of mediated learning during which objects, events and processes are selected, analyzed, emphasized, and interpreted to the child by parents, teachers and other significant persons. The insufficient amount or type of mediated learning experience (MLE) leads to the child's reduced ability or/and efficiency of direct learning. At the same time, enrichment of the MLE, even in older children and young adults may result in the significant improvement of their cognitive functioning and learning ability.

By including the MLE-rich phase into the cognitive assessment procedure called Learning Potential Assessment Device, Feuerstein et al., (1979) radically changed the goals, techniques and interpretations of cognitive testing, and by implication also cognitive research. Instead of selecting cognitive tasks that have high stability, i.e., that show the same result over multiple administrations, Feuerstein selected tasks that have greater sensitivity to learning, i.e., will show different results depending on successful (or unsuccessful) learning during the MLE phase of the assessment. The impartial and neutral style of standard psychometric testing was replaced by active interaction between the evaluator/mediator and the child during the MLE phase. The results of the assessment are interpreted as indices of the cognitive and learning change rather than scores to be compared to the age norms. Feuerstein also dispensed with the entire philosophy of labeling and classifying students and called for an ongoing evaluation of the child's learning potential with the aim of formulating an optimal educational intervention for each individual child.

If a philosophical label is needed, then Feuerstein's approach is close to that of existentialism. For him each individual, particularly a child or adolescent, harbors an indeterminate capacity or propensity for change. The goal of assessment is to provide an ongoing evaluation of the qualitative and quantitative discrepancy between the children's manifest functioning and their modifiability and to suggest appropriate intervention. There is no attempt on the part of Feuerstein to predict the future functioning of the child or to compare the child's learning potential with that of other children. The child in Feuerstein's systems serves as his or her own system of reference. In his more recent papers, Feuerstein et al. (2002) went even further claiming that individual cognitive functioning can best be described in terms of a changeable "state" and that there is no reason attempting to find its more permanent traits.

The case studies that served as an illustration of Feuerstein's method (Feuerstein et al., 1979; Feuerstein, Rand, and Rynders, 1988) portray low functioning children, classified at best as educable mentally retarded, who, in the course of lengthy assessment-cum-intervention, start displaying isolated instances of higher learning ability. These instances then become consolidated and at the end of the assessment period, the children themselves as well as their teachers and psychologists change their opinion about the children's true abilities. The next stage includes placing these children in a new, more advanced educational setting and providing them with a remedial cognitive program based on the method of Feuerstein's et al. (1980) *Instrumental Enrichment*. Often a case study is concluded with the child successfully graduating from regular high school, and acquiring a gainful profession or trade.

In his non-reductionist orientation, Feuerstein is probably more radical than any of the approaches reviewed in this paper. From his point of view, not only can cognitive and learning functions not be treated as stable objects, but even the measure of cognitive modifiability is sufficient only for planning the ongoing educational intervention rather than for predicting the children's future functioning. Two of the main principles of a standard research paradigm are challenged here, replication and prediction. The highly interactive character of LPAD practically precludes exact replication because the type and amount of help is attuned to the needs and the progress made by an individual child in the course of the assessment. The prediction of the children's future functioning also seems to be rejected by the Feuerstein et al. (2002) theoretical model. As a result a new paradigm should be formulated, that is not dependent on replication and prediction.

Such a paradigm may actually be closer to art rather than to the natural science. In the work of art, precise replication is not considered a desirable goal. Instead, each piece of art is expected to be different reflecting its intimate and unique connection to its object and the technique. In a somewhat similar way, the emergence of cognitive functions revealed during the LPAD procedure is a unique event engendered by the interaction between the mediator and the child. As such a precise replication of the same interaction and the same result is neither possible nor desirable. In the artwork, prediction is not expected in a sense that a picture of an object executed in a certain technique does not predict the future depiction of similar objects by the same artist. A given work of art allows us rather to expect from the artist a certain range of possibilities that may become realized in the next picture. In the same way cognitive modifiability revealed during an LPAD session does not predict the future performance of the child, but indicates certain possibilities that might be realized in the future in his or her work with other tasks. Such an alliance of psychological study with artistic rather than natural-scientific orientation inevitably reminds us of early attempts of Vygotsky (1971; see also Kozulin 1990; 1998) to set the creation (authoring) and appropriation (reading) of literary texts as a general model of human psychological activity.

We may thus tentatively formulate an alternative non-reductionist paradigm independent of the standard postulates of replication and prediction. In such a paradigm, the "experimental" situation is aimed not at creating the product that can be veritably reproduced under similar conditions, but rather to develop a new cognitive process leading to such psychological products that were beyond the reach of the child before the experimental encounter. Internalization of these new processes, their generalization and deployment in the new problem solving situations constitute the criteria of an experimental success.

References

Chaiklin, S. (2003). The Zone of Proximal development in Vygotsky's analysis of learning and instruction. In A. Kozulin, B. Gindis, V. Ageyev & S. Miller (eds.), *Vygotsky's educational theory in cultural context*. New York: Cambridge University Press.

Davydov, V. (1988). Problems of developmental teaching. Part 1-3. *Soviet Education*, 30, Nos. 8-10.

Feuerstein, R., Rand, Y., and Hoffman, M. (1979). *The dynamic assessment of the retarded performer*. Baltimore, MD: University Park Press.

Feuerstein, R., Rand, Y., & Hoffman, M., & Miller, R. (1980). *Instrumental Enrichment: An intervention program for cognitive modifiability*. Baltimore, MD: University Park Press.

Feuerstein, R., Rand, Y., and Rynders, J. (1988). *Don't accept me as I am*. New York: Plenum.

Feuerstein, R., Rand, Y., Falik, L., & Feuerstein, Ra. (2002). *Dynamic assessment of cognitive modifiability*. Jerusalem: ICELP Press.

Greenfield, P., Maynard, A. and Childs, C. (2003). Historical change, cultural learning, and cognitive representation in Zinacantec Maya children. *Cognitive Development*, 18: 455-487.

Holmovskaja, V.V (1976). Genesis sposobnosti k zritel'noj ozenke proporzij (Genesis of the ability of visual evaluation of ratios. In L.A. Venger, *Genesis sensornyh sposobnostej* (Genesis of sensory abilities), pp. 135-161. Moscow: Pedagogika.

Kozulin, A. (1990). *Vygotsky's psychology: A biography of ideas*. Cambridge, MA: Harvard University Press.

Kozulin, A. (1998). *Psychological tools: A sociocultural approach to education*. Cambridge, MA: Harvard University Press.

Kozulin, A. (2005). Who needs metacognition more: Teachers or students? Paper presented at the Annual Meeting of American Educational Research Association, Montreal, 2005.

Lave, J. (1988). *Cognition in practice*. New York: Cambridge University Press.

Luria, A. (1976). *Cognitive development*. Cambridge, MA: Harvard University Press.

Minick, N. (1987). Implications of Vygotsky's theories for dynamic assessment. In Lidz, C. (ed.), *Dynamic assessment*, pp. 116-140. New York: Guilford.

Marti, E. and Majordomo, R. (2001). How to use a cell phone? Children's and adults' written instructions. Paper presented at the conference of the European Association for Research in Learning and Instruction. Padua, Italy.

Rey, A. (1934). D'un procede pour evaluer l'educabilite, *Archives de Psychologie*, 24: 297-337.

Sakharov, L. (1930/1994). Methods for investigating concepts. In R. van der Veer and J. Valsiner (eds.), *The Vygotsky reader*, pp. 73-98. Oxford: Blackwell.

Scribner, S. and Cole, M. (1981). *The psychology of literacy*. Cambridge, MA: Harvard University Press.

Sternberg, R. (1985). *Beyond the IQ: A triarchic theory of human intelligence*. New York: Cambridge University Press.

Sternberg, R. and Grigorenko, E. (2002). *Dynamic testing*. New York: Cambridge University Press.

Towsey, P. (2006). *In search of Vygotsky's blocks*. M.A. thesis. School of Education, University of Witwatersrand, Johannesburg, South Africa.

van der Veer, R. and Valsiner, J.(1991). *Understanding Vygotsky*. Oxford: Blackwell.

Venger, L.A. (1969). *Vosprijatie i obuchenie* (Perception and teaching/learning). Moscow: Prosveschenie.

Vygotsky, L. (1971). *Psychology of art*. Cambridge, MA: MIT Press.

Vygotsky, L. (1934/1986). *Thought and language*. Cambridge, MA: MIT Press.

Vygotsky, L. (1930/1979). Instrumental method. In J. Wertsch (ed.), *The concept of activity in Soviet psychology*, pp. 134-143. Armonk, N.Y.: Sharpe.

Vygotsky, L. and Luria, A. (1930/1993). *Studies on the history of behavior*. Hillsdale, N.J.: Lawrence Erlbaum.

Zuckerman, G. (2004). Development of reflection through learning activity. *European Journal of Psychology of Education*, 19: 9-18.

3

Creating the Future: Vygotsky as an Experimenter

René van der Veer

Introduction

It has repeatedly been argued that Vygotsky's actual empirical investigations did not live up to his own standards for doing empirical psychological research. In this essay I will pay attention to both Vygotsky's reasoning about the aims of empirical research in psychology and to several empirical studies that he supervised or discussed approvingly. That will allow us to gain more understanding of Vygotsky's aims in psychological research and to answer the question whether the research projects he favored reached these aims or whether there exists some tension between Vygotsky the theorist and Vygotsky the researcher, as has been claimed. I shall begin by outlining in some detail Vygotsky's theoretical views concerning the proper way to do empirical research.

Theoretical Considerations

On several occasions Vygotsky discussed the role of properly conducted empirical research in psychology. He clearly was well aware of the ongoing discussions between behaviorists, introspectionists, and so on, and at times referred to explicitly methodological studies such as Lewin (1927). The most elaborate considerations about the role of theory and experiment in psychology can perhaps be found find in Vygotsky's analysis of the causes of the crisis in psychology (Vygotsky, 1997). In that essay, written in 1926, Vygotsky argues that we should try to investigate the essence of a phenomenon, its ideal form. However, in practice this essence will never be found as such, because it cannot be separated from all sorts of other phenomena and factors. Nevertheless, Vygotsky argued, it makes sense to attempt to reveal the inner mechanism of phenomena through analysis and experiment. Vygotsky then elaborated on the similarities between theoretical analysis, on the one hand, and experiment, on the other hand, and wrote that the similarity of theoretical analysis to the experiment:

> resides in the fact that in the experiment as well we have an artificial combination of phenomena in which the action of a specific law must appear in its purest form; it is like a snare for nature, an analysis *in vivo*. In analysis we create a similar artificial combination of phenomena, but then through mental abstraction. This is particularly clear in its application to artificial constructions. Because they are not aimed at scientific but at practical goals, they rely upon the action of some specific psychological or physical law. Examples are a machine, an anecdote, lyrics, mnemonics, a military command. Here we have a practical experiment. The analysis of such cases is an experiment with finished phenomena. The experiment's significance comes close to that of pathology—this experiment arranged by nature itself—to pathology's own analysis. The only difference is that disease causes loss or the demarcation of superfluous traits, whereas here we have the presence of necessary traits, a selection of them—but the result is the same.

> Each lyrical poem is such an experiment. The task of analysis is to reveal the law that lies at the basis of nature's experiment. But also when analysis does not deal with a machine, i.e., with a practical experiment, but with any phenomenon, it is in principle similar to the experiment. One could show how infinitely much our equipment complicates and refines our research, how much more intelligent, stronger, and more perspicuous it makes us. Analysis does the same.

> It may seem that analysis, like the experiment, distorts reality by creating artificial conditions for observation. Hence the demand that the experiment should be close to life and naturalistic. If this idea goes further than a technical demand—not to scare off what we are searching for—it leads to absurdity. The strength of analysis is in abstraction, just like the strength of the experiment is in its artificiality. Pavlov's experiment is the best model: for the dogs it is a *natural* experiment—they are fed etc.; for the scientist it is the summit of artificiality—salivation takes place when a specific area is scratched, which is an unnatural combination. Likewise, we need destruction in the analysis of a machine, imaginary or real damage to the mechanism, and in the [analysis of] aesthetic form we need deformation.

> If we remember what was said above about the indirect method, then it is easy to observe that analysis and experiment presuppose *indirect* study: from the analysis of the stimuli we infer the mechanism of the reaction, from the command the movements of the soldiers, and from the form of the fable the reactions to it (Vygotsky, 1997, p. 320; Vygotsky, 1982, pp. 406-407).

This lengthy quote deserves some comments and clarification. To refer to pathology, machines, anecdotes, lyrics, mnemonics, military commands, and fables as practical experiments that lay bare some fundamental physiological or psychological law is certainly original. What Vygotsky suggested was that by analyzing the inner structure, or form, of such "artificial constructions" we can infer the reaction they provoke in the recipient. Elsewhere Vygotsky explained that fables, for example, evoke contradictory emotions that are finally resolved in the denouement or punch line, which Vygotsky compared to a short circuit. He discussed one of Krylov's fables in which a lamb defends itself against a wolf's accusations. The more successful the lamb becomes in its plea, the more one feels approaching its imminent death. In the end, the tension between the feeling of increasing hope (caused by the lamb's successful arguments) and the feeling of growing danger is resolved by the wolf's words: "You are guilty, because I am hungry" (Vygotsky, 1986).

Vygotsky explained that one way to investigate the role of the structure of a fable, anecdote, or poem, is to change elements of its structure and see whether the effects it produces in the recipient are preserved or spoiled. This method of "experimental deformation" he considered to be one of the most fruitful methods of psychology (Vygotsky, 1986, p. 121). The method of deformation is an example of what Vygotsky held to be a general rule, namely that we can only fully understand a certain phenomenon by changing it. Vygotsky believed that the key to understanding complex phenomena is to trace their history. Thus, he emphasized a research approach that was focused on processes rather than outcomes. The study of finished phenomena is often not very revealing and we do better to trace their genesis. In arguing a genetic or historic approach Vygotsky relied both on Marxist thinking and on the work of Darwin (Van der Veer & Valsiner, 1991). Vygotsky repeatedly pointed to Darwin's theory of evolution and its advantages over the views of predecessors. Before evolutionary theory, animals and plants would be classified according to external properties, similarities, and differences. After evolutionary theory was advanced, biologists discarded classification according to static external properties and attempted to demonstrate kinship on the basis of dynamic development (lineages). Plants or animals that superficially, i.e., as observed by the human eye, seem similar or related may not be related at all and vice versa. Genuine kinship relations can only be found by doing developmental analyses. The more recent attempts at determining the age of species on the basis of their DNA is no more than a more advanced application of this viewpoint. So, the proper understanding of a phenomenon requires us to trace its development in time.

The methodological demand to do historical, developmental analyses in psychology was also connected with Vygotsky's theory of the origin of the higher cultural functions. The core of this theory can be outlined as follows. Vygotsky believed that conceptually we can make a distinction between natural and cultural mental processes. Natural mental processes have a genetic basis and develop through maturation and not on the basis of a teaching-learning process. Therefore, in the case of natural mental processes, we do not see differences between people from different cultures and sometimes not even across species. One of Vygotsky's favorite examples was that of natural memory. There is no doubt that animals have memory and that young children develop their memory without any explicit teaching-learning process. Cultural mental processes result from the mastering of some cultural tool that may be specific to a certain culture. One of these cultural tools, and in fact the most important one, is human language. The mastering of a human language changes the mental processes in a fundamental way and makes them cultural. For example, memory changes qualitatively after the child has mastered his native language. If asked to memorize a set of objects, the child can now memorize them on the basis of their names or a superordinate label. For instance, the child may realize that some of the objects can be classified as furniture and others as kitchen utensils and this helps the child to memorize and reproduce the items. Of course, such a form of memory is not innate, cannot be found in very young children, and may differ across human cultures to the extent that their languages differ. Now, according to Vygotsky natural and cultural mental processes do not exist side by side, but what happens is that basic natural abilities are transformed through the mastering of cultural tools such as language. If, however, by dint of some disaster, that cultural tool is damaged, such as in the case of brain damage and resulting aphasia, we may witness a return to a pre-cultural stage of development, so to speak.

Vygotsky argued that all complex human mental processes are higher cultural functions in that they rely on the use of symbols, notably language. Vision, to give another example, is highly determined by language and previously acquired verbal knowledge in that we tend to see categorical objects, not dots or flashes of light. For feeling holds the same. Wundt's blindfolded subjects were inclined to say they felt the impact of a needle on their skin, not a sharp radiating sensation. Because Wundt believed in the existence of "immediate sensation" he had to train his subjects not to give answers based on the knowledge of a categorized world of verbally designated objects. For a Vygotskian, this was a rather strange procedure: we experience the world in terms of verbal categories or concepts acquired in a specific culture. To try to go back to a pre-categorical stage—if at all possible—would be to attempt to undo large part of our mental development.

The great challenge for Vygotsky and his colleagues was to demonstrate that this view on human mental development was indeed a plausible one and they tried to amass evidence in its favor. But how to trace the genesis of mental functions? As was mentioned in the long quote given above, sometimes nature in the form of pathology may reveal something of the development of mental processes, but more often we must take recourse to microgenetic or ontogenetic studies in which we follow or create the developmental process. One of the mental functions Vygotsky and his colleagues investigated most thoroughly was that of memory. In a typical experiment, the child would be requested to memorize a long list of words. The list was too long for the child to remember without any help. However, the child was also supplied with a set of pictures of scenes or objects that had nothing to do with the words to be memorized and he or she was told that these pictures might be of some help. The task of the child was to actively construct a situation in which the pictures played some helpful role. For example, if the child was to remember the word "bike" and he or she found a picture of the sun, it would be possible to imagine a child biking in the sun. Looking at the picture of the sun, the child would then come up with the word "bike." For all the other words to be remembered, the child would also form associations with the pictures and by consulting the pictures in front of him or her it would be possible to reproduce the original list of words.

It is important to reflect on the properties of this type of empirical investigations. First, it is quite clear that Vygotsky expected the children to play a very active role in the experiment. As far as we know the instruction to the subjects was minimal. The children were told that they might use the pictures to aid their performance, but not in what way. Second, this implies that the children themselves had to change the supplied material into effective means that might help to solve the problem. Vygotsky used the terms then available in empirical psychology and spoke of them as "stimuli" that the situation presents. However, in line with his whole theoretical approach and his emphasis on the active role of the subject, he distinguished between stimulus-objects and stimulus-means. In our fictitious example, the words to be remembered were the stimulus-objects and the pictures (or other objects) the stimulus-means. It is the subject, however, who him- or herself had to grant some stimuli the role of means. In other words, it is the subject who redefines some of the presented stimuli as stimulus-means, i.e., in cases where the subjects were presented with a variety of objects that might be used the subjects themselves had to select some of these objects and re-conceptualize them as means to be used in the task solution.

Vygotsky and his colleagues and students did very many of these little investigations with children of various ages and various mental abilities and handicaps, but most of them are only mentioned in passing (and not or only very inadequately described) and it is actually quite hard to find clear examples of actual Vygotskian research. Most clearly described are the experiments that formed part of Vygotsky's colleague Leontiev's dissertation research, which will now be briefly described.

Leontiev's Memory Research

The task in Leontiev's memory research was to play a well known game (Leontiev, 1931; Van der Veer, 1994; 2008). The experimenter asked 18 questions to which the subject had to reply with one word. Seven of these questions regarded the color of an object. However, in answering to these color questions the subject had to avoid the names of two specified colors. In addition, the subject had to avoid repeating a color name. Thus, to give an example, if the experimenter asked "What color is grass?" and the colors "green" and "red" were forbidden, then the subject should avoid answering "green." In addition, if the subject had already answered "blue" to some question and the experimenter asked "What color is the sea?," then the subject should avoid answering "blue" for the second time. This task is quite difficult for children and even for adults, because one has to avoid the forbidden colors and the repetition of colors, even while the experimenter is asking "innocent" questions that do not require a color answer at all. Leontiev tested children of different ages and adults repeatedly and found that they could not perform the task without making mistakes. However, he then supplied the subjects with colored cards and suggested them to make use of them in some way. Moreover, if subjects proved unable to make any spontaneous use of the colored cards, Leontiev would show them how to do it and observe whether they were able to follow his example. The colored cards, then, might be used as stimulus-means to enhance performance. The results of these experiments were intriguing. What Leontiev found, was that the youngest children (5-6 years old) could not make use of the colored cards. Older children (8-13 years old) used them quite consistently, however, and as a result their number of mistakes decreased substantially. One strategy the older children used, for example, was to turn over the two cards with colors that corresponded to the forbidden colors and then turn over colored cards when the corresponding color had been used in an answer. In this way, the subjects could avoid mentioning a forbidden color or repeating colors by consulting the still available cards. Other strategies were also noted. The important thing for Leontiev and Vygotsky was that children, when they grow older, become capable of using cultural tools (in this task in the form of colored cards) to enhance their performance in a memory task. This they judged to be an important result in itself. Even more intriguing was the finding that adults did not make use of the supplied color cards, but still performed better than the children of various age groups. Apparently, the adults no longer relied on external aids to improve their performance, but instead relied on other strategies. Leontiev noted, for example, that adults might simply look at the color cards and then give the answer. In subsequent research (cf. Van der Veer, 1994) it was noted that adults frequently relied on verbal strategies. Rather than say that an object is red, one can say that it is scarlet, for example. And instead of answering truthfully, one may give patently false answers. Both strategies would be in line with Vygotsky's and Leontiev's thinking in that we see a progressive shift from reliance on external tools to reliance on internal verbal tools when the subject grows older.

Much can be said about the merits of Leontiev's memory experiments (Van der Veer, 1994), but to Vygotsky and Leontiev they illustrated the idea that mental growth consists in mastering various cultural tools and that children shift from external to internal tools as they grow older. And it is exactly this developmental perspective that makes Vygotsky's approach unique.

To illustrate that point we can reflect on similar experiments from Vygotsky's contemporaries. Vygotsky took inspiration, for example, from Köhler's seminal chimpanzee research. The chimpanzees were supplied with different tools (e.g., a box, various sticks) and had to grasp themselves that these might be used to reach the solution of a problem (e.g., reaching a banana). Several of Vygotsky's experiments were clearly modeled on this experimental setup. Or, take Maier's equally famous experiments with the two-cord problem and other problems (Maier, 1930, 1931, 1933). There we also have a situation where a problem has to be solved (tying the two cords) and different materials or potential tools are supplied (e.g., a hammer) without any clear instruction how to use them and the subject has to re-conceptualize the situation and has to see that some of the stimuli can be used as stimulus-means to solve the problem.

The subject has to realize that the hammer can be used as a dead weight to give one of the cords a pendular movement.

There is one fundamental difference, however, between Vygotsky's research and that of these contemporaries. It is the following. In both Köhler's and Maier's and Vygotsky's experiments we can witness micro-genetic changes. The subjects suddenly realize that a colored card can be used to memorize an answer, that a stick can be used to grab a banana, that a hammer can serve as a tool in order to be able to tie two cords. All three researchers assumed that subjects within the constraints of the experimental setup can in principle actively restructure the situation. All three researchers did not hesitate to interfere in the problem solving process if necessary. Köhler wrote, for example:

> Clever apes can even be "taught." By all possible means you may draw their attention to the color of two boxes (to their difference) and you may show at the same time that inside the box of one color there is nothing; whereas behind the walls of the other color there is a banana. Whenever I proceed so, forgetting the rule that an experimenter shall not play any direct role in experiments with animals, a striking increase of right choices used to be the immediate effect (Köhler, 1928, p. 152).

Likewise, Leontiev would show a way to make use of the cards or other materials if children failed to use them. Finally, Maier would "accidentally" touch one of the cords and bring it into a pendular movement if the subjects failed to find the solution of the problem spontaneously. Often that subtle hint was enough for the subjects to get onto the right track.

Incidentally, by actually giving hints or prompts or teaching the subjects the solution these researchers were indeed going against a conception of experimental research that was prevalent at the time. That conception involved that reality is out there waiting to be discovered or detected and that the experimenter should not interfere with his topic of research. In Danziger's words, this model is

> reminiscent of the tale of Sleeping Beauty: The objects with which psychological science deals are all present in nature fully formed, and all that the prince-investigator has to do is to find them and to awaken them with the magic kiss of his research (Danziger, 1990, p. 2).

Danziger added that

> in truth scientific psychology does not deal in natural objects. It deals in test scores, rating scales, response distributions, serial lists, and innumerable other items that the investigator does not just find but constructs with great care. Whatever guesses are made about the natural world are totally constrained by this world of artifacts (ibid., p. 2).

In Danziger's view the experimental situation is inherently social and the fact that social effects are regarded as artifacts is due to the misunderstanding that psychological experimentation is like natural scientific research. Puzyrej (1986) has observed that the "Sleeping Beauty" view of psychological science is particularly unfit for Vygotsky's cultural-historical theory. After all, that theory presupposes that mental development consists in mastering cultural tools. Consequently, there is no such thing as pure, uncontaminated natural mental development. But if mental development is equivalent to mastering cultural tools in a teaching-learning process (and Vygotsky attached a significant role to schooling in this context), then there is nothing wrong to study such a teaching-learning process within the constraints of the experimental setup. The findings that one produces then are not experimental artifacts, but form a model for genuine mental development or become part of that same mental development. This is why Vygotsky, his associates, and his followers made use of what has also been called "teaching experiments."

That brings us to the distinction between Köhler's and Maier's experiments, on the one hand, and Vygotsky's and Leontiev's, on the other hand. The distinguishing feature is that Vygotsky held that the microgenetic changes he produced and witnessed were of ontogenetic relevance. All of the mentioned researchers observed and to an extent produced microgenetic shifts in the mindset of their subjects, but Vygotsky claimed in addition that the microgenetic transformations he observed were what mental development is all about. Cognitive development *is* the mastering of relevant cultural tools like language and if we manage to teach subjects how to use certain tools then we have promoted their cognitive development. From the cultural-historical viewpoint, then, showing the way how children of different ages create and master specific cultural tools to improve their performance in task settings is showing how natural abilities become "culturized." It is showing what human mental development essentially is.

There is another example of Vygotskian reasoning that is intimately related to what we have discussed here, although it is never mentioned in this context. It is Vygotsky's thinking about the zone of proximal development. In a way, the dual testing model favored by Vygotsky comes quite close to the teaching experiments he and his associates actually performed.

The Zone of Proximal Development

By the end of his career, Vygotsky argued that IQ-scores can be raised by offering children stimulating school instruction. In his view, in order to achieve the right instruction the school must do two things. First, we must carefully establish the individual child's intellectual level. Second, we must establish the range of tasks and problems that are above the child's intellectual level, but not too far above it. It was in this context that Vygotsky mentioned the new method of measuring children's intellectual potential. Formerly, he said, we measured the child's intellectual level by establishing the number and type of problems the child could solve independently. This gave us an indication of the child's mental age and we tried to adjust the level of instruction to that mental age. However, the new method is to test the child twice: first, when the child solves the problems independently and then when the child solves the problems together with a more able partner. This second procedure yields a score that proves to be the more revealing one. In Vygotsky's own words:

> I show them [the children] different ways to solve the problem.... The children are fully shown how to solve the problem and they are asked to do it again; or the beginning of the problem solving process is shown and the children are asked to finish it, or the children are asked leading questions. In a word, in various ways we ask the child to solve the problem with our help (Vygotsky, 1935, pp. 41-42).

Of course, when we apply this procedure, we will see that children solve more problems with assistance than they would independently. However, the interesting thing is that different children are capable of profiting from the hints and helps of others to a different degree. Some children will be able to gain one year of mental age with help, others two or more. In Vygotsky's view, these differences were far from accidental: a child who profits more from the help of a more able partner has more intellectual potential. This is so because the ability to grasp or imitate the actions of the more able partner tells us something about the child's own intellectual understanding. We cannot just grasp and imitate anything, we cannot imitate things that are beyond our comprehension, we can only grasp and imitate things that are within our reach. Conversely, the things we can understand and imitate indicate our intellectual horizon. In Vygotsky's words:

> Let us explain this concept of the zone of proximal development and its meaning. Let us call, as this is becoming more and more generally accepted in contemporary pedology, that level which the child reached in the course of his development and which is established with the help of tasks solved by the child independently the level of actual development. Consequently, the level of actual development is the mental age in the

usual sense in which it is used in pedology. We now in pedology refrain from calling exactly this the mental age, because, as we saw, it does not characterize mental development. The zone of proximal development of the child is the distance between the level of his actual development, established with the help of problems independently solved, and the level of the child's possible development, established with the help of problems solved by the child under the guidance of adults or in cooperation with his more intelligent partners. What is the level of actual development? When we from the viewpoint of the most naïve person ask what the level of actual development is—in simple words, what the problems that the child independently solves mean—the most usual answer will be that the level of the actual development of the child is determined by the functions that have already matured, the fruits of development. The child can independently do this, that, and that, thus the functions needed to independently do this, that, or that have matured. And the zone of proximal development, established with the help of problems which the child cannot solve independently, but can solve with help, what does that signify? The zone of proximal development refers to functions that have not yet matured, but are in the process of maturing, functions that mature tomorrow, that now are still in their embryonic form; functions that cannot be called the fruits of development, but the buds of development, the flowers of development, i.e., that which is only just maturing. The level of actual development characterizes the successes of development, the results of yesterday's development, but the zone of proximal development characterizes tomorrow's mental development (Vygotsky in a talk delivered on December 23, 1933. See Vygotsky, 1935, p. 42).

What Vygotsky was arguing here was that testing children twice, first without help and subsequently with help, gives us the lower and upper boundaries of the zone within which proper school instruction should move. The teacher should ideally present the child with problems that the child cannot yet fully solve independently, but is capable of solving with help. Such problems will be new and stimulating to the child and will propel the child's intellectual development forward. In order to solve these problems the child will have to use skills that are only just maturing. Of course, after enough time of practice even these new tasks and problems will become a matter of routine and will no longer be challenging to the child. The child has now realized its (former) zone of proximal development and it is time to move on and to offer new and more difficult tasks. These new tasks must lie within the child's next zone of proximal development. In this view then, mental development constitutes a process of shifting boundaries: what once was a task within or even beyond the zone of proximal development, has now become a task within the zone of actual development. What once could only be accomplished with help can now be accomplished independently. Viewed in this way, the concept of the zone of proximal development has three aspects that we must look at specifically. First, there is the dimension of time and the prognosis of mental development. Second, there is the dimension of the social-individual transition. Third, there is the idea that instruction is the leading factor in mental development.

As to the time dimension and the prognosis of mental development we can note the following. The researchers whom Vygotsky referred to and Vygotsky himself were clearly interested in using mental tests as a prognostic device for individual children. Children were tested to get an idea about their future performance in school. The researchers found that their new method of dual testing (once without and once with help) was more indicative of the child's learning potential or intelligence than the standard procedure of just looking at the mental age or IQ scores. After all, children with the same IQ might have a different zone of proximal development as determined by the dual testing procedure. Thus, the new procedure allowed psychologists to make finer distinctions between children and to give better predictions of their future performance. Such information was viewed by the adherents of mental tests as vitally important for teachers at both primary and secondary school. This concept of repeated testing was partly rediscovered and partly reinvented in our time and led to a new trend in the mental testing tradition (Van der Veer, 2007).

The second point to note is that the dual testing procedure involved the social-individual dimension. After all, what is claimed is that what the child can do now in cooperation, it will be able to do tomorrow independently. In other words, it is suggested that joint problem solving actions precede and partially create individual problem solving behavior. And we can now see clearly why the idea of the zone of proximal development must have appealed strongly to Vygotsky. After all, for Vygotsky all higher mental functions originate in social interaction. He even stated a so-called sociogenetic law:

> In general we might say that the relations between higher mental functions once were genuine relations between people.... Every function in the cultural development of the child appears twice, in two planes, first, the social, then the psychological, first between people as an interpsychological category, then within the child as an intrapsychological category (Vygotsky, 1931/1983, pp. 142/145).

This sociogenetic law essentially stated that higher mental processes and self-regulation originate in social interaction with a more able partner. What the child can do in cooperation now, it can do independently tomorrow. The stage of joint performance precedes that of autonomous performance. Now, the concept of the zone of proximal development seems a perfect illustration of that law. The test performance with help indicates the interpsychological stage of problem solving, the test performance without help the intrapsychological stage. What may have appealed to Vygotsky in the concept of the zone of proximal development was that it seemed a transposition of the idea of the sociogenetic law to the domain of prognosis. In that respect, the helps and hints provided in a joint problem solving situation are similar to the colored cards in the forbidden colors task. Both are essentially cultural tools provided by more able partners that the child utilizes to solve a problem. As the child grows older it will internalize these tools or shift to others in order to be able to solve the task independently. Because joint problem solving precedes and partially creates individual problem solving (the sociogenetic law) the one can be used to predict the other (the concept of the zone of proximal development).

Finally, we should note that Vygotsky discussed the idea of the concept of proximal development in the context of education and, particularly, as a means to ensure good instruction. Ideally, instruction should be geared to the individual student, i.e., the instruction should fall into the zone of proximal development of the particular student. Instruction should not follow mental development (as determined by traditional tests), but create it. In Vygotsky's words:

> Only that instruction is good that runs ahead of development ... the correctly organized instruction of the child leads the child's mental development, calls into life a whole series of developmental processes that without instruction would have been altogether impossible (Vygotsky, 1933/1935, pp. 15/16).

This was a view of the relationship between instruction and cognitive development that was not generally shared at the time. It fitted perfectly well with the general orientation of the theory of the higher cultural functions that Vygotsky had been elaborating in the previous years. That theory stated that seemingly private intellectual abilities originate in social interactions with adults or more able peers. In these social interactions, children learn to master specific cultural tools that enable them to solve intellectual problems and master their own behavior. Instruction at school is a special and privileged form of social interaction. Teachers introduce children to the scientific way of thinking by teaching them coherent systems of scientific concepts in specific areas. These scientific concepts are dependent upon the children's everyday concepts, but will also restructure and enrich them. The rational scientific approach will spread to the child's everyday thinking and will allow the child to carry out his actions in a conscious and deliberate manner. This means that school instruction creates something over and above normal social interaction. Formal instruction is necessary to lift the child to the level of systemic scientific thinking. Instruction in the zone of proximal development creates new levels of cognitive development that would not have been reached otherwise.

Conclusions

There is a recurrent pattern in many of Vygotsky's empirical investigations: the child was supplied with semiotic or material means and was encouraged to use these means to solve certain tasks. If the child proved able to do so, he or she had reached a higher level of mental functioning and Vygotsky had shown that the development toward such higher mental functioning might in principle take place in exactly that way. For example, a child who was taking an intelligence test was given hints and prompts and his or her gain in IQ score as compared to a previous independent IQ score was then seen as similar to or prognostic of normal cognitive development. Or, in order to improve memory in a paired-associates task, the child was provided with beans or counters. If the child was capable of using them this was seen as a model of normal memory development. In fact, what happened was that the researcher provoked the very development he wished to study. This approach was unique in that it posited the relevance of microgenetic shifts for ontogeny. Its methodology was process-oriented and truly developmental. It presupposed an active subject who does not passively "respond" to so-called "stimuli," but creates his or her own environment. In this sense, Vygotsky's empirical research was also emancipatory. The subjects in Vygotsky's research were as it were creating their own future.

References

Danziger, K. (1990). *Constructing the subject: Historical origins of psychological research*. New York: Cambridge University Press.

Köhler, W. (1928). Intelligence in apes. In C. Murchison (ed.), *Psychologies of 1925* (pp. 145-161). Worcester, MA: Clark University Press.

Leontiev, A.N. (1931). *Razvitie pamyati: Eksperimental'noe issledovanie vysshikh psikhologicheskikh funktsiy*. Moscow-Leningrad: Gosudarstvennoe Uchebno-Pedagogicheskoe Izdatel'stvo.

Lewin, K. (1927). *Gesetz und Experiment in der Psychologie*. Berlin: Weltkreis-Verlag.

Maier, N.R. F. (1930). Reasoning in humans I. On direction. *Journal of Comparative Psychology, 10*, 115-143.

Maier, N. R. F. (1931). Reasoning in humans II: The solution of a problem and its appearance in consciousness. *Journal of Comparative Psychology, 12*, 181-194.

Maier, N.R.F. (1933). An aspect of human reasoning. *British Journal of Psychology*, 144-155.

Puzyrey, A.A. (1986). *Kul'turno-istoricheskaya teoriya L.S. Vygotskogo i sovremennaya psikhologiya*. Moscow: Izdatel'stvo Moskovskogo Universiteta.

Van der Veer, R. (1994). The forbidden colors game: An argument in favor of internalization? In R. van der Veer, M.H. van IJzendoorn, & J. Valsiner (eds.), *Reconstructing the mind: Replicability in research on human development* (pp. 233-254). Norwood, NJ: Ablex Publishing Corporation.

Van der Veer, R. (2007). *Lev Vygotsky*. London: Continuum Publishers.

Van der Veer, R. (2008). Multiple readings of Vygotsky. In B. van Oers, W. Wardekker, E. Elbers, & R. van der Veer (eds.), *The transformation of learning* (pp. 20-37). Cambridge: Cambridge University Press.

Van der Veer, R., & Valsiner, J. (1991). *Understanding Vygotsky: The quest for synthesis*. Oxford: Blackwell.

Vygotsky, L.S. (1931/1983). Istoriya razvitiya vysshikh psikhicheskikh funktsiy. In l.S. Vygotsky, *Sobranie sochineniy. Tom tretiy. Problemy razvitiya psikhiki* (pp. 6-328). Moscow: Pedagogika.

Vygotsky, L.S. (1935). *Umstvennoe razvitie detey v protsesse obucheniya*. Moscow-Leningrad: Gosudarstvennoe Uchebno-Pedagogicheskoe Izdatel'stvo.

Vygotsky, L.S. (1982). Istoricheskiy smysl psikhologicheskogo krizisa. In *Sobranie sochinenij. Vol. 1. Voprosy teorii i istorii psikhologii* (pp. 291-436). Moscow: Pedagogika.

Vygotsky, L.S. (1986). *Psikhologija iskusstva*, Moscow: Iskusstvo.

Vygotsky, L.S. (1997). The historical meaning of the crisis in psychology: A methodological investigation. In R.W. Rieber., & J. Wollock. (eds.), *The collected works of L.S. Vygotsky.. Vol. 3. Problems of the theory and history of psychology* (pp. 233-343). New York: Plenum Press.

4

Baldwin's Quest:
A Universal Logic of Development

Jaan Valsiner

There are many unfinished projects in science. When viewed historically it is as if the social realities trim off many productive juvenile branches from our tree of knowledge. Whether in the middle of wars, emigrations, moral scandals, or funding cuts—scientists struggle to nourish their ideas—often to no avail. Ideas live in the middle of everyday life activities—where they sometimes thrive precisely at times when the rest of scientists' lives is hard, or even cruel. Scientists are ordinary human beings—who think in ways that transcend the immediate everyday life contexts. Most of the ideas—productive or not—become abandoned as the lives of the scientists move on. What remains are social-institutional narratives about the histories of the sciences—usually to promote the glory of the survived, and to designate the forgotten to the dustbins of history. Institutional histories of sciences or societies serve social—rather than epistemological—goals.

The intellectual legacy of James Mark Baldwin is a good example of how we forget the ideas of our predecessors—while honoring them in the special discursive domain—that of "history of the discipline." Writing history of a scientific discipline is as much a revelation as it is an act of hiding. Usually we present the latter by claims that a narrative about the intellectual *impasses* of the scientist is of no use for anybody. Yet aside from futile pursuits, there were also fruitful beginnings which were not brought to flourish. Thus, an inquiry into the "aborted intellectual fetuses" in a discipline is of use for the conception of new ones—in this day and age of fascination with "in-vitro fertilization." Thus—history of sciences is a powerful refrigerator of ideas from where new intellectual generative materials may emerge for the sciences at our time. History fuels the future.

In What Ways Do We Know James Mark Baldwin?

We know Baldwin—as a foremost developmental psychologist, founder of psychology laboratories in different universities in North America, co-founder of the organic selection perspective in evolutionary thought, and *connoisseur* of the pleasures of living (Broughton, 1981; Cahan, 1984; Cairns, 1980, 1983, 1992; Richards, 1987, Wozniak, 1982). Yet, at the same time we do not know him. One hundred years have passed since Baldwin (1906, 1908, 1911, 1915) outlined his "genetic logic"—logic of development—yet we are as far from creating adequate models of development as were his contemporaries. Psychology has been in a methodological crisis ever since its establishment as a separate social institution. It is particularly in the case of study of development, that is, the investigation of real emerging phenomena brings to the attention of developmentalists the full extent of that crisis. At the same time, Baldwin's quest would have fitted well into the realm of formal logics that branched of from philosophy into mathematics over the twentieth century. Baldwin's aesthetic synthesis—*pancalism*—may be a formal net of concepts to map onto the realities of affective processes in contemporary psychology (Laird, 2007). So, we really do not know Baldwin—or know only one of his many facets.

Limits to Knowing within Psychology: Vulnerability to Social Positioning

Science—as *Wissenschaft*—is an inherently non-democratic exercise. In it, axiomatic assumptions fully determine the realms and ways in which a particular kind of knowledge can be created. Of course, these axiomatic bases may be selected in ways that renders the whole research direction futile—yet there is no alternative than to strive for assuming appropriate—as judged by fit to the phenomena—basic axioms. Such axioms are taken as bases for knowing—following them proceeds without doubt. Yet choice of one's axioms is always deeply filled with doubt—this distinguishes the act of axiom construction from religious conversion. The scientist literally "floats" in the middle of various ideas that surround him or her—sometimes to become influential through reading a book outside of one's field,[1] at times overhearing neighborhood gossipers or reacting to politicians' verbiage on TV screens—not to speak of good ideas appearing in dreams. Thus—the scientist is always interdependent with the social world. The social and intellectual tension of the scientist's environment is crucial for the ideas (Valsiner & van der Veer, 2000)—both for their creation, and for their abandonment. The latter is regulated through a system of social selection that is often based on current social norms of what constitutes appropriate scientific knowledge in the given area at the given time (Toomela, 2007). In terms of Thomas Kuhn—the "normal" and "revolutionary" streams of science are constantly in tense relations with one another—under the influence of course of history of the societies within which the scientists are embedded.

Baldwin's Context

The turn of the twentieth century was a fertile period for the sciences in the United States. The country was under the stress of rapid industrial development—linked with bursts of urbanization and immigration (Commager, 1950, chapter 2). The "American" and "non-American" histories of persons, languages, and ideas were in direct contact both in daily lives of ordinary people, and in the academic domain. Baldwin was at the center of world's philosophical and developmental discourse at his time—of course in his time that discourse was carried forth by few core people—his peers (like Charles S. Peirce, G. Stanley Hall, William James, John Dewey, and others)—whom we now easily consider "classic thinkers." Psychology had only recently emerged—from philosophy and physiology—as an independent area of science. Its roots in Germany were rather quickly imported into North America, where Baldwin was on the forefront in introduction of psychology laboratories in the New World. The backlash of the restoration of the socio-moral rigidity that rooted in the isolationism of the rural world in new (urbanized) form—called the "Progressive Movement" (Hofstadter, 1963) had not yet started. That period of rapid social transformations—followed by equally rapid counter-actions to curb growth—in the history of the United States set the stage for the social sciences for high productivity.[2]

Baldwin was the product of his time—when the curious geographically challenged label "American psychology" was not yet invented, and all of the developing new discipline was one around the World. By being that, of course, it was a European invention that sent young aspiring students from North America to study in Germany—and in German. They managed to bring back to the New World a discipline that could become transformed in the context of U.S. society into an "American version" over some decades (Dolby, 1977). Baldwin and his contemporaries—G.H. Mead, J. Royce, and others—were thinkers of no international boundaries. In fact, he (and others) were largely unwilling witnesses of the emergence of "the American way" in psychology—that of behaviorism.

Behaviorism was an artifact of the "Progressive Era"—with the increasing focus on control and prediction of the free flow of human conduct. As it grew on the basis of proliferation of the pragmatist philosophical lore (see Baldwin, 1904), it created a border of values that separated the first decades of psychology in the U.S. from the emergence of "American psychology."[3] From William James' will to believe (Valsiner, 2000) to our present day will to "measure" ever new kinds of psychological features of practical value and conceptual obscurity, pragmatism has had a deeply ideological and non-pragmatic impact on psychology in the U.S. Even today, pragmatism's major themes

> of evading epistemology-centered philosophy, accenting human powers, and transforming antiquated modes of social hierarchies in light of religious and/or ethical ideals makes it relevant and attractive. The distinctive appeal of American pragmatism in our post-modern moment is its unashamedly moral emphasis and its unequivocally ameliorative impulse. In this world-weary period of pervasive cynicisms, nihilisms, terrorisms, and possible extermination, there is a longing for norms and values that can make a difference, a yearning for principled resistance and struggle that can change our desperate plight (West, 1989, p. 4).

Baldwin was a generalist—and hence he did not find much value in the behaviorist ways of analyses of "objective" phenomena, criticizing that orientation for its reduction of psychological phenomena to biological levels. Looking back at his work and its social contexts, he was mildly sarcastic:

> Another theory popular in America, the country of intellectual fads and the worship of new words, is that of "behaviorism." It is a refined and, in itself, valuable recourse to the objective method proper to physiology and biology, of which, in fact, it forms a legitimate chapter… But it is not psychology; it is biology, and, at the best, physiology. To be available to the psychologist, its results must *be interpreted by introspection of the reagent; for none of the results of the method could be applied in psychology if we did not already know from the experience the conscious connotation of the terms used* (Baldwin, 1930, p. 29, emphasis added).

Baldwin's criticism of psychology's vulnerability to fashions—given in his autobiographical retrospect—paralleled that of Lev Vygotsky (van der Veer & Valsiner, 1991) and Karl Bühler (1927/1978). Fashions were—and are—dangerous for the development of ideas since they may eliminate productive emerging "idealings" not letting them to grow to maturity. In a way—fashions perform the social selection of thinking in the development of scientific ideas. Baldwin's own theory of development emphasized selection (Baldwin, 1898, 1902b, 1902c) makes an attitude of irreverence to fashions in science valuable.

The key idea thus lost from focus was that of the nature of the whole— and its relations with its parts. Clearly, the whole (water) is qualitatively different from hydrogen and oxygen[4]—hence it would make sense to undertake an "analysis-into-units" (rather than into elements) in psychology's methodological claims. Yet despite pointing this mismatch of levels in data and of phenomena out from time to time, psychology through the twentieth century continued to construct methods that unabashedly reduced complexity to its elementary constituents—without restoration of the whole. It is obvious that a score—be it "high" or "low"—on a scale of X (where X may be any of "neuroticism," "intelligence," "collectivism," etc.) does not re-create the psychological system that makes it possible for the person to act in ways describable as X.

Of course, there has always been a branch of psychological knowledge that has never reduced complexity to trivial elements—but rather attempted to maker sense of complex phenomena by reference to complex explanatory systems. Psychoanalysis has been built on complex process ideas that are fortified by historically maintained myths. Baldwin was also clear about the ambivalent role psychoanalysis played in psychology:

> Based on sometimes unreal and always extravagant presuppositions, as in the theory of the libido and in the interpretation of dreams, Freudism, nevertheless, is an instrument of some value when divorced from the applications made of it by the parlor psychologist and the charlatan.... The place of sound hypothesis is too often taken by wild analogy such as those drawn from sex, and instead of sober scientific interpretation we have fanciful inferences seen at their climax in the "Oedipus complex" and in the interpretation of dreams (Baldwin, 1930, pp. 28-29).

In his estimation of the sexual overemphasis in psychoanalysis, Baldwin could have found an ally in another dissenter within the movement—Carl Gustav Jung, who could not pass by without commenting wryly:

> Scientifically, the theory of infantile sexuality is of little value. It is all one to the caterpillar whether we say that it eats its leaf with ordinary pleasure or with sexual pleasure (Jung, 1966, p. 36).

The issue at stake here for science is general—where do its general ideas come from? What kind of abstracted generalizations—be these libido, causal determinacy by genes, or explanation of phenomena by reference to abstract processes (attachment, learning, cognitive computing, heuristics, etc.)—are usable for developmental science? The generalized concepts to which causality for development regularly becomes attributed are static causal entities, rather than generic dynamic process descriptions. Explaining away adult psychological phenomena by juvenile life events does not capture the processes of development—because of the constant feed-forward loops between the person and the social others.

The Personal Uniqueness of the Thoroughly Social Self

By personal uniqueness Baldwin proves the social nature of the self. At first moment this direction of thought may be counterintuitive—if we operate within the confines of the classical logic. Within that system of thought it would be impossible to accept statements "an individual is unique and not-unique at the same time." The person is either uniquely subjective being (and not social), or the person is a social being (and not unique and subjectivity-ridden). The declared opposites cannot be true at the same time.

Baldwin could transcend the limits of such static *ontology of being* either "unique" (individual) or "common" (social) by assuming a stance of *becoming*. The psychological uniqueness of each person is the proof of the social origins of the self that develops through relating with others:

> *a man is a social outcome rather than a social unit.* He is always in his greatest part, also some one else. Social acts of his—that is, acts which may not prove anti-social—are his *because they are society's first*; otherwise he would not have learned them nor have had any tendency to do them (Baldwin, 1897, p. 87).

Baldwin's consistently developmental perspective made it possible to reconcile the uniqueness of person—who imitates socially given models constructively—and the knowledge base of the *socii*. He evoked the image of a boomerang in the relations of the person and the society ("When he acts quite privately, it is always with a boomerang in his hand; and every use he makes of his weapon leaves its indelible impression both upon the other and upon him"—ibid, p. 88).

The notion of self-as-boomerang-thrower fits with the basic developmental ethos that Baldwin carries systematically through in all of his thinking. The self and the others continuously relate with one another, feeding forward into one another's individual development. According to Baldwin, such dialectic relation could de described like this:

> my thought of self is in the main, as to its character as a personal self, *filled up with my thought of others, distributed variously as individuals; and my thought of others, as persons, is mainly filled up with myself.* In other words ... the self and the alter are to our thought one and the same thing (Baldwin, 1897, p. 343, emphasis added).

Being "one and the same thing" is not an ontological statement of being—but a dynamic statement of directed movement. In order to "be myself" I "fill my thinking" with what "others" might—or do—think of me, and in return I communicate to them what I happen to think of them. The "boomerang of thought" is thrown towards the "alter" in order to return to myself—and the myriads of similar communicative "boomerangs" are thrown from all others towards me—only to return to their "throwers."

Based on his observations of the play of his own young children (Baldwin, 1895), and extrapolated to the abstract notion of "organic evolution" (Baldwin, 1902c), Baldwin's theory recognizes the reality of irreversible time that frames any notion of development. A developmental approach—similarly to any dynamic one—cannot be set up within an axiomatic system that excludes time. Yet the class of dynamic approaches can be built upon varied time concepts—including circular time. However, an inherently consistent developmental perspective is only possible on the basis of recognition of irreversible time. Such recognition creates very complex conceptual problems for developmental science. Baldwin's theoretical efforts can be considered to be the most elaborate—even if unsuccessful—efforts to address these problems over the past century.

Developmental Science and Genetic Logic

Baldwin understood the uselessness of importing the non-developmental notions of causality into the new "genetic [=developmental] science":

> We must be free from all constructions drawn from the strictly a-genetic sciences in which the causal sequence is the typical one. The birth of a new mode in the psychic life is a *"progression" from an earlier set of conditions, not the effect of these conditions viewed as cause*; and this is equally true of any new genetic mode, just so far as the series in which it appears is really genetic at all (Baldwin, 1906a, p. 29, emphasis added).

Baldwin was caught in-between the glorifiers of the expressivity of natural language for psychology and those who would prefer the precision of mathematics (Charles S. Peirce, for one). While recognizing the confusions coming from the common language, Baldwin was not ready to give in to full formalization either (cf. Baldwin, 1930, p. 26). Thus, in his presentation

> logic … may be applied to the processes of mind in general, all recognized as being parts of one's continuous movement. This had analogies in expressions already in

use, such as "logic of experience," logic of history" etc. *Genetic logic was, in my usage, the term adopted to designate the body inside or psychic process in which mental development takes place. Within this logic, all the varied special motives of adaptation, opposition, assimilation, etc. uncovered in the detailed researches, show themselves in the phenomena of personal and social progress* (Baldwin, 1930, pp. 11-12, emphasis added).

In his system—published in three volumes of *Thought and Things* and the fourth—*Genetic Theory of Reality*—he addressed questions of three kinds of logic: *functional logic*—operations of the mind in concrete terms (Baldwin, 1906), *experimental logic* (Baldwin, 1908)—laws in discursive operations in thought, and *reality-logic* (*Logique réal* - Baldwin, 1911). The reality-logic (or real logic) included his treatise of genetic epistemology (Baldwin, 1911) and genetic morphology (Baldwin, 1915). The four-volume *oeuvre* was originally meant to be published in French,[5] yet the English publishers managed to get ahead in their production of the book.

Baldwin's focus in logic

consists essentially in the *experimental* erection of an object already made up in consciousness, and its treatment as having a meaning or value which *it has not yet been found to have*, with the expectation and intent that in the result it may be found to have it (Baldwin, 1908a, p. 4).

Thus, the cognitive activity entailed in the logic is oriented towards further construction of meanings. He made a conscientious effort to re-define many of the crucial terms of classical logic (e.g., disjunction, proposition, implication, inductive and deductive inference; Baldwin, 1908). Nevertheless, his elaboration of logical concepts can be seen as a frivolous step in the area of language philosophy, and is not well connected with the foundations of genetic logic.

Genetic logic for Baldwin implied the study of emergence, rules of use in bringing by further emergence, of meanings. In this respect, Baldwin's "genetic logic" can be viewed—in our time—as an effort to develop a system of developmental semiotics. The centrality of schemas—existing generalized meanings—and their application towards the possible future state through imagery of feeling-into the present-moving-towards-future were the core of Baldwin's theory. He was closely connected with the semiotics of Charles S. Peirce—particularly in their joint wok on the *Dictionary of Philosophy and Psychology* (1901-1906). The principles of development that were elaborated by Baldwin in this work in the 1890s (and laid the foundation of the "organic selection" theory of evolution), were taken and applied to the realm of the philosophy of language in general, and of language use in particular. Any general system of such a kind needed explicit basic axioms.

Axioms and Postulates of the Genetic Science

Baldwin formulated four "axioms" of genetic science (1902, p. 323; 1906a, p. 20), which fortified the irreducibility of the developmentally more complex phenomena to their preceding (less complex) counterparts. This effort can be viewed as a counter-action to the reductionist habits that were coming into vogue at his time.

The first two axioms deal with the relation of levels:

> [Axiom 1]. [T]he phenomena of science at each higher level show a form of synthesis that is not accounted for by the formulations which are adequate for the phenomena of the next lower level. ["Lower" here denotes a developmental antecedent, "higher" an emerging subsequent.]

> [Axiom 2]. [T]he formulations of any lower science are not invalidated in the next higher, even in cases in which new formulations are necessary for the formal synthesis which characterizes the genetic mode of the higher.

Axioms 1 and 2 specify the non-reducibility of the newly emergent levels to the previous ones. They also specify the continuing viability of the previously existing levels, after the novel level has emerged. This "vertical decalage" (as later emphasized by Jean Piaget) guarantees the range of adaptability of the organism.

For example—consciousness of *Homo sapiens* is an emergent new level of phenomena that cannot be explained by reducing it to physiological principles that governed the functioning of the nervous systems of pre-human species. Consciousness requires explanation in terms of its own principles, even as the phenomenon itself is an outgrowth from the previous ("lower") physiologically regulated processes. These "lower" levels remain in their full function, providing support for the new "higher" ones—yet do not determine the latter. The new level of explanation—which fits consciousness—does not invalidate the physiological mechanisms that keep regulating the continuously existing "lower" processes.

In Axiom 3, Baldwin restricted the use of analogies:

> [Axiom 3]. [T]he generalizations and classifications of each science, representing a particular genetic mode, are peculiar to that mode and cannot be constructed in analogy to, or *a fortiori* on the basis of, the corresponding generalizations or classifications of the lower mode.

Axiom 3 restricts the transferability of scientific models by way of analogy. It is consistent with the other axioms—if each new level of phenomena is new, unique emergent, then surely a model that fits that uniqueness is not transferable to other phenomena (and levels) merely on the basis of analogy. Rather, the principles (the models) need to be constructed from the study of the emergent phenomena themselves (Axiom 4).

> [Axiom 4]. [N]o formula for progress from mode to mode, that is, no *strictly genetic* formula in evolution or in development, is possible except by direct observation of the facts of the series which the formulation aims to cover or by the interpretation of other series which represent the same or parallel modes (Baldwin, 1906, p. 20).

Following these axioms, specific elaborations of the methodology of the developmental science were in order. Baldwin specified two "postulates of method." It is here that his full interest in development comes through.

Postulates for Developmental Science

The first (or "negative") postulate emphasized the irreversibility of time in development:

> *the logic of genesis is not expressed in convertible propositions.* Genetically, A = (that is, *becomes,* for which the sign ((is now used) B; but it does not follow that B = (becomes, (( ) A (Baldwin, 1906, p. 21).

The first postulate specifies the realm of possible relations that are allowable among the formulae of "genetic logic"—namely, each proposition includes a temporal directionality vector. Thus, the reversal (i.e., B ((A) is not implied by the notion of A becoming B. If we were to use a better-known terminology (of Piaget's talk about operations), Baldwin's genetic logic is set up using non-operational terminology. Thus, the issue of thinking at the level of "concrete" or "formal" operations (in Piaget's sense) is not part of Baldwin's logic.[6] The symmetry of transformation between A and B is broken by the irreversibility of time, and of the very transformation. Contemporary tense logic operates with notions *before* and *after*—but not with notions of *becoming*.

The second (so-called "positive") postulate was given as:

> that series of events is truly genetic which cannot be constructed before it has happened, and which cannot be exhausted backwards, after it has happened (Baldwin, 1906, p. 21).

The "positive" nature of this postulate is in its focusing of the study of development on that of the unfolding novel processes, rather than their prediction, or retrospective explanation. The phenomena of emergence, becoming, and transformation become the objects of investigation. This fitted well with what was to come in the 1920s—the invention of the

Aktualgenese (or microgenesis) orientations (Ipsen, 1926; Sander, 1927; Werner, 1927) and reaches into our times in new versions of semiotic microgenesis (Abbey and Diriwächter, 2008). Such investigation would entail preserving the irreversible time sequence in the data, and analyses of events of synthesis of novelty within these processes.

Baldwin's "Canons" and "Postulates of Method"

Baldwin's "canons" were expected to "regulate the method," especially in the sense of the avoidance of "fallacies," which were set up as counter-points to each of the given canons. By creating such dialectical opposites, Baldwin could map out his developmental perspective on the background of the regular non-developmental one.

> Canon of *Continuity*. All psychic process is continuous. The fallacy of discontinuity "consists in treating of any psychic event as *de novo*, or as arising in a discontinuous series" (Baldwin, 1906, p. 23).

Baldwin had a biological scenario of his time in mind—that of "divergence" of change. Continuity is the basis for development—the arena that enables the emergence of novelty. No novelty is emerging on an empty place.

Canon of *Progression*. All psychic process is genetic, not a-genetic, expressed by the formula A becomes B whether or not it is ever true that B becomes A. The birth of a new mode (B) is a progression from the previous state (A), which entails specific conditions. However, the latter are not "causes" for the new mode (B), causality is a way of discussing phenomena that is fit for a-genetic sciences. The opposite Fallacy of Composition (or "cause and effect" fallacy)

> "consists in treating a psychic event as compounded or made up of or caused by other psychic events: so the fallacy of treating the sensation purple as made up of the sensations blue and red, or as caused by them" (Baldwin, 1906a, p. 23).

In this canon, the contrast between developmental phenomena (which operate in irreversible time, hence the reversal of development—B → A—is not possible), and non-developmental phenomena (where one can, time-freely, assume reversibility of A → B and B → A) is played out. In the case of dynamic, organismic processes, the developing novel state cannot be reduced to causes which are conditions of the immediate past. Neither can the complexity of the new state be reduced to elementaristic causes. Baldwin here opened the door for a theoretical system where discussion about specific (independent) causes is replaced by analysis of the process of emergence (of B from the set of conditions A).

Canon of *Quality*. Every psychic event is qualitatively different from, not equal to, the next antecedent and the next succeeding event and also from its own earlier or later case. This canon emphasizes the constant emergence of novelty within the developmental process. If a developmental series of events entails a sequence of A → B → C, then there exists a qualitative difference not only between A and B and B and C, but also within each of the states (A, B, C—i.e., the formulation of difference "also from its own earlier or later case"). The fallacy of this canon—"Fallacy of Equality"—entails treating any two psychic events as equal, or any one as identical with itself when repeated.

The Canon of Quality brings the uniqueness of the lived-through psychological events to the core of method construction for developmental science. Any aggregation of similar events over time and space constitutes a captivation by the Fallacy of Equality. If such aggregation is accomplished, it leads to the construction of a fuzzy category of similarity, which cannot be interpreted as that of sameness. There is no sameness (other than our mentally constructed illusion) in the world of developmental phenomena, and all similarity is of a fuzzy kind. That aspect of human living is frequently forgotten (Sovran, 1992).

Modal Relevancy. No psychic event can be taken out of its mode and treated as belonging in or with events of another mode. This is opposed by the Fallacy of Modal Confusion, i.e., treating an event or meaning characteristic of one mode as remaining what it was, when it is used in a synthesis of another mode.

Modal Unity. No psychic event or meaning can be treated as being what it is except in the entire context of the mode in which it arises. Here the context-specificity of development is emphasized: any developmental event emerges only in the given context, and none other. The opposing Fallacy of Division or Abstraction consists of treating an event or meaning as a static and separable "element" or "unit."

Through the modal unity canon, Baldwin attempted to keep the research effort focused on the unique psychological phenomena united with their context of emergence. In each unique phenomenon—when observed—we arrive at some generalization already through the very act of reflection. Our reflection upon us in action moves us away from that very action.

Actuality. No psychic event is present unless it be actual. A corollary from this Canon requires us to identify first the clear and unambiguous case, rather than the "first case" at which the given state can be said to have evolved in some minimalist form. According to Baldwin, this canon

checks the rage for the "simplification" of what in its concrete occurrence is rich with shadings of complex meaning (Baldwin, 1906, p. 24).

A fallacy of this canon (Fallacy of the Implicit or Potential) consists of treating something as implicitly or potentially present when it is not actual (e.g., claiming that implicit logical processes are present in the pre-logical mode of thinking, or the "potential self" is present in the impersonal mode of thought). The focus here is on being present, as contrasted with becoming. Thus, if a psychologist claims that "intelligence" is implicitly present in a child who fails to solve a given mental task (e.g., as implied by "production deficiency"), then this kind of a statement exemplifies the fallacy. If, instead, a claim is made that "intelligence" emerges from the failures to solve a problem, then the canon is upheld (since talking of emergence does not entail projection of a hidden ontological state onto the present phenomenon).

> *Revision.* No psychic event or meaning is to be treated as original or unrevised except in its first appearance, since its reappearance may be in a mode in which it is essentially revised. This canon is another way to emphasize the uniqueness of each observable phenomenon. Its fallacy—that of Consistency—consists of holding the psychic process to any consistency *except what it shows*.

Baldwin's Epistemological Goals

Baldwin's formulation of the canons of the method was an effort to overcome the tendencies that existed in his contemporary sciences to reduce all phenomena to static, causal explanatory entities. Thus, he claimed:

> We have all been hypnotized by the thought of cause of the type of impact, transfer of energy fixed in quantity, with a formulation of effect in terms of an equation... We are told that nothing can be in the effect that is not already in the cause. All this is a partial and forced interpretation of nature. If science deals only with such causation series, then the great body of what we may in the large case call, "conditioning," or "sequence," remains uninterpreted. The Adaptations, Growths, Novelties, in nature are as much in evidence to the scientific observer as are the Identities, Conservations, and Effects....
>
> The genetic progression recognizes *all the characters* of the event, allows the causal interpretation as an abstraction, but attempts to reconstitute nature in the fullness of her processes of change from the mode that conditions to a richer mode... that succeeds[7]. The psychology that does not do this makes a fetish of physics, and sells her birthright for a mess of pottage (Baldwin, 1906a, p. 25).

This direction of Baldwin's thought antedates our contemporary focus on emergence, and of biological transformation (e.g., Beloussov, 1998). The abstraction notion of causality is a tool for looking at the complex dynamics of real—cyclical and hyper-cyclical—developmental processes. From abstractions like "genes and environment cause our functioning" or even from Kurt Lewin's general scheme B= f (P, E) we are led to not merely repeating the obviously true general statements as if considering them causal, but to the investigation of the particular. The abstracted models of processes that regulate the co-production of concrete examples of human lives are our target of investigation—"attempts *to reconstitute nature in the fullness of her processes* of change." What is at stake is the question of "*how does* it (development) happen?" rather than "*how much* of it is caused y A—'*nature*'—or B—'*nurture*'?"

Baldwin's preservation of developmental processes is evident in the case of each canon. Thus, instead of viewing an event as without predecessors he insists upon its continuity with previous states (Canon of Continuity), while the continuity entails constant transformation of the state of the event (Canon of Revision). This state of affairs is brought about by irreversibility of developmental processes (Canon of Progression), and that entails transformation of the qualitative re-organization of the events (synthesis; Canon of Quality). Finally, all the uniqueness of developmental psychic events is context-bound: hence, Baldwin demands that scientific analysis maintain the linkages with the context (Canon of Modal Relevancy) and is not transposed to another context (Canon of Modal Unity).

The difficulty of developmental logic is the need to make the *processes of synthesis* explicit. The issue of synthesis was crucial in Baldwin's times—it was part of the notion of "growing Gestalts" (Ehrenfels, 1890/1988) as well as in Wilhelm Wundt's and Felix Krueger's *foci* in the two "Leipzig Schools" (Abbey and Diriwächter, 2008). The demonstration of the actual ideational synthesis moments—the *Aha Erlebnis* as documented by Karl Bühler (1908/1951) showed the reality of synthesis within the stream of consciousness. On the side of "higher psychological processes," the philosophers and psychologists of the time paid serious attention to experiences of art, and of religious sentiments.

Singular phenomena and community of experience. Any developmental logic has to face the difficult problem of referential generalizability. In principle (given the irreversibility of time) each and every particular phenomenon can occur only once, in its absolute individual uniqueness. Nevertheless, any general formal system needs to refer to phenomena in general, as the general laws for the phenomena transcend each and every special occasion. This generalization is in some way performed by any user of language in everyday contexts, as well as by scientists in their categorization of phenomena. Yet that generalization occurs within the mental construction by a person. In order to obtain understandability it needs to be communicated to others.

Baldwin formulated two principles:

identity of indiscernibles—"in the absence of discernible difference, two or more objects are judged to be one and the same recurrent experience.... [W]e have here the process of individuating as one, objects which do not give experience of difference."

difference of discernibles—"A single object is rendered, by reason of differences discerned in its several appearances, as more than one" (Baldwin, 1907, p. 399).

The making of the "identity of indiscernibles" as a regular feature of our meaning construction has been demonstrated clearly by Sovran (1992). Different strategies here may lead to different results, as Baldwin himself described:

A paranoic declares that everybody is persecuting him, because he generalizes recurrent experiences as all fit to excite his fear of others; he is working under the principle of "identity of indiscernibles." At the other extreme we may cite the individual we call "subjective," who sees always in our conduct, however uniformly kind, new and varied signs of change. He in turn is magnifying the "difference of discernibles" (Baldwin, 1907, p. 400).

We regularly create similarity classes (crisp sets) or experiences that are always in some sense novel—yet recognizably belong to the same class (which is a fuzzy set). Through such "defuzzification" our common sense gets rid of the excessive recognition of temporal instabilities of the stream of experience.

The process of generalization operates at the opposition between the identity and difference principles, always moving away from the absolute objectivity of being (i.e., that of the singulars as such). As Baldwin pointed out, human language provides its users vehicles to assist the generalization in either directions. With language, knowledge becomes relational and communicable. Fuzzy quantifiers are always available to create indeterminate (yet realistic) reflections upon the reality:

"This woman is always vain" is a universal in appearance; it is quantified in community; just as "women are always vain," equivalent to "all women are vain," has universal quantity in extension. Proposition in "sometimes" are particular in community (as "this woman is sometimes vain") or in extension (as "women are sometimes vain") or in both (as "some women are sometimes vain") (Baldwin, 1907, p. 400).

A critical issue in Baldwin's conceptualization of sameness of phenomena lies in the equalization of intra-personal and inter-personal spheres of application of the principles described above. In order to detect "sameness" of A and A, the opposite comparison (A with non-A) must be possible. If we cannot make a distinction A *versus* non-A, then detection of "sameness" of "this A" and "that A" is logically impossible. Thus, he claimed:

> The process whereby the meaning of "sameness" attaches to an object is the same whether the recurrences of the meaning thus identified as the same be in one mind or in more; for there is either actual reference [or: conversion] or the presupposition of it, from one experience to another in both cases alike.... [A] judgment of singular identity is possible on the basis of a single person's recurrent experience; and ... it is a judgment in community, having the force of commonness for all thinkers alike (Baldwin, 1907, p. 397).

The adaptation of organisms to irreversible flow of lifetime guarantees the active move by organisms into the making of novelty—and comparisons of the novelty with the previously existing. This simple idea was at the root of the "organic selection" theory. The phenomenological basis for seeing the relevance of the detected "non-sameness" in biological life was his observation of children's play (Baldwin, 1895) and—later—his treatment of the aesthetic experience in art.

Sembling through Play

In play, children rise beyond their current developmental level and create their own "zone of proximal development." In terms of implication for thinking, play (and its intra-psychological parallel—imagination) allows for different ways of combination of materials—unification of opposites making of third classes (beyond "A vs. non-A"). Play is constructed without end—an earlier form becomes substituted by new ones.

Baldwin was an ardent observer of children's play—feeling into it as a parent, and observing how the children—his own two daughters—feel into the socially organized environment of their own. Language is our main—but not the only—way of inquiry, that unites the personal with the social. Language is a

> testimony to the *falsity of any individualistic theory of thought*. Thought must be social in order to be adequately personal.... [L]anguage summarizes and demonstrates this necessity (Baldwin, 1908a, p. 167).

In order to know, one has to explore—into the meanings of the others as these refer to commonly shared objects. Thus, *feeling into* the other—where the interiors of the other's mind are never known—occurs through the reference to objects that can be socially referenced.[8]

By the end of the nineteenth century, the notion of *Einfühlung* was developed in the context of German aesthetic philosophy from where it moved into psychology (Groos, 1902; Lipps, 1903; Witasek, 1901—see Pigman, 1995 on the history of the concept). Baldwin warned his readers that his affective logic "is distinctively French in its origin, as the theory of 'Einfühlung,' also accepted and utilized in its fundamental meaning, is distinctively German" (Baldwin, 1911, p. x). It was clear for Baldwin that imagery, fantasy, and *Einfühlung* ("sembling") play the crucial role in human development. Every object that a person encounters is

> either one of knowledge, recognized as part of the actual, the external, the true; or it is one of assumption, "semblance," or make-believe, one to be toyed with, "sembled" or *Eingefühlt*, one to get satisfaction from, to image for personal purposes and selective handling (Baldwin, 1911, p. 4).

For Baldwin, sembling entailed the person's establishing inner control over the object by way of persistent imitation—the ideational experimenting with the potential properties of the object (Baldwin, 1906a, p. 122). In general terms,

> the process of Sembling consists in the reading-into the object a sort of psychic life of its own, in such a way that the movement, act, or character by which it is interpreted *is thought of as springing from its own inner life* (Baldwin, 1906a, p. 124, emphasis added).

By "feeling into" the other the projection of the affective contents into the other is taking place—the person feels *as if* the other "possesses" the characteristics that the feeler-in assigns to the other. This is the personal act of the construction of the other in the social universe—"inserting" meaning "into" the other. In a way, it is a highly functional "attribution error" that becomes a crucial moment in the development of the social relations through shared make-belief conditions.

The act of sembling works for the sembler. When exploring an object—and inserting meaning into it—the person sets that object up to be put into some constructed, desired imaginary role, and leads to the establishment of its internalized counterpart—the schema:

> The semblant or make-believe use of an object having merely inner character as image or fancy, whereby it is treated for playful or other personal purposes as having further meaning or reference. The object thus becomes a "scheme," a *Schema*, charged with further meaning which it has not as yet been found in its own right (Baldwin, 1908a, p. 5).

Thus, the actual thing, passes into the instrumental image, becoming a mere "schema" of the further intent read in and through it, to be again "tried-on" in the actual struggle with the world. (Baldwin, 1911, p. 6). The result is a never-ending forward-oriented construction cycle where established schemas lead to new created roles for new objects of exploration, while the latter lead to establishment of ever new schemas.

The dialectics of personal development requires the **self ←→ other** op-
positions consistently and persistently.

Syndoxic and Synnomic Orientations

Baldwin introduced his specific terms "syndoxic" and "synnomic" to
characterize the process of relations between inter-individually coordi-
nated and intra-individually uniquely reconstructed meanings. Within the
field of socially promoted (syndoxic) "truths and usages," the developing
person establishes his or her exploratory (i.e., experimenting) relationship with some sub-areas of that field, within which the constructive
internalization of the syndoxic, by transforming it into the synnomic,
then takes place. Nevertheless, the loci of these regions of personal
experimentation are themselves dependent upon the syndoxic field, and
effectively set up by it.

For instance, a person may be guided to establish a completely idiosyn-
cratic (maximally synnomic) way of thinking about the political system
of the given country, yet the very same person would never question his
or her own patriotic feelings towards the country as a whole (accepting
the syndoxic). The possibility for such "split" is natural given the socially
interdependent nature of the self and the other. It becomes visible in the
context of interaction with others—through application of self/other
separation (let us call it *hetero-synnomicity*) about assumptions. Consider
Baldwin's example:

> [W]hen I say "I believe my grandfather's ghost to exist, but I don't expect you to
> believe it," it is the second clause that asserts the privacy of the meaning. This second
> clause may express either two meanings: the one, "the evidence would not convince
> you," which removes the presupposition of a control sphere from my own belief; the
> other, "this is not a matter of evidence, but of personal acceptance," which in turn
> makes the meaning one of selective force. Fully stated the two meanings are, (1) I
> accept this ghost, but not as a case of a class of which you might also find an illustra-
> tion of your acceptance… and (2) I accept the ghost because I elect to—because it
> satisfies my interest and purpose so to do (Baldwin, 1908a, p.66).

The self and the other are linked—but not fused. The boundaries of
what the self considers not part of the other's context are made as the
communicative efforts proceed. Baldwin's focus on the functional role
of construction of meanings led him to the formulation of a schema notion—a syndoxic pattern—as an extension of an image—a synnomic one.
The image "must be treated *as if* it held, in order to find out *whether* it
holds" (Baldwin, 1908a, p. 83).

The construction of possibility of the future—through play or imagination—creates for Baldwin the need to transcend Aristotle's "law of

excluded middle"—the cornerstone of classical logic. The foundations for thinking—and any rules that govern that thinking—are in the person's constant movement of what is (=what is made to be, by creating a given meaning), towards what-is-not-yet. This focus got a coverage about hundred years later—in temporal logic (Anisov, 2002, 2004). The future and the past differ in their structure—the past is an outcome of uncertainties, while the future is characterized by uncertainties.

The *past and the future are not symmetric* (Figure 1). All the possibilities that existed in the past (when that time period was still future) have been turned into actualities (which are singular). In contrast, while facing the future, the possibilities are open. This structural asymmetry of the classes of past (occurred) events (given without their context of those possibilities that were there in the past, but were not used), and future (potential) events. It leads scientists to probabilistic predictions of the actualization of the future potentials into the continuous past. Yet precisely because of the past—as a sequence of resolved uncertainties—it is impossible to predict the ways in which future potentialities are being turned into actualities. This temporal-logical condition gives substance to Baldwin's "positive" and "negative" postulates, eliminates the utility of frequentist practices of probability calculations,[10] and requires the open-endedness[11] of the future development.

Affective Logic in Contrast with Rational Cognition

Baldwin was eager to solve the problem of relations between human affective and rational sides. He was eager to look at processes of affective generalization, ejection, and idealization (as parts of the affective processes) in relation to their rational-logical counterparts:

> Affective logic is a process proceeding by the mediation of ends through means; *its result is always in the domain of an interest or value.* On the other hand, that of cognition is in the domain of truth. But there are all sorts of criss-crossings and interferences between the two, the process of truth-seeking rarely being free of influence from the tendencies of feeling and interest which assert themselves when most unexpected. *Here the "will to believe" shows itself actively, by the intrusion of interest; it finds value at the end of a process which claims to issue solely in the establishment of truth* (Baldwin, 1930, p. 18, emphases added).

Baldwin's dialogue here is with William James' pragmatism—taken to the extreme in the manifesto of "the will to believe"[12] (James, 1896, 1979, see also Valsiner, 2000). By recognizing the inevitable nature of the affective side of human beings to be the framework of the rational side—"interest" intrudes the cognition to undermine its movement to

Figure 1

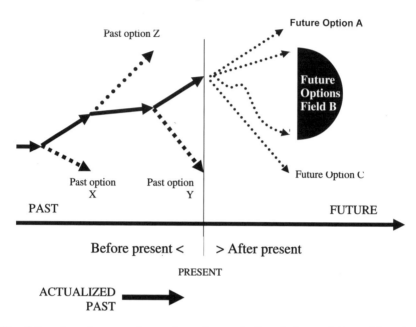

"truth" and produce another value—instead of truth (or—claims of "truth of X" are values-laden)—Baldwin antedates the invention of "cognitive heuristics" in the 1970s.

Affective processes are teleological, i.e., they express desired values and beliefs in ways that relate the presently established belief with one desired for the future, or that are simply considered true. This teleology can occur through processes of affective generalization, ejection, and idealization affective generalization entails the distribution of a particularly established emotional tone from the object (or context) of its original emergence, to other objects (and contexts). This process is complemented by ejection:

> "the self ... embodied in ... mass of general interests, ejects itself semblantly or imaginatively into other selves, and so establishes meanings of common interest, conformity and practice" (Baldwin, 1911, p. 94).

Thus—a person is social not by way of "succumbing" to "social influences" from outside, but by actively feeling into the "social others" on the basis of one's own affective understanding of the world. It involves idealization—which is a by-product of constructive internalization. In the process of establishing personal meanings of objects, the object becomes "charged with further unfulfilled meaning" (Baldwin, 1906a, p. 233).

Persons always create ideal meanings of objects, aside from—and on the basis of—their commonly shared meanings. These ideal meanings orient the person in relation to the given object, as well as to other objects:

> the ideal meaning resides (1) in the objects constructed out of certain materials—these materials... *not allowing any construction which does not have something of the ideal meaning*—and (2) in the treatment of other materials in the same way, that is, *as if they also had the characters which normally take on this meaning* (Baldwin, 1906a, p. 235).

The person establishes an idealized view of one object in his or her encounters with it, and then transfers it to further encounters with other objects. In its function, the idealized meaning limits the set of possible affective relations to these objects. It serves as the mediating device that imbalances any equally-valenced disjunctive situation ("X is equally either Y or Z"), turning it into a case of affective dismissal of one of the options ("X *must be* Y, even if it can be both Y or Z").

Logical Operations within Developmental Realities

Baldwin emphasized that affective logic is closely intertwined with the cognitive logic, at the level of particular content-filled versions of those operations. Baldwin's elaboration of the operation of disjunction illustrates that connection very well:

> We customarily say, "It is this or that," meaning "It may be this, <u>but is probably that</u>"; and often also, "It may be either of these, <u>I have no means of deciding</u>"; and sometimes, again, "It may be that, <u>but let us try this</u>." While, that is, the circle of determinateness closes around the entire group of alternatives, it does not in just the same sense hold aloof from each of them. On the contrary, *it has its points of emphasis, its selections, its preferences, due to the attitude—the selective interest, the dispositional character, etc.,—of the thinker*. Some disjunctions should read, "It may be that, <u>but I hope it is this</u>" (Baldwin, 1908a, p. 50, italics emphases added).

The subjective future-orientation, as well as personal volition at the given time ("let's try this" and "I hope it is this") link the affective and cognitive sides in the logical form of disjunction. In reality, Baldwin's efforts to elaborate logical terms amounted to construction of a synthetic philosophy of language (on the basis of schemata of the classical logic), where the meanings entered into logical forms have both representational semantic structure, and personal-desire or -preference quality.

Baldwin's *Genetic Logic* in the Context of Development of Logics

Why was Baldwin framing his theoretical synthesis in terms of logic? At his time the "gold standard" of science was classical logic—Aristotelian as explicated by George Boole in mid-nineteenth century and for-malized by Gottlob Frege in the 1870s. The rigor of logical thinking was viewed as cornerstone for *Wissenschaft*—yet as in any growing science the top-down normativeness of classical logic was found unproductive. New formal systems emerged—and logic became increasingly emulated by mathematics, moving away from philosophy. It was precisely at Baldwin's creative high times—1900s to 1915—that logic was moving into new domains of inquiry.

Baldwin's work has been tied with a number of streams of thought in philosophy and logics of his time. His intention was to develop a logic—a developmental logic—that would be the basis for developmental science. A century later we still do not have such logic—and we attempt at times to re-establish developmental science in the middle of our contemporary a-theoretical, non-mathematical,[13] and hyper-empiricistic child psy-chology (e.g., Carolina Consortium on Human Development, 1996). In some sense, Baldwin has failed—or maybe we all have, overlooking his generalizing quest.

Development of logic has also bypassed Baldwin's efforts over the twentieth century. In these past hundred years, logic as a framework of thinking has gradually moved from the realm of philosophy to that of mathematics (Betti, 2002; Karpenko, 2000). It has become fragmented into a myriad of different systems of logics—where a particular key idea is taken to develop a set of axioms. Most of the effort has gone to the deductive work proving different theorems—rather than map the formalized system onto the functioning of human beings in their minds and activity contexts. Table 1 is an attempt to locate Baldwin's thinking about "genetic logic" on a general mindscape of various logics.

The move of logics from philosophy to mathematics seems to follow a general line of gaining freedom from the prescriptive limits of the static dominant forms of the classical Aristotelian logic, and branching off to a variety of new formal systems that capture one or another specific aspect of human thought. First—in the 1910s-1920s—we see the move to tran-scend the "law of excluded middle" and open the door to the development of multi-valued logics. Jan Lukasiewicz's revolution of transcending Aristotle's bi-valent logic and allowing for the "third, indeterminate" truth value led the way. Yet the acceptance of the "indeterminate third" did not open the way to developmental logic—since the "law of excluded fourth" was in place, limiting the horizon for further development.

Baldwin's developmental perspective needed this "third zone"—in-determinacy—in conjunction with development (cf. Baldwin's "second postulate," above). It can be claimed that Baldwin de facto developed the notion of multi-valued logic at least in parallel with Lukasiewicz, if not before.[14] Yet Baldwin needed to move quickly beyond the basic idea of multi-valued logic—which in Lukasiewicz's version remained static. Multi-valued logics since the 1920s have not provided a logical system that captures development—as their axiomata do not allow that.

In Baldwin's developmental scheme, the triadic system *{A that was}—{no more A but not yet non-A}—{non-A that could be}* necessarily requires the abandonment of the "law of excluded middle." So far it concurs with multi-valued logics. However, that was not sufficient—he had to integrate the notion of temporal logic into his multi-valued scheme. There was no version of a logic that would take time into account available in Baldwin's time The temporality of human thinking did not escape the attention of logicians either. The *tense logic* (Prior, 1957, 1967) brought the temporality into the center of attention.

In tense logic the truth value of a statement varies by different times. At the moment "now" the previous state of affairs no longer exists—while the one to come does not yet exist (Anisov, 2002, p. 7). While a statement "it was raining yesterday" can be bi-valent (either true or false), the statement "it will rain tomorrow" is indeterminate. This is guaranteed by the difference between the time structures:

> In the branching time structure the past has no alternatives, however, there are a lot of ways of a realization of the future. Alternative possibilities of a realization of the future are called possible futures. However, usually we assume, that among all possible futures only one is realized (Surowik, 2002, p. 91).

By breaking the symmetry of time, logics in the twentieth century opened the door to consider the regularities of human thought about what is not yet—but could, and even should (ought) to be. The system of *deontic logic* (Mally, 1926; von Wright, 1951, 1981) was to be the logic of obligations—and thus transcended the world of "as is" to that of "as-it-ought-to be."

It could be claimed that the invention of the deontic logic was a result of Mally's intellectual heritage within the tradition of Alexius Meinong, together with the impacts of World War I and its aftermath where questions of ethics (the "ought") became emphasized in the wider societal discourses in Europe. Mally sought to formalize a "pure ethic"—yet he was not interested in what such ethic may imply for action. Rather, he tried to capture the "state of affairs" in their a-temporal and non-actional senses. Yet—when taken to its limits—a*ny deontic logic presupposes*

Table 1
Historical contexts of logics for Baldwin's "genetic logic"

Time period	Kind of Logic	Basic features
< 1880s	Classical (**Aristotelian Logic**) with elaborations by George Boole and Gottlob Frege	strict acceptance of the Law of Excluded Middle ("if A then not non-A")
	Hegel's philosophy	notion of dialectics in thinking
1860s-1900s	Emergence of C.S, Peirce's **Semiotic logic**	triadic system where **"the interpretant"** grants constant openness to novelty
1890s-1915	Baldwin's "Genetic logic" under construction	rejects Law of Excluded Middle introduces temporality introduces value unity of opposites pancalist synthesis
1910-1913	Whitehead and Russell's *Principia Mathematica*	
1910-1920	Lukasiewicz introduces **Multi-valued logic** Lewes introduces **Modal logic**	rejects Law of Excluded Middle accepts multiple states between "true" and "false" focus on possibilities (**"A could be X"** rather than **"A is X"**)
	Intuitionist logic (Brouwer)	Law of Excluded Middle rejected in strict form Instead: "A **if and only if** not { non-A}"
1920-1930	Mally formalizes **Deontic logic**	introduces value by emphasis on "ought"
1927-1945	Nishida develops *zettai munjunteki jikodoitsu*	logic of dynamically united opposites that lead to hyper-generalized *nothingness*
1937-1960s	Black and Zadeh Introduce **Fuzzy logic**	introduce idea of inherently vague nature of the world
1960s-2000	temporal logics Introduced— Prior's **Tense logic**, Burgess' and Anisov's **Temporal logic**	past/future distinction central, future is not isomorphic with the past but branches off with uncertainty
1980-1990s	Herbst (1995) develops **Co-genetic logic**	formalized developmental logic parallel to Baldwin's
2006	Foundations for **Ambivalence logic** (Rudolph, 2006a, b,c)	emphasis on unity of opposites as the basis for psychological functions

temporality—tense logic—as any statement of moral or evaluative kind is oriented towards future possibilities (Thomason, 1981).

Baldwin (1906a, 1908a, 1911, 1915) antedated Ernst Mally (1926—see also Zecha, 2001) in the invention of *deontic logic*[15]—in dialogue with their common roots. All through *Thought and Things* the reader can find footnotes referencing different aspects of Meinong's *Gegenstandstheorie*. Last—but not least—the inclusion of *things* in the main title of the three-volume book—alongside with thought—can be seen as a dialogue with Meinong (cf. Baldwin, 1906, p. viii) whose conceptualization was non-developmental in its core, yet abstractive in its intention.[16] The questions of "ought"—seen developmentally, in terms of actions, were very much in Baldwin's mind when he created his genetic logic. Hence it may be adequate to see Baldwin as one of the co-founders of deontic logic.

In all of the systems of logic covered here—multi-valued, tense, and deontic—the terms used are assumed to be precise. Even the notion of "indeterminate" is taken in its precise form—as a third counterpart to "true" and "false." There is no possibility that the meaning of "true" smoothly—without qualitative breaking point—"moves into" the state of "indeterminate" (nor from "indeterminate" to "false." The crisp categorization is pre-given, even if at times indeterminate. Such way of categorization may be a means for our cognitive economy in dealing with the world—but need not reflect the world itself. Since 1937 our contemporary world views have had a place for thought systems that accept the inherent vagueness of reality (Black, 1937). The "fuzzy set theory" of Lofti Zadeh, developed in the mid-1960s, has led to the challenge to our world view to accept inherent vagueness, and to develop a new version of *fuzzy logic* (Rosenthal, 2004).

However—all these features of logics—fuzzy inherent nature of terms, temporal conditionality of truth or falseness, and the multi-valued nature of the range "true"-"false"—lack the focus on development. In general, the "kidnapping" of logics from the realm of philosophy by mathematics and making the different logics into highly formalized mathematical systems may have brought with it increasing impossibility of looking at time-dependent phenomena of change and development. In existing mathematics, "temporal factors do not intrude" (Burgess, 1979, p. 566)—yet in all biological, psychological, and social sciences they not only do "intrude," *but such "intrusion" is the central feature of any kind of general logics of development.* Baldwin understood that acutely in the beginning of the twentieth century. Very few efforts to follow can be found (van Haaften, 1998).

A consistently developmental logic would require explicit coverage of qualitative transformation of form—in the form of sudden ("mutation") or gradual contour change. Modeling such change is relevant in embryogenesis (Beloussov, 1998). The logic of development can be built on inherent rules of monotonic transformation of form (conditional rule-based synthesis), or on the basis of *dialectical logic* that attributes the transformation to the contradiction of opposing parts of the whole that results in the emergence of new form (Marková, 1990, 2003). Ruptures are central in development (Zittoun, 2006)—and making sense of those requires explication of the processes involved in dialectical synthesis. Mere labeling of a rapid emergence of new quality of form as a "dialectical leap" silences our curiosities of how such emergence happens. In this respect, the dialectic orientation—well-known in Eurocentric knowledge through Hegel's philosophy—has its intellectual charms as well as imprecision.

By emphasizing the construction of novelty—in dialectical synthesis—the use of reference to "dialectical leap" blocks the analysis of the precise process of such construction. The "dialectical leap" is an appealing theoretical idea—yet one that cannot be grasped before it has happened (and explained afterwards—cf. Baldwin's "postulates" above). Theodor Adorno captured that feature of dialectics in a sensible way:

> By ways of logic, dialectics grasps the coercive character of logic, hoping that it may yield—for that coercion itself is the mythical delusion, the compulsory identity. But the absolute, as it hovers before metaphysics, would be the nonidentical that refuses to emerge until the compulsion of identity has dissolved. Without a thesis of identity, dialectics is not the whole; but neither will it be a cardinal sin to depart from it in a dialectical step (Adorno, 1973, p. 406).

Thus, the deductive rigor of logic is taken to its limits when a *deductive system that is open to transcending its own bases* is being contemplated under the label of a logic. This difficulty was faced already by Charles S. Peirce in his efforts to explain the notion of abduction. The unity of opposites in their dynamic relation was the extension of Hegelian dialectics in the work of Kitaro Nishida's dialectical "logic of nothingness" (Axtell, 1991, Wargo, 2005). In our contemporary work where relations of ambivalence (Rudolph, 2006a, 2006b, 2006c) are taken as the basis for topological models the question of transforming these ambivalences into a new form is raised—but not solved.

The person—constantly embedded in ambivalent situation of experiencing the new and unknown on the basis of the previously known—builds up the *cognitive schemata*. The present content (presently established schema) is set up in a tensional relation with present *intent for the immediate future state* of the thinking process. The schema is anticipatory as to the desired—yet indeterminate—future state. Thus,

> The different stages of experimental meaning called, from the psychic point of view, schematic, are those in which an established recognitive context, accepted for what it is, *is also read for what it may become* (Baldwin, 1908, p. 11).

Baldwin saw the act of "persistent imitation"—trying something in some direction, and trying again—as the center for all of human development. Persistent imitation—experimentation with what might could become out of the different possible future trajectories that are desired—leads to accepting *constructive* nature of all human endeavors. Yet not all acts of construction are examples of dialectical synthesis—most of our lives is spent in re-combining existing parts of already established wholes into new wholes. These new wholes are synthesized—but not through any dialectical leap that breaks their previous quality in a rupture. New qualitative wholes can be created through finite sets of components.

However, the moments of dialectical synthesis occur—and Baldwin's genetic logic was attempting to capture such synthesis in domains where it is most visible—that of aesthetic experience. While mathematical formalizations of such synthesis do not exist, descriptions of trajectories towards it do. The development of human cognitive functions, according to Baldwin, entailed three stages: *prelogical*, *logical*, and *hyperlogical*. The first two have found their way into developmental science in the form of the differentiation theory of Heinz Werner (see Valsiner, 2005a) and in the myriads of cognitive "stage theories" which either follow or dispose of the descriptive aspect of Jean Piaget's genetic epistemology. Baldwin himself saw the solution to human social (and personal) problems in the realm of aesthetic synthesis.

Baldwin's LAS: Logic of Aesthetic Synthesis

Baldwin had good intuitions at the start—but circumstances of his career did not facilitate his developing his system of logic further. Had he done so he would have been seen as the originator of both deontic logic as well as tense logic (Prior, 1957, 1967). Undoubtedly he would have been a pioneer in the realm of multi-valued logics (known by the work of Jan Lukasiewicz[17]) and to dialectical logic.

Baldwin's canons of "genetic logic" were not developed further as a formalized logical system that would be a foundation for a consistently developmental methodology. It may have been that Baldwin's general direction of intellectual pursuits at the time of formulating the canons of genetic logic was already such that productive further development of that logic was impossible.

Pancalism. Baldwin's final synthetic solution to the problem of the social nature of human psychological functions took the form of an aesthetic synthesis. He labeled this focus "pancalism," or "constructive affectivism," as it was claimed to unite aesthetic feeling with a distanced view of the object. Aesthetic synthesis entails retaining the object-subject differentiation (i.e., the subject does not "fuse" himself with the object), yet it simultaneously entails the emergence of a novel feeling that overwhelms the subject. In Baldwin's terms:

> What we are justified in taking the real to be is that with which the free and full aesthetic and artistic consciousness finds itself satisfied. *We realise the real in achieving and enjoying the beautiful* (Baldwin, 1915, pp. 276-277).

> The object of art does not tolerate any strictly private motives or purposes; it is detached from the individual self, at the same time that it embodies what is common and essential to the life of all (Baldwin, 1915, p. 298).

In aesthetic experience, the singular event (a person's encounter with a particular art object in a here-and-now situation) becomes generalized by the person to represent something at the level of great abstraction. The aesthetically-operating person relates to the object in terms that are generic, even as the actual encounter is not different from a mundane one.

The person's arrival at the aesthetic synthesis is made possible by the process of tension between the aesthetic and mundane areas of reflection. Thus, for instance in watching a theater performance,

> there is a certain vibration of the mind between the ordinary and prosaic system of actualities and the dramatic situation depicted on the stage. The mind's eye, open in turn to each of the two spheres of actual and semblant, prosaic and ideal, enhances the value of the latter by allowing itself from time to time to lapse into the former. And after the play is over, after the intense concentration of the mind on the depicted situation, there is a violent return, a reaction amounting sometimes to a shock, to the partial interests and concerns of every-day life.... [I]t is simply the return from the ideal completeness of a fully organized aesthetic whole to the sphere of relativeness, opposition, incompleteness (Baldwin, 1915, pp. 281-282).

Pancalism retains the structure of the generalized affective (aesthetic) process, and constitutes (for Baldwin) the highest form of psychological synthesis. Even within the pluralist set of aesthetic experiences, some of them serve as anchoring points.

> The logical erects classes and establishes facts and truths, by its methods of proof; the teleological issues in affective interests and defines ends and values. Now, in the

religious life we find the object, God, looked upon as *really existing, as if* established by processes of knowledge, while, at the same time, it is determined by the religious interest *as an ideal or end*. Religion claims to present both a system of truth and a system of personal and social values. God is *both fact and ideal*; not merely in the common way of a value attaching to a fact or truth, as utility attaches to my inkstand, but in the peculiar way in which a meaning attaches to that which symbolises it (Baldwin, 1915, p. 108).

The development of higher psychological functions entails the creation and extension of personal life philosophies—be these linked with religious, ideological, or socio-moral thought systems that are co-present in a society. The double feed forward—*"meaning attaches to that which symbolises it"* guarantees that human psychological worlds become inevitably projected into the object world. If meaning X symbolizes object Y than Y becomes saturated with X (beyond the previous presentation), and feeds into further transformation of X, and so on. Here we see continuity of Baldwin's thought with Peirce's notion of the interpretant.

Baldwin emphasized the negative aesthetic—"the ugly." There was an interesting resistance to the construction of meaning that this notion provided:

> We can play with anything; anything can be selected to take on the playful sort of semblance. But with art it is not so; the ugly is not beautiful, and nothing can make it so; it embodies materials *in which the sort of semblance operating in the aesthetic cannot go forward*. Some materials are always ineligible or unfit for aesthetic or artistic treatment. Let the term "ugly" to cover all cases of this—to include all objects which are positively unaesthetic—and inquire why they are so (Baldwin, 1911, p. 179, emphasis added).

Of course the historical movements in the European arts after 1911 proved this point of Baldwin's wrong—after World War I many aspects of reality previously seen in terms of "ugly"—dead or mutilated bodies, animal or human excrements, toilet bowls attached to walls, etc.—became experimented with in various branches of modern visual art.

However, perhaps Baldwin understood the dynamics of constraining in meaning transition—if a particular currently "ugly" object manages to move to the area of "non-ugly" (but this is not—yet—an area of "beautiful"!), then the "previously ugly" enters the domain of "potentially beautiful." It is here that the Aristotelian logical principle of the "excluded middle" (if A—then not—non-A), and the need for multi-valued logic (e.g., triadic logic {A, neither A nor non-A; non-A[18]}) would be necessary starting point for any developmental science. All developmental phenomena—as they are emerging—belong to the indeterminate "zone" of {neither-a nor non-A}[19] at the given time. Jan Lukasiewicz was about to develop his rejection of the "law of excluded middle" around the time when Baldwin was creating his genetic logic (Betti, 2002).

General Conclusions

The newly (re)emerged developmental science (Cairns, Elder, & Costello, 1996)—built on the historical grounds of the legacies of James Mark Baldwin, Lev Vygotsky, George Herbert Mead, and Urie Bronfenbrenner—brings to psychology a new look at the history of developmental ideas in psychology (Cairns, 1983 and later printings). The role of Baldwin plays a crucial role in that new look (Valsiner & van der Veer, 2000, chapter 5)—yet there are many leads that could be picked up and developed further when looking into Baldwin's consistently developmental thought.

It was clear to Baldwin that developmental science could not develop using the inferential tools of non-developmental sciences. Thus, he understood the futility of the acceptance of quantitative methodology in psychology:

> The ... quantitative method, brought over into psychology from the exact sciences, physics and chemistry, must be discarded; for its ideal consisted in reducing the more complex to the more simple, the whole into its parts, the later-evolved to the earlier-existent, thus denying or eliminating just the factor which constituted or revealed what was truly genetic. Newer modes of manifestation cannot be stated in atomic terms without doing violence to the more synthetic modes which observation reveals (Baldwin, 1930, p. 7).

Baldwin's understanding of thinking and the relating with the world of objects—his focus on aesthetic objects as the highest level of development—was the obvious rationale for abandoning the quantitative method. In psychology, that method has been the major tool for creating misplaced and illusory precision of knowledge about non-existing objects—such as intelligence, personality, etc. Instead, it is the processes of meaning construction—persistent construction of new nuances of meaning—that need to be investigated—as those are presented within generalized feelings about the world.

> There is, in the aesthetic object, first the character of imaginative semblance, which suggests the ordinary dualism between idea and fact; there is, second, the character of idealization, which suggests the dualism between fact and end; there is, third, the character of self-embodiment or personalization, suggesting the dualism between the self and non-self; and finally, fourth, there is the character of singularity, suggesting the dualism between singular and universal. All these shadings of meaning are positively present in the genuine appreciation of any work of art. It remains to show, however, *that instead of developing themselves, these strains of dualism lose themselves in the rich synthesis of immediate contemplation. With all its varied suggestions, no state of mind is more fully one and undivided than that of aesthetic enjoyment, when once it is fully entered into* (Baldwin, 1915, p. 232, emphasis added).

Aesthetic synthesis is a form of "meaning<u>ful</u> <u>nothing</u>ness"—hy- pergeneralized feeling field that lacks object reference (= "nothing") while being filled with meaningfulness—the "no-thing" is filled with "some-(thing)-meaning." The experiencer may remain silent—yet filled with overwhelming feeling of totality of meaningfulness (see Valsiner, 2005 on hypergeneralized fields as field-like signs). This is the level of higher[20]—or maybe *highest*—psychological functions. Their importance in human lives has been recognized by religious systems and military leaders who manage to send young people to demise under the banners of holy wars or defending of the mother/fatherland (Senyavskaya, 1999, 2006). Yet the science of psychology has only meager understanding of how such basic processes function

Pancalism has dramatic implications for methodology. Baldwin's developmental scheme IMMEDIACY → MEDIATION → NEW IM- MEDIACY (=dialectical synthesis) proves the "misplaced concreteness" nature of efforts in psychology to "measure" its "variables." What psy- chologists construct as "variables" belong to the MEDIATION phase of Baldwin's developmental scheme—these are differentiated (from original immediacy field) objects—"data points"—that can be detected, counted, accumulated (re-assigned to configurations different from their original context), and—conventionally "analyzed." It is clear that through such operations the "data" lose their links with the original immediacy of the psychological processes—captured by James Gibson's focus on "infor- mation flow," and never gain access to the new immediacy of affective constructivity—that of highest psychological functions.

If we were to accept Baldwin's developmental scheme, then the claim by Lee Rudolph (2006c)—*psychological phenomena are best not to be represented by real numbers*—acquires new meaning. The framework of number systems that can be used is by far wider than that of real numbers, and mathematics of our contemporary times is qualitative in its main nature. Furthermore—there is simply no way to "assign numbers" to the developing affective synthesis of a person who enjoys the moonlight, Mona Lisa, or a military parade, so as to capture the "quantity" of such enjoyment. It is the higher Gestalt quality (Ehrenfels, 1890/1988) that is emerging in the process of creating such new immediacy. There can be other formal methods for modeling such holistic emerged phenom- ena—but "measurement" of some presumed quantities of elementary qualities would be superfluous. Psychology needs to get its thinking straight—before starting to "measure" ephemeral elementary constructs that are projected into the others. Our objects of investigation—the subjective realities of our behavioral worlds—may easily vanish and remain mysterious beyond the horizon of markers of symbolic significance on the pages of publications.

Acknowledgments

I am grateful to Lee Rudolph for his persistent efforts to educate me in contemporary mathematics, and Pina Marsico for her highly caffeinated suggestions at the critical moment of finishing this chapter.

Notes

1. For example, Niels Bohr's theory of complementarity in physics is traced to his reading of William James' *Principles of Psychology* (Holton, 1988, pp. 125-126).
2. Analogical periods of social tensions leading to inovations in sciences can be seen in other countries at other times—in Russia in the 1920s (ending in early 1930s—van der Veer & Valsiner, 1991), in Germany (same period). It speaks in favor of coordination of social ruptures with the opportunities for "revolutionary science" in the sense of Thomas Kuhn.
3. It is quite interesting that two major figures of psychology—Baldwin and G.H. Mead—exited from, the increasingly experimentally oriented psychology roughly around the same time—first decade of the twentieth century.
4. All major thinkers on that theme at the end of the nineteenth century used the same general argument (i.e., the non-reducibility of the properties of a molecule—say, water—into its atomic components. That example can be dated back to J. S. Mill's *Logic of the Moral Sciences* and to Hans Driesch (1893). It was widely used in the beginning of the twentieth-century discussions about the whole being not equal to the sum of its parts. Baldwin (1930, p. 8)—H and O are not just elementary components of water, but as emergent phenomena—H and O *become water*.
5. This explains Baldwin's dedication in volume 1 of *Thought and Things*—"to his friends who wrote in French—Janet, Flournoy, Binet, and to the lamented Tarde and Marillier this Book is inscribed by the author in testimony to the just criticism and adequate appreciation his other books have had in France" (Baldwin, 1906, p. iii). The French publication occurred with delay, and was partial (Baldwin, 1908b, 1918).
6. Interestingly, Piaget spent his efforts in the 1920s precisely to give empirical material for some kind of developmental logic—even making passing references to Baldwin—yet in his later work he moved into formalized frameworks of non-developmental logical systems. Piaget's notion of concrete operations is a non-developmental constituent within his developmental system of genetic epistemology.
7. Baldwin's effort was in direct opposition to his contemporary efforts to reduce psychology to physics, especially through the use of the notion of energy (propagated by Wilhelm Ostwald; see Hakfoort, 1992). The obvious energy-allusion continues to proliferate at the end of twentieth century (e.g., the notion of cognitive "processing capacity"). The transfer of the energy concept from physics to psychology has created a conceptual obstacle for the latter, similar to the role "phlogiston" notions in earlier physics.
8. These include non-existing objects, in Meinong's sense—the objects ("fountain of youth," "golden mountain") need not exists in reality, but can be communicated about in terms of shared "as-if" rules.

9. "To semble"= to *make like by imitation* (Baldwin, 1906a, p. 122)—Baldwin's rendering of *Einfühlung* into English. Later it was replaced by Titchener's and Ward's suggestion of "empathy" (Baldwin, 1911, p. 167). The latter term is void of any inherent reference to the psychological processes of "feeling in" that would result in acting through the "feeling into the other" within the psychological domain of the "feeler-in"—"sembling" preserves that interdependence.

10. Obviously, the frequentist notion would be adequate only if the accumulated frequency of the past be imperative for the actualization of a future option—a kind of "slavery of history," rather than oportunity of the future that is informed—but not repeated—by the uses of the past.

11. This open-endedness is organized. If one assumes that an infinitely generated sequence of numbers X=X+y where y>0 where y is randomly generated is being run, the developmental progression of the number series is strictly determined—even if its actual sequence at every new run is completely unique.

12. In his glossary of terms, Baldwin describes the will-to-believe as "readines to accept one alternative in preference to others, in the absence of logical proof or strong rational presumption" (Baldwin, 1915, p. 321).

13. The over-use of statistics in psychology does not count as mathematics here—for reasons, see General Conclusions.

14. Cf. Baldwin's claim (1908a, p. 280) "Excluded middle is merely the act of exhaustion."

15. *Deontic logic* is a formal logical system that operates with normative terms—*obligatory, permitted, forbidden* (von Wright, 1951, p. 1). It is time-free, yet embodies indeterminacy. Its immediate history is presented as initiate by Ernst Mally in his *Grundgesetze des Sollens: Elemente der Logik des Willens* (1926)—for overview see Lokhorst, 2004—yet its pre-history is traced back to Leibniz and Bentham (von Wright, 1981) and to the social discourses of moral being in fourteenth-century Europe (Knuuttila, 1981).

16. However, Baldwin noted that *Thought and Things* ended up as the main title at the insistence of the publishers for a title "less severe, although, if taken literally, still suficiently descriptive" (Baldwin, 1906a, p. vii). The French title was to be *Le Jugement et al Connaissance: Logique fonctionelle* (ibid., p. xi)—no reference to "things" or objects (yet the publicatiuon restored it—Baldwin, 1908b). Baldwin himself would have opted for *Genetic Logic* as the main title. Still, in the German translation of *Thought and Things* (Baldwin, 1908d, 1910, 1914) used the term *Dinge* for things—rather than *Gegenstand* (which would have directly pertained to Meinongian discourse—and which was used in explaining the title in the first sentence of the Foreword (ibid, p. vii). By the apearance of the fourth volume—with the original publisher already bankrupt—he did set the notion *genetic* into the main title—yet no longer paired with *logic* but with *theory* (Baldwin, 1915, 1918)

17. While Lukasiewicz formalized it, the roots of multi-valent logics go back to the work of Hugh McCall in the nineteenth century and Charles S. Peirce and Nikolay Vasilev at the beginning of the twentieth century—Rescher, 1968, pp. 55-56. Peirce of course was one of Baldwin's closest intellectual interlocutors.

18. Note that N-valued logic is an extension of the bi-valent logic, and operates by the rule of exclusion of N+1 version, e.g., in triadic logic of three possibilities any fourth is ruled out, in quadratic logic of four posibilities any fifth is ruled out, etc. Thus all multi-valent logics have inherent restrictions that make their applicability to processes of development not possible. As development entails the emergence of new possible states, i.e., the emergence of N+1th condition—ruled out by each N-iadic logic.

19.   or better—{*no longer* A andf *not yet* non-A}—see Josephs, Valsiner & Surgan, 1999. The whole isue of Vygotsky's "zone of proximal development" is that of such intermediate state of afairs unfolding in time (Valsiner & van der Veer, 1993).
20.   Along the lines of Vygotsky—"higher psychological functions" are intentional, signs-mediated psychological processes.

References

Abbey, E. A., and Diriwächter, R. (eds.) (2008). *Innovating genesis.* Charlotte, N.C.: Information Age Publishers.

Adorno, T. W. (1973). *Negative dialectics.* New York: Continuum.

Anisov, A. M. (2000). *Temporal'nyi universum I ego poznanie* [The temporal universe and its perception]. Moscow: RANIF.

Anisov, A. M. (2002). Logika neopredelennosti i neopredelennost' vo vremeni [The logic of indeterminacy and indeterminacy in time]. *Logical Studies, 8,* 1-27.

Anisov, A. M. (2005). Time as a computation process. In A. N. Pavlenko (ed.), *Zamysel Boga v teoriakh fiziki i kosmologii. Vremya* (pp. 72-88). St. Petersburg.

Axtell, G. S. (1991). Comparative dialectics: Nishida Kitaro's logic of place and Western dialectical thought. *Philosophy East and West, 41,* 2, 163-184.

Baldwin, J. M. (1895). *Mental development in the child and the race.* New York: Macmillan.

Baldwin, J. M. (1897). The genesis of social "interests." *Monist, 7,* 340-357.

Baldwin, J. M. (1898). On selective thinking. *Psychological Review, 5,* 1, 1-24.

Baldwin, J. M. (1902a). *Social and ethical interpretations in mental development.* 3rd ed. New York: MacMillan.

Baldwin, J. M. (1902b). *Fragments in philosophy and science.* New York: Charles Scribner's Sons.

Baldwin, J. M. (1902c). *Development and evolution.* London: MacMillan.

Baldwin, J. M. (1904). The limits of pragmatism. *Psychological Review, 11,* 30-60.

Baldwin, J. M. (1906a). *Thought and things: A study of the development and meaning of thought, or genetic logic.* Vol. 1. *Functional logic, or genetic theory of knowledge.* London: Swan Sonnenschein & Co.

Baldwin, J. M. (1906b). Introduction to experimental logic. *Psychological Review, 13,* 388-395.

Baldwin, J. M. (1907). Logical community and the difference of discernibles. *Psychological Review, 14,* 395-402.

Baldwin, J. M. (1908a). *Thought and things: A study of the development and meaning of thought, or genetic logic.* Vol. 2. *Experimental logic, or genetic theory of thought.* London: Swan Sonnenschein & Co.

Baldwin, J. M. (1908b). *La Pensée et les choses: La logique fonctionelle.* Paris: Librairie Doin.

Baldwin, J. M. (1908c). Knowledge and imagination. *Psychological Review, 15,* 181-196.

Baldwin, J. M. (1908d). *Das Denken und die Dinge, oder Genetische Logik.* Vol. 1. *Funktionelle Logik oder genetische Erkentnistheorie.* Leipzig: J. A. Barth.

Baldwin, J. M. (1910). *Das Denken und die Dinge, oder Genetische Logik.* Vol. 2. *Experimentelle Logik oder genetische Theorie des Denkens.* Leipzig: J. A. Barth.

Baldwin, J. M. (1911). *Thought and things: A study of the development and meaning of thought, or genetic logic.* Vol. 3. *Interest and art being real logic.* London: Swan Sonnenschein & Co.

Baldwin, J. M. (1914). *Das Denken und die Dinge, oder Genetische Logik.* Vol. 3. *Eine Untersuchung der Entwicklung und der Bedeutung des Denkens.* Leipzig: J. A. Barth.

Baldwin, J. M. (1915). *Genetic theory of reality.* New York: G. P. Putnam's sons.

Balfwin, J. M. (1918). *Théorie génétique de la réalité—le pancalisme.* Paris: Librairie Félix Alcan.

Baldwin, J. M. (1930). James Mark Baldwin. In C. Murchison (ed.), *A history of psychology in autobiography.* Vol. 1 (pp. 1-30). New York: Russell & Russell.

Belousov, L. V. (1998). *The dynamic architecture of a developing organism.* Dordrecht: Kluwer.

Betti, A. (2002). The incomplete story of Lukasiewicz and bivalence. In T. Childers and O. Majer (eds.), *The Logica Yearbook 2001* (pp. 21-36). Praha: Filosofia.

Black, M. (1937). Vagueness: an exercise in logical analysis. *Philosophy of Science, 4,* 4, 427-455.

Broughton, J. M. (1981). The genetic psychology of James Mark Baldwin. *American Psychologist, 36,* 4, 396-407.

Burgess, J. P. (1979). Logic and time. *Journal of Symbolic Logic, 44,* 4, 566-582.

Bühler, K. (1908). Tatsachen und Probleme zu eine Psychologie der Denkvorgänge. II, III *Archiv für die gesamte Psychologie, 12,* 1-92.

Bühler, K. (1927/1978). *Die Krise der Psychologie.* Frankfurt-am-Main: Ullstein.

Bühler, K. (1951). On thought connections. In D. Rapaport (ed.), *Organization and pathology of thought* (pp. 39-57). New York: Columbia University Press (partial translation of Bühler, 1908).

Cahan, E. D. (1984). The genetic psychologies of James Mark Baldwin and Jean Piaget. *Developmental Psychology, 20,* 1, 128-135.

Cairns, R. B. (1980). Developmental theory before Piaget: the remarkable contributions of James Mark Baldwin. *Contemporary Psychology, 25,* 6, 438-440.

Cairns, R. B. (1983). The emergence of developmental psychology. In W. Kessen (ed.), *Handbook of child psychology. Vol. 1. History, theory and methods* (pp. 41-102). New York: Wiley (4th edition—repeated in 5th ed. 1998 and 6th ed. 2006).

Cairns, R. B. (1992). The making of a developmental science: the contributions and intellectual heritage of James Mark Baldwin. *Developmental Psychology, 28,* 1, 17-24.

Cairns, R. B., Elder, G. E., & Costello, E. J. (eds.) (1996). *Developmental science.* New York: Cambridge University Press.

Carolina Consortium on Human Development (1996). Developmental science: A collaborative statement. In R. B. Cairns, G. Elder & E. J. Costello (eds.), *Developmental science* (pp. 1-6). New York: Cambridge University Press.

Commager, H. S. (1950). *The American mind: An interpretation of American thought and character since the 1880s.* New Haven, CT: Yale University Press.

Dalmedico, A. D. (2004). Chaos, disorder, and mixing: a new fin-de-siècle image of science? In M. N. Wise (ed.), *Growing explanations: Historical perspectives on recent science* (pp. 67-94). Durham, NC: Duke University Press.

Dolby, R. G. A. (1977). The transmission of two new scientific disciplines from Europe to North America in the late 19th century. *Annals of Science, 34,* 287-310.

Driesch, H. (1893). *Die Biologie als selbständige Grundwissenschaft.* Leipzig: Verlag von Wilhelm Engelmann.

Ehrenfels, C. von (1988a). Über "Gestaltqalitäten." In R. Fabian (ed.), *Psychologie, Ethik, Erkentnistheorie* (pp. 128-167). München: Philosophia Verlag. English version: On 'Gestalt Qualities'. In B. Smith (ed.), *Foundations of Gestalt theory* (pp. 82-117). München: Philosophia Verlag.

Groos, K. G. (1902). *Der aesthetische Genuss.* Giessen: J. Ricker'sche Verlagsbuchhandlung.

Hakfoort, C. (1992). Science deified: Wilhelm Ostwald's energeticist world-view and the history of scientism. *Annals of Science, 49,* 525-544.

Herbst, D. (1995). What happens when we make a distinction: An elementary introduction to co-genetic logic. In T. Kindermann & J. Valsiner (eds.), *Development of person-context relations*. Hillsdale, NJ: Lawrence Erlbaum Associates.

Hofstadter, R. (1963). *The Progressive Movement 1900-1915*. Englewood Cliffs, N.J.: Prentice-Hall.

Holton, G. (1988). *Thematic origins of scientific thought*. Chicago: University of Chicago Press.

Ipsen, G. (1926) Zur Theorie des Erkennens: Untersuchungen über Gestalt und Sinn sinnloser Wörter. *Neue Psychologische Studien, 1*, 3, 283-471.

James, W. (1896). The will to believe. *New World, 5*, 327-347.

James, W. (1979). *The will to believe, and other essays in popular philosophy*. Cambridge, MA: Harvard University Press.

Josephs, I. E., Valsiner, J., & Surgan, S. E. (1999). The process of meaning construction. In J. Brandtstädter and R. M. Lerner (eds.), *Action & self development* (pp. 257-282). Thousand Oaks, CA.: Sage.

Jung, C. G. (1966). Sigmund Freud in his historical setting. In C. G. Jung, *Collected Works*, Vol. 20 (pp. 33-40). Princeton, NJ: Princeton University Press.

Karpenko, A. S. (2000). Logika na rubeze tysjachiletii [Logic at the boundary of millennia]. *Logical Studies, 5*, 1-39.

Knuuttila, S. (1981). The emergence of deontic logic in the fourteenth century. In R. Hilpinen (ed.), *New studies in deontic logic* (pp. 225-248). Dordrecht: Reidel.

Laird, J. L. (2007). *Feelings: The perception of self*. New York: Oxford University Press.

Lipps, T. (1903). Einfühlung, innere Nachahmung, und Organempfindungen. *Archiv für die gesamte Psychologie, 1*, 185-204

Lokhorst, G.-J. (2004). Mally's deontic logic. In *Stanford Encyclopaedia of Philosophy*. Internet resource.

Marková, I. (1990). A three-step process as a unit of analysis in dialogue. In I. Marková & K. Foppa (eds.), *The dynamics of dialogue* (pp. 129-146). Hemel Hempstead: Harvester.

Marková, I. (2003). *Dialogicality and social representations*. Cambridge: Cambridge University Press.

Moutafakis, N.J. (1987). *The logics of preference*. Dordrecht: D. Reidel.

Mueller, R. H., (1976). A chapter in the history of the relationship between psychology and sociology in America: James Mark Baldwin. *Journal of the History of the Behavioral Sciences, 12*, 240-253.

Pigman, G. W. (1995), Freud and the history of empathy. *International Journal of Psycho-Analysis, 76*, 237-256.

Prior, A. N. (1957). *Time and modality*. Oxford: Clarendon Press.

Prior, A. N. (1967). *Past, present, and future*. Oxford: Clarendon Press.

Rescher, N. (1968). *Topics in philosophical logic*. Dordrecht: Reidel

Rescher, N. and Urquhart, A. (1971). *Temporal logic*. New York: Springer.

Richards, R. J. (1987). James Mark Baldwin: evolutionary biopsychology and the politics of scientific ideas. In R. J. Richards, *Darwin and the evolutionary theories of mind and behavior* (pp. 451-503). Chicago: University of Chicago Press.

Rosenthal, C. (2004). Fuzzyfying the world: social practices of showing the properties of fuzzy logic. In M. N. Wise (ed.), *Growing explanations: Historical perspectives on recent science* (pp. 159-178). Durham, NC: Duke University Press.

Rudolph, L. (2006a). The fullness of time. *Culture & Psychology, 12*, 2, 169-204.

Rudolph, L. (2006b) Mathematics, models, and metaphors. *Culture & Psychology, 12*, 2, 245-259.

Rudolph, L. (2006c). Spaces of ambivalence: qualitative mathematics in the modeling of complex fluid phenomena. *Estudios de Psicologia, 27*, 1, 67-83.
Sander, F. (1927). Ueber Gestaltqualitäten. *Proceedings of the 8th International Congress of Psychology, 1926.* (pp. 183-189). Groningen: P. Noordhoff.
Senyavskaya, E. S. (1999). *Psikhologia voiny v 20 veke* [Psychology of war in the 20th century]/ Moscow: ROSPEN.
Senyavskaya, E. S. (2006). *Protivniki Rossii v voinakh 20 veka* [Rusia's opponents in the wards of 20th century]. Moscow: ROSSPEN.
Sovran, T. (1992). Between similarity and sameness. *Journal of Pragmatics, 18*, 4, 329-344.
Surowik, D. 2002). Tense logics and the thesis of determinism. *Studies in Lkogic, Grammar and Rhetoric, 5* (18), 87-95.
Thomason, R. H. (1981). Deontic logic as founded on tense logic. In R. Hilpinen (ed.), *New studies in deontic logic* (pp. 165-176). Dordrecht: Reidel.
Toomela, A. (2007). Culture of science: strange history of the methodological thinking in psychology. *Integrative Psychological & Behavioral Science, 41*, 1, 6-20.
Valsiner, J. (2000). Thinking through consequences: the perils of pragmatism. *Revista de Historia de la Psicologia, 21*, 4, 145-175.
Valsiner, J. (Ed) (2005a). *Heinz Werner and developmental science.* New York: Kluwer.
Valsiner, J. (2005b). Affektive Entwicklung im kulturellen Kontext. In J. B. Asendorpf (ed.), *Enzyklopädie der Psychologie.* Vol. 3. *Soziale, emotionale und Persönlichkeitsentwicklung* (pp. 677-728). Göttingen: Hogrefe.
Valsiner, J., & Van der Veer, R. (1993). The encoding of distance: The concept of the zone of proximal development and its interpretations. In R. R. Cocking & K. A. Renninger (eds.), *The Development and Meaning of Psychological Distance* (pp. 35-62). Hillsdale, NJ: Lawrence Erlbaum Associates.
Valsiner, J., & Van der Veer, R. (2000). *The social mind.* New York: Cambridge University Press.
van der Veer, R., & Valsiner, J. (1991). *Understanding Vygotsky: A quest for synthesis.* Oxford: Basil Blackwell.
van Haaften, W. (1998). Preliminaries to a logic of development. *Theory & Psychology, 8*, 3, 399-422.
Werner, H. (1927). Über Pysiognomische Wahrnehmungsweisen und Ihre experimentelle Prüfung. In *Proceedings and papers of the 8th International Congress of Psychology, 1926,* Groningen (pp. 443-446). Groningen: P. Noordhoff.
West, C. (1989). *The American evasion of philosophy: A genealogy of pragmatism.* Madison, WI: University of Wisconsin Press.
Witasek, S. (1901). Zur psychologischen Analyse der ästhetischeb Einfühlung. *Zeitschrift für Psychologie und Physiologie der Sinnesorgane, 25*, 1-49.
Wolf, K. (1971). Ernst Mallys Lebensgang und philosophische Entwicklung. In K. Wolf and P. Weingartner (eds.), *Ernst Mally Logische Schriften* (pp. 3-15). Dordrecht: D. Reidel.
Wargo, R, J, J. (2005). *The logic of nothingness.* Honolulu, HI: University of Hawaii Press.
Wozniak, R. (1982). Metaphysics and science, reason, and reality: The intellectual origins of genetic epistemology. In J. M. Broughton & D. J. Freeman-Moir (eds.), *The cognitive-developmental psychology of James Mark Baldwin* (pp. 13-45). Norwood, NJ: Ablex.
Wright, G. H. von (1951). Deontic logic. *Mind, 60*, No. 237, 1-15.
Wright, G. H. von (1981). On the logic of norms and actions. In R. Hilpinen (ed.), *New studies in deontic logic* (pp. 3-35). Dordrecht: D. Reidel.

Zecha, G. (2001). Ernst Mally (1879-1944). In L. Albertazzi, D. Jacquette and R. Poli (eds.), *The school of Alexius Meinong* (pp. 191-203). Aldershot: Ashgate.

Zittoun, T, (2006). *Transitions.* Greenwich, CT: Information Age Publishers.

5

Ecological Psychology's Struggle to Study Perception at the Appropriate Level of Analysis: Examining the Past, Guessing the Future

Eric P. Charles

The perceptual process cannot just be unconscious information processing (as cognitivists tend to assume) because this leaves out of account the dynamic, intrinsically motivated aspects of looking, listening, feeling, and so on…. The psychology of exploratory activity—the psychological analysis of the process of and motives behind looking around one's world-has made almost no progress in the intervening three decades since Gibson's Senses Considered [as Perceptual Systems] (Reed, 1996, p. 258).

James J. Gibson left a legacy of research and theory that challenges researchers to study perception as an activity driven, dynamic interaction between individuals and their meaning laden environments. This legacy guides the field of ecological psychology, and mandates the rejection of many reductionistic elements of traditional "perceptual" research. That position owes much to Gibson's intellectual heritage from the non-experimental tradition of E. B. Holt's New Realism. From that starting point, Gibson's system developed out of the interplay between theory, experimentation, and application. While ecological psychology currently represents a thriving field of research, many potential areas of research remain virtually uninvestigated. Ecological psychologists struggle to devise experiments that do justice to the antireductionist nature of their beliefs, and it is likely that the future of research in ecological psychology will involve a rediscovering its theoretical legacy.

Perception

There are two obvious ways in which the ecological approach to perception is less reductionistic than traditional approaches. Both involve assumptions about what the basic state of perception entails. First, the ecological approach considers the most basic perceptual situation to involve a goal-directed, active organism moving through an environment filled with objects and energies. Second, the ecological approach considers the most basic result of perceptual activity be the registering of affordances, not merely the firing or not firing of sensory neurons. By "basic situation" I mean both most natural and most straightforward to analyze. When experimenters restrict participants so that these activities are not possible, the systemic properties operating on the higher level are not visible: Under restriction the original and natural function of perception becomes obscured; the perceptual system's functions become fractionated into pieces that give little insight into the whole.

Skipping the lengthy justifications: *Perception*, to an ecological psychologist, is best described as a resonance between information in the environment and the perceptual system of the organism (Gibson, 1966, 1979). *Information* is defined as patterns in the energy arrays that surround us, be they light, sound, chemical, etc., which specify (i.e., are specific to) the objects and events that structured them. For example, an illuminated sphere creates patterns of reflected light different from those created by an illuminated cube. If one *moved through* the environment properly, one could detect the difference. Because perception thus entails active exploration, the *perceptual system* includes all parts of the body involved in such explorations. Given the dependence of perception on the coordination of movements in an intentional fashion, the reduction of perception to sensation (or similarly the processing of "sensory information") can be easily rejected. Hence, the ecological approach is clearly less reductionistic than traditional reflex-oriented, sensation-oriented, or cognitive perspectives on perception.

It is further postulated (again skipping the lengthy theoretical justification), that perception is usually, if not always, perception of affordances. *Affordances* are opportunities for interaction created by the complementarity of properties of the organism and properties of the environment. Thus people can, in at least a limited sense, directly perceive meaning in their environment (cliffs can be fallen off, stairs can be walked up, etc.). This makes ecological psychology's view of perception less reductionistic than both views that assume we can only perceive a stationary, instantaneous scintillation of nervous activity, and views which assume all meaning must be added to perceptions in some post-hoc dualistic fashion.

Ecological Psychology's Distant Past

Ecological psychology's most direct intellectual predecessor was New Realism, from which it inherited much of its antireductionist attitude. While the debt to this tradition is obvious on the theoretical side, it is not yet obvious on the experimental side. New realism did not generate a strong experimental tradition. However, as ecological psychologists attempts to understand how perception functions in ever more complex situations, their approach starts to look much like what an experimental New Realism might have been. Thus understanding ecological psychology's past may be important for understanding ecological psychology's future.

New Realism

E.B. Holt, a student of William James and dissertation advisor to James J. Gibson, was a leader in the philosophical movement known as New Realism (Holt, et al., 1910, 1922). New Realism resulted from collaboration amongst a group of philosophers who could agree on some basic premises, but who ultimately failed to create a fully unified program. Holt's work with the New Realists framed his molar behaviorism and ideas about consciousness, which in turn greatly influenced his students. Three points seem particularly worth noting:

First, New Realists, as the name would imply, thought that people experienced the world as it was—they thought the world was composed of observable things and that people observed them. The relics of this line of thinking can be found in Gibson's prioritization of veridical (accurate) perception. Mainstream study of perception, both then and now, often seems to focus on illusions and other errors produced by unusual or restricted circumstances. Gibson felt this was backwards, that most perception was startlingly accurate, and that it was the overwhelming accuracy that begged for explanation, not the rarer mistakes. If asked to explain *perception,* Gibson would argue, your primary obligation is to explain how people correctly respond to the objects and events of the world. As more evidence would accrue that this accuracy resulted from higher-level interactions between perceiver and environment, Gibson would increasingly reject reductionistic experimental methods.

Second, proponents of New Realism argued strenuously that relations were real, that relations between relations were real, etc. The issues seem obscure out of context, but Gibson's analysis of perception makes clear its value. Perception is a relation between the observer and the environment. The necessary next question is "What type of relation is perception?" Though Gibson's approach would deviate greatly from the New Realist approach, this influence of this question is clear: Much of Gibson's theoretical innovation resulted from trying to find a way to explain all kinds of perception, of all organisms in all situations, as examples of a single type of relation.

Third, proponents of New Realism argued that psychological phenomenon were perceivable. This relates closely to the first two points: If psychological phenomenon are relational, and we can accurately perceive relations in the external world, then we should be able to detect whether or not a person is in one of those relations. This is probably the most radical of the New Realist's claims, at least from the traditional psychologist's perspective. To a limited extent, it is obvious that Gibson's analysis of perception (a psychological phenomenon) lends itself to this analysis: If perception can be explained as an organism's acting correctly towards surrounding objects as a result of a particular type of interaction with environmental energy, then we, as outside observers, should be able to see whether or not *others* are perceiving. In the bigger picture, however, it is not obvious how this principle relates to the work of ecological psychologists more broadly. I believe this will soon change. As ecological psychology tries to tackle issues of social perception adequately, researchers must take a stance on the visibility of a broad range of psychological phenomenon. It is unclear what the result would be if ecological psychology moves broadly in a New Realist direction, but a preview of the possibility can be illustrated by examining the only other major attempt to extend New Realism.

Purposive Behaviorism

E. C. Tolman, now hailed as a pioneer of cognitive psychology, was also a student of Holt. The influence of the New Realist movement is very visible in Tolman's early work, especially as he was first developing his "purposeful behaviorism." In particular, he argued that "purpose" described a type of higher-order matching between an organism's behavior and environment, and, hence, that purpose could be empirically observed. For example, placing the result of Thorndike's escape-box experiments on par with other forms of intentional behavior he argues that:

> Thorndike's kitten in the puzzle-box went through a series of random "trial and error" acts—clawing, bighting, squeezing—*until* by a chance clawing at the loop of string

connected with the catch it got out…. The child tries hiding behind this chair, that chair, and the other, until he gets from the sight of the stranger. In each case the trials (and errors) *keep on until* some particular objectively discoverable end-object or situation is got to or from…. The cat's trials are quite objectively exhibiting the purpose to *get to* the outside of the cage; the rat's runnings-about [in a maze] that to get *to* the food-box; the man's examining of successive cars [*to find* his own]; the child's hidings that to get [*away*] *from* the stranger. These purposes to get to or from are part of the very descriptive texture of the act…. The purposes we have here observed, these purposes which exhibit themselves in trial and error, these *persistences-until,* are not mentalistically defined entities at all, but behavioristically defined ones…. [Purpose] is not a mentalistic entity supposed to exist parallel to, and to run along side of the behavior. It is *out there in* the behavior (Tolman, 1926, pp. 354-355).

Here, Tolman is clearly asserting that we can perceive the intentionality of the others. In a very New Realist way, he claims their intentionality is "out there" to be seen in the relation between their circumstances and their actions. While Gibson's research on object and event perception dealt with much more mundane claims than these, the style of argument is similar—For example, Gibson would claim that for a suitably fit person the walk upable-ness of the stairs was visible, out there, in the environment. Further, when discussing ecological psychology's future, I will argue later that our best hope of making a coherent transition to dealing experimentally with interpersonal and cultural phenomenon will be to extend ecological theory back towards a New Realist approach.

First, however, it is necessary to discuss the present state of the field and how it came about.

Ecological Psychology's Recent Past

James J. Gibson began his career as a fairly orthodox researcher of human vision. Through his constant struggle to make sense of experimental findings and to create theories of ever-broader applicability, Gibson influenced a large number of peers and students. Perhaps most importantly, for this volume, his theoretical innovations were intimately tied to empirical problems.

Early Rejection of Reductions

As did most all of his generation, Gibson began his professional career as a behaviorist, and with a firm belief that perception was built up from sensations. However, his move away from that position began early, and was characterized by theoretical movement spurred by experimental results that contradicted "established" reductions. For example, Gibson's first experiment in conjunction with his later to be wife Eleanor Jack Gibson involved conditioning subjects to lift their finger off a shock grid

(Gibson, Jack, & Raffel, 1932). They were tying to show that training a finger of one hand quickened training of a finger of the opposite hand. To their surprise, they showed that the response transferred from one hand to the other hand with no additional training. From this, they concluded that subjects' learning could not be reduced to a "specific response," in the reflexive or stimulus-response sense, and that, even in a very simple situation, subjects were learning about the relation between themselves and the environment (E. Gibson, 1980).

Around the same time, Gibson's early work on adaptation to prismatic distortion (which established his experimental reputation) yielded further dissociations with traditional thinking. Among other things, the prisms initially made straight lines appear curved. However, after only a short time wearing the glasses while doing normal activities the wearer adapted, coming to see straight lines as straight again. Perhaps most intriguingly, after adaptation had occurred, removing the prism-glasses produced an after-effect, straight lines now appeared curved in the opposite direction (Gibson, 1933, etc.). Aspects of this experience seemed to question the explanations for perception popular at the time. In particular, current explanations for after effects required that they only occur as a result of so-called simple sensory experiences, such as color. If those theories were correct, then prism-wearer's experiences must be the result some associative process due to their wearing the glasses when engaged in activity, rather than a true physiological after-effect. Gibson's initial instinct was to try to save this way of thinking, but his tests only lead him to question more:

> I thought of a control experiment that would surely put the doctrine of sensory empiricism back on its feet. I would look at a field of *actually* curved lines equivalent to the prismatic distortion... and show that no change in apparent curvature would then occur. But to my astonishment it did....
>
> This result was shocking to an empiricist. How could sensory experience be validated except against other sensory experience? It might, of course, be validated against behavior... but there had *been* no behavior in my experiment. I could only conclude that perception of a line must be like the sensation of a color or temperature in being susceptible to the negative afterimage caused by some process of physiological normalization. This was equally puzzling, however, for it called in question the very notion that perceptions were based on physiological sensations (Gibson, 1967, p. 133).

The results of the ensuing series of experiments began the experimental support for Gibson's rejection of the reduction of perception into sensation. It was clear that his experiences could not be attributed to the simple firing or not firing of individual sensory neurons, explanation required *something* of much higher order. Gibson began to believe that the fault in the old stimulus-response formula was largely due to its dismally reductionistic view of stimuli.

Perceiving the World

Gibson further broke with traditional perceptual theory while working for the Air Force during World War II. He researched (among other things) perception related to the skills necessary to pilot planes, and "gradually came to realize, nothing of any practical value was known by psychologists about the perception of motion, or of locomotion in space, or of space itself" (Gibson, 1967). That is, perceptual research performed up to that point focused on people whose exploratory abilities had been restricted (head on a chin rest, etc.) and focused on verbal report of perceptions almost exclusively. It offered little insight into how people moved through and interacted with the world, little insight into normal, natural, straightforward perception. This is problematic, as (we know from ecological psychology's distant past) the burden of a perceptual researcher is to explain people's accuracy in interaction with the world.

Slowly and steadily, Gibson began adding more of the real world into his work. Rather than have people judge distance to and size of objects represented in a picture, he had them judge the size and distance of *actually* far away objects. He also innovated using motion pictures for psychological experiments to create controlled moving stimuli. (Gibson, 1967). As this happened, he became more enamored with light in the ambient environment. He came to feel that peoples' accuracy in perception could be explained by their having access to the complexity of available ambient energy. Traditional perceptual psychologists had spent so much time trying to break apart aspects of a stagnant retinal image, they had ignored the larger pattern, the ways in which those patterns changed as people moved, and the ways in which those patterns could change if they moved in different ways; by focusing on the parts, perceptual psychologists had lost track of the wholes. Of course, Gibson did not go so far as the Gestaltists who influenced him (Koffka and Gibson overlapped in their tenure at Smith College) to speak of fundamental principles of organization, nor of the mind as organizer. He "merely" hypothesized that the patterns in ambient light itself contained higher-order variables, previously neglected, of the type that his prior research suggested *must* support perception.

> [Fifteen] years of research having to do with the perception of moving things or processes and with the control of locomotion ... point to the general conclusion that the flow of stimulation, its transformations, reveals the activity of perception better that the unchanging form, the picture, that we generally use as a stimulus....

> We found that continuous optical transformations can yield quite simple percep-
> tions, but that they yield two kinds of perception at the same time, one of change and
> one of nonchange. (4) The perspective transformations of a rectangle, for example, was
> always perceived as both something rotating and something rectangular. This suggests
> that the transformation as such is one kind of stimulus information, for motion, and
> that the invariants under transformation are another kind of stimulus information, for
> the constant properties of the object (Gibson, 1966, pp. 144-145—"(4)" cites Gibson
> and Gibson 1957).

Because people are sensitive to transformations, to change itself, the role of their activity in perception becomes emphasized. Some transformations are due to the movement of objects (as in the experimental example given), but surely most optical transformations that people experience are the result of self-movement, of exploratory activity.

Moving on in Research

The traditional model for perception is a photographic camera (and before that, the camera obscura, which provided an almost identical analogy). As Gibson's understanding of perception changed, he offered up a model of perception as resonance, like that found in a crystal radio: When the radio is tuned properly, the crystal's vibrations reveal structure in the surrounding environment. Similarly, when the perceptual system is tuned properly, it reveals structure in the surrounding environment. This tuning can involve adjustments of all parts of the organism, and adjustments in how the organism moves through the world. Thus, perception involves loop-like qualities with no clear beginning or end. It can be just as sensible to start descriptions of perception with the activities of the organism as with the nervous system, the light in the retina, the light in the world, or the objects and events which structure the light:

> [My approach to] perception can begin to talk about activity before sensations have
> been aroused by stimuli, an activity that orients the organs or [sic, "for"] perception,
> explores the ambient array, and seeks an equilibrium. For example, the adjustments
> stabilizing the eyes, fixating them, turning them, converging them, accommodating the
> lens, and modulating the pupil are surely activities (Gibson, 1976, pp. 235 & 237).

The importance of activity in perception extends from these simple physiological adjustments to movement of the whole body through the world. Some ways of moving would reveal some patterns in the light, while other movements would reveal different patterns. Studies of haptic perception (active touch) also showed the importance of active exploration. One important study demonstrated that perceptions differed when the same stimulation was gained through active exploration or passive presentation (i.e., the subject moving his hand on an object versus the experimenter moving an object on the subject's hand, Gibson, 1962). This proved that it is not mere movement that is important, but subjects controlled movement.

This creates a complicated burden for the perceptual researcher. Presumably, to study perception proper, the researcher must allow for all the adjustments involved in perception. As a result, much of the trappings of standard perceptual research must go by the wayside and new methods must be come up with to capture the bigger, expanded picture. Gibson was well aware of this dilemma:

> Experimental studies that display optical information are not so easy to perform as the old-fashioned experiments that expose a stimulus to a fixed eye. The experimenter cannot simply apply a stimulus. Instead, he must make available an optical invariant that he expects will specify something about the world on grounds of ecological optics. This takes ingenuity....
>
> The experimenter should not hope, and does not need, to display *all* the information in an ambient optic array, let alone all the information in a transforming ambient optic array. He is not trying to stimulate reality. He could not create the illusion of looking around and walking through the countryside in any case, for he would have to create the countryside. He should not want to deceive the observer. The observer who begins to be fooled should be allowed to make the standard tests for reality, such as getting up and looking behind the screen of the display....
>
> The experimental psychologist should realize that he cannot truly *control* the perception of an observer (Gibson, 1979, p. 305).

By the end of his career Gibson's standards for experiments on perception had become quite high.

Ecological Psychology's Present and Future

The topic of this volume is very apropos. The future of ecological psychology will either be grim or glorious depending on its ability to reconcile its antireductionist attitude with its empirical obligations.

The difficulty of experimentation within Gibson's system is, I believe, at least partially responsible for the continued semi-obscurity of the system. As I see it, the two major problems are: First, the difficulty of creating good experiments can lead ecological psychologists to spend a great deal of time criticizing other people's research on seemingly obscure philosophical grounds—what is seen as "obscure" criticism from the perspective of the other, is quite a central flaw for the ecological psychologist. Given that such criticisms often sound like "You have not seen the light" speeches, it is unsurprising that this behavior often alienates interested, but trepid potential collaborators.[1] Second, the high expectations make it very difficult for ecological psychologists to do research. As the readers and contributors to this volume will no doubt attest, methods for pursuing reductionistic research are better developed than methods for systems-level research. Further, it is difficult in the current academic climate to do the very risky research needed to develop alternative methods—risky in the sense that there will be failures, and in the sense that even the successes will be difficult to get published, accepted, and understood. As such, it is not surprising that most of the research done in ecological psychology is the most easily reducible research, that is, the parts of the problem that require the least modification of previous methods.

Reed lamented this state in 1988, saying that even amongst ecological psychologists "The empirical study of perceiving for its own sake, and for the sake of how perceiving connects to other psychological processes, is almost extinct."

From the perspective of this volume, the present state of experimentation in Ecological Psychology offers little reason for excitement. The defining characteristic of current research is its narrowness of focus. I do not mean to be too disparaging; there is a great deal of research being done, much of it is of very high quality, and the field *is* moving forward. However, the majority of research focuses upon aspects of Gibson's thinking most easily fit into standard experimental methods. Much attention is given to 1) the identification of affordances, e.g., determining relation between body and environment that makes a chairs sit-onable, stairs walk-upable, etc.; and 2) measuring people's accuracy in perceiving affordances in controlled conditions, i.e., judging gap cross-ability, judging doorway walk-through ableness, etc. Readers will recognize that, though these research topics are definitely specialized to suit a specific theoretical agenda, they are only slightly less reductionistic versions of human factors work and psychophysics.

The future is not entirely dim however. Ecological psychology continues to be developed theoretically and empirically. Gibson asserted that the major function of an experiment was to demonstrate an unexpected result.[2] That is, the purpose was not to test a theory, or iron out a nuance, but to show that something interesting does indeed happen. In that sense, ecological psychology is doing reasonably well, slowly spreading out into other fields to demonstrate that things are not as simple as they seem, that systems can be analyzed at higher levels, and that perception and action can be treated in more complex ways. However, just because ecological psychologists are helping others be less reductionistic does not mean that they, themselves, are pushing the envelope. In that vein I want to conclude by pointing out some recent advances in ecological psychology, and highlighting the areas of research I believe still cry out for investigation. These areas cry out because they are the places where ecological psychologists can demonstrate the existence of interesting phenomenon that other systems of psychology do not consider. Unsurprisingly, pursuing these projects will require the creation of less reductionistic methods of research.

Future Areas of Research

Expanding the mathematics of invariants. First, ecological psychologists would benefit from expanding the types of mathematics they use to identify information. While it is important to continue identify more examples of algebraic invariants in optics, acoustics, and haptics, there is no reason to think that all interesting types of patternings can be reduced to fit that model. We should try to incorporate new ways of characterizing stability and change, to help find and describe patterns that would otherwise remain hidden. Gibson did a bit of this himself (see Gibson, Kaplan, Reynolds, & Wheeler, 1969, appendix), but he admitted lacking the mathematical sophistication necessary to pursue it in depth. Good prospects can probably be found within theoretical geometry, and some work has been done in this regard by Rudolph (2006a, 2006b, 2008a, 2008b), and similar recommendations are made by Kadar and Effken (2006, etc).

The identification of new types of invariants will most likely also be key for expanding ecological psychology into the social realm. To repeat the New Realist's almost tautological premise, anything perceived must be an observable. In this sense, any integration of social psychology with ecological psychology will have to include a determination of the types of observations made possible by being in a social setting. How does watching people interact, or interacting with them, make visible my behavioral possibilities? Given the logical parallels, I believe that working in such a direction will inevitably bring ecological psychologists back towards their New Realist roots. It will have to be claimed that certain psychological phenomenon are visible in others, and that social psychological phenomenon are visible in other's interactions with each other and in groups' interactions with the world. Suggestions to this effect have been made for many years by Dr. Thompson (summarized in Thompson, 1997) and a non-mathematical feel for the style of the resulting science can be found in a recent tribute to him (Charles, 2008).

If this line of researching is followed qualitative differences between social interaction and physical interaction will start to seem fuzzy: We will start to understand people who are able to "work crowds," expert storytellers, expert "readers" such as poker players, and the like as keen observers, sensitive to information we often miss, but that is out there for any to see. We will understand them as people who have become attuned to their environment in the exact same manner that we understand skilled athletes or mechanics as having become attuned.

For an ecological psychologist (rather uniquely), answering these challenges *requires* determining what types of mathematical relations "out there" distinguish between situations in which different outcomes are possible. Surely, if situations can be distinguished in that way, it will have to be as the result of combinations of many different factors. The challenge is to find the mathematics suited to describe our phenomenon of interest, rather than forcing our phenomenon to reduce (or expand) to fit a particular mathematical analysis.

Physiological mechanisms of information extraction. Given the current importance of neuroscience both in the public and professional view of psychology, ecological psychology would benefit from better articulating its view of the role of physiology in the perceptual process. An essential part of creating a less reductionistic psychology is articulating the roll of lower level functions within the bigger picture. What is it that happens within an organism when said organism is "resonating" with the environment? Gibson laid the foundation for such thought in *The Senses Considered as Perceptual Systems* (1966), yet, 40 years later, ecological psychologists still have no good way of talking about the role of physiology in the perceptual process, particularly the central nervous system. Work along these lines has been done (for example by Reed, 1989, and by Schöner, 1995 and colleagues, 1998), but a systematic vocabulary is still lacking.

It is clear what is rejected, the computational/information processing model. It is also clear the flavor of answer desired, something resembling current dynamic systems work; however, much greater specificity will eventually be needed. Unfortunately, this task is very difficult to begin, as the vocabulary with which neuroscientists and psychologists interact is that of "cognitive neuroscience," steeped in dualism and inseparable from many of the assumptions that ecological psychologists reject. As it stands, neuroscientists are finding more and more data that is compatible with the ecological psychologists' way of thinking, and incompatible with the cognitive psychologists'. However, because ecological psychologists lack a vocabulary to offer them, neuroscientists interested in psychology play procrustean games with cognitive terms—they mutilate the terms beyond all recognition, but because they ultimately use the cognitive term, their work is falsely believed to affirm the standard paradigm.[3]

Any acceptable vocabulary created in this endeavor will entail empirical claims about the roll of the brain in keeping us connected with the world. It must make it more intuitive to describe our ability to interact with the world accurately, accommodate discussion of situations in which we react inaccurately, and only secondarily account for our ability to articulate about the world. Notice that this is in the opposite of the priority order of the most cognitive psychologists. An action oriented accounting of the brain, rather than a "knowledge"-oriented accounting of the brain, would need to contextualize neural function as part of the activities of organisms within a dynamic environment.

The behaviors of perception. If information exists in the environment to be discovered, then how we move around in the world is a primary determinant of what we can perceive. Ecological psychologists know little about what types of movements are necessary to extract particular types of information. There is good work on a number of related topics: work on where people look when performing certain tasks, for example while driving (i.e., Rogers, Kadar, & Costall, 2005a, 2005b); work showing that some unknown aspect of movement is important to perception, for example, that amount of postural sway can correlate well with judgment accuracy, (i.e., Stoffregen, Yang, & Bardy, 2005); and work suggesting that people trying to attempt certain tasks behave in ways that generate certain optical patterns, for example, that moving in way that cancels the acceleration of optic expansion leads to intercepting a baseball (i.e., Michaels & Oudejans, 1992). However, we should be able to go much further: We still know almost nothing about how our exploratory movements expose us to information necessary for almost any of the thousands (millions?) of perceptually guided behaviors each of us performs on a daily basis. Part of the difficulty in beginning such studies may be that most activities do not seem to require specific motions (as catching the baseball might). Gibson claimed that "Perceiving is flexible, opportunistic, and full of multiple guarantees for detecting facts" (Gibson, 1967, p. 136). This flexibility means that in any natural case there will be many ways to move that facilitate any given perception. As ecological psychologists tend focus on tasks where it seems reasonable to hypothesize a single correct method of motion, I assume the natural redundancy in everyday tasks is seen as intimidating or limiting in some way, rather than as indicative of a plethora of untapped possibility.

We know even less about how we learn to make such movements. How do children and young animals develop the ability to extract invariants? Broadly, if we create situations that require specific types of movement in order to extract the invariants, how do people come to make those movements? How is ability-to-learn-the-correct-movement related to ability-to-make-proper-judgments? Are there other factors that affect the way perceptual systems move through the world? How do the different factors coordinate? This is probably the area in which ecological psychologists could most readily demonstrate unexpected phenomenon, if the experimental barriers could be overcome. Alas, in this instance the antireductionist theory has far outpaced the empirical ability.

Conclusions

The ecological approach, at least in psychology, is known for its antireductionist stance. On the other hand, that has also lead it to be thought of as quirky, strange, and even sometimes mystical. From his origins in the lineage of William James and E. B. Holt, Gibson tried to explain perception in a way that acknowledged the complexity of the ever-flowing interactions between organisms and their environment, and sought to explain how that complexity lead to organisms startling accuracy in acting towards the world. Along the way, there was a constant interplay of empirical and theoretical work, and that tradition remains alive and well in the field today. On the other hand, the challenges of conducting research on unreduced phenomenon are great, and many have yet to be overcome. While this difficulty can be somewhat disparaging at times, it is also inspiring to think of the possibilities that yet await us when those challenges are overcome. In summary, I wish to give what little sage advise I believe ecological psychology has to offer those wrestling with similar problems.

Offerings

Ecological psychologists do have some lessons to offer others who find themselves rejecting traditional reductions, but they may not have much in the way of deep insight. The lessons learned seem, at least in hindsight, like common senses:

1. *Look for signs that your explanations are too simplistic and then emphasize these problems rather than discounting them.* Sometimes further examination will reveal your current model to be adequate, sometimes further examination will force you to modify your model.

The history of ecological psychology contains important incidences in which discrepancies that could easily have been swept under the rug lead to innovation, almost always in the form of movement further away from traditional reductions.

2. *When you pick a phenomenon of interest, try to examine the whole phenomenon, at as large a scale as possible.* Try to determine the full range of things to be explained, and keep the range in mind when trying to form explanations. It is easy to become egocentric, anthropocentric, or just laboratory-centric. The drive to create an explanation for perception that could hold outside of the lab, and hold for organisms without the camera-like human eye, were very influential in pushing ecological psychology's antireductionism.

3. *Be sure, at least occasionally, to do experiments that find things other approaches would not predict, or cannot account for.* This is the only empirical bullet that non-reductionistic approaches can deliver to reductionistic approaches—the simple demonstration of nonreducable phenomenon. Most experimental data can be easily accommodated by multiple approaches, but early ecological psychologists emphasized the data that could not, convincing themselves, and others of the inadequacy of their previous views.

Reflections

Perhaps a crucial part of "being in awe" of your subject matter is being unwilling to pretend you are studying the phenomenon of interest when you are really studying some lesser, limited, or degenerate case. If that is the true, then the future of ecological psychology is largely in the hands of innovators. There are holes to be filled; areas of theoretical interest that have not been empirically investigated, or have only had the surface scratched. To explore these areas researchers must codify their previous methodological insights and push themselves to find new ways of studying phenomenon without reducing them. This volume will, no doubt, place these struggles in a much larger context of similar struggles in other areas of psychology. With luck, it will also help point a direction for the future.

Acknowledgments

Preparation of this manuscript was supported by a National Science Foundation Predoctoral Fellowship. An early draft of this work was presented to the Social, Evolutionary, Cultural Group at Clark University. Dr. Craig was very patience and provided helpful feedback on previous drafts. Also, much of the historical work would not have been possible without many hours of discussion with Dr. Thompson, perhaps the world's only remaining New Realist, over the previous years.

Notes

1.   I do not wish here to add citations or name names. I ask the reader to believe that I have A) seen this in response to talks at conventions, in which well meaning researchers tried to incorporate ecological concepts into their more cognitiv.ely oriented research, B) read it in peer reviews for both my own and other's journal articles, and C) read it at least a few published back and forths.

2   This has been confirmed to me anecdotally by multiple sources. The most easily cited confirmation was from participants in a discussion session on experiences of Gibson's graduate students, held at the 2005 Biannual Convention of the International Conference on Perception and Action in Monterey, CA.

3.   Again, I do not wish to add critical citations or name names, here because the practice is so widespread. To hear one prominent example, attend any current cognitive neuroscience conference and you will hear presenters saying that a given change in a given neuron "is" learning, "is" memory, etc.

References

Charles, E. P. (2008). Describing and explaining animal minds. In. R. Sokal & E. Abbey (eds.), *A Man of Many Hats: A Festschrift for Nicholas S. Thompson*. In Press.

Gibson, E. J. (1980). Eleanor J. Gibson. In L., Gardner (ed.), *A History of Psychology in Autobiography, Volume VII* (pp. 239-271). San Francisco: W. H. Freeman & Co.

Gibson, J. J. (1933). Adaptation, after-effect and contrast in the perception of curved lines. *Journal of Experimental Psychology, 16*, 1-31.

Gibson, J. J. (1957). Optical motions and transformations as stimuli for visual perception. *Psychological Review, 64*, 288-295.

Gibson, J. J. (1962). Observations on active touch. *Psychological Review, 69*, 477-490.

Gibson, J. J. (1966). The problem of temporal order in stimulation and perception. *Journal of Psychology, 62*, 141-149.

Gibson, J. J. (1967). James J. Gibson. In G. Lindzey (ed.), *A History of Psychology in Autobiography* (Vol. 5, pp. 125-143). New York: Appleton-Century-Crofts.

Gibson, J. J. (1976). The myth of passive perception: A reply to Richards. *Philosophy and Phenomenological Research, 37*, 234-238.

Gibson, J. J. (1979). *The Ecological Approach to Visual Perception*. Boston, Houghton Mifflin.

Gibson, J. J., & E. J. Gibson (1957). "Continuous perspective transformations and the perception of rigid motion." *Journal of Experimental Psychology, 54*, 129-138.

Gibson, J. J., Jack, E., & Raffel, G. (1932). Bilateral transfer of the conditioned response in the human subject. *Journal of Experimental Psychology, 15*, 416-421.

Gibson, J. J., Kaplan, G. A., Reynolds, H. N., JR., & Wheeler, K. (1969). The change from visible to invisible: A study of optical transitions. *Perception & Psychophysics, 5*, 113-115.

Holt, E. B., Marvin, W. T., Montauge, W. T., Perry, R. B., Pitkin, W. B., & Spaulding, E. G. (1910). The program and first platform of six realists. *Journal of Philosophy, Psychology, and Scientific Methods, 7*, 393-401.

Holt, E. B., Marvin, W. T., Montauge, W. T., Perry, R. B., Pitkin, W. B., & Spaulding, E. G. (1922). New Realism: Cooperative Studies in Philosophy. New York: The MacMillan Company.

Kadar, E. E., & Effken, J. A. (2006). Beyond good and evil: Prelude to a science of the future. *Ecological Psychology, 18*, 319-363.

MacLeod, R. B. (1974). A tribute to J. J. Gibson. In R. B. MacLeod, & H. L. Pick, Jr. (eds.), *Perception: Essays in Honor of James J. Gibson*. Ithaca, NY: Cornell University Press.

Michaels, C. F., & Oudejans, R. R. D. (1992). The optics and actions of catching fly balls: zeroing out optic acceleration. *Ecological Psychology, 4,* 199-222.

Reed, E. S. (1988). *James J. Gibson and the Psychology of Perception*. New Haven, CT: Yale University Press.

Reed, E. S. (1989). Neural regulation of adaptive behavior. *Ecological Psychology, 1,* 97-117.

Reed, E. S. (1996). James J. Gibson: Pioneer and Iconoclast. In G. A. Kimble, C. A. Boneau, & M. Wertheimer (eds.), *Portraits of Pioneers in Psychology, Vol. II*. Mahwah, NJ: Lawrence Erlbaum Associates.

Rogers, S. D., Kadar, E. E., & Costall, A. (2005). Gaze patters in the visual control of straight-road driving and braking as a function of speed and expertise. *Ecological Psychology, 17,* 1-38.

Rogers, S. D., Kadar, E. E., & Costall, A. (2005). Drivers' gaze patterns in braking from three different approaches to a crash barrier. *Ecological Psychology, 17,* 39-53.

Rudolph, L. (2006). Mathematics, models, and metaphors. *Culture and Psychology, 12,* 245-265.

Rudolph, L. (2006). Spaces of ambivalence: Qualitative mathematics in the modeling of complex fluid phenomena. *Estudios de Psicología , 27,* 67-83.

Rudolph, L. (2008a). A unified topological approach to umwelts and life spaces. Part II: Constructing life spaces from an umwelt. *From Past to Future*.

Rudolph, L. (2008b). A unified topological approach to umwelts and life spaces. Part I: Umwelts and finite topological spaces. In R. I. Sokol (ed.), *Relating to Environments: A New Look at Umwelt*. Charlotte, NC: Information Age Publishers.

Schöner, G. (1995). Recent developments and problems in human movement science and their conceptual implications. *Ecological Psychology, 7,* 293-314.

Schöner, G., Dijkstra, T. M. H., & Jeka, J. J. (1998). Action-perception patterns emerge from coupling and adaptation. *Ecological Psychology, 10,* 323-346.

Stoffregen, T. A., Yang, C., & Benoit, G. B. (2004). Affordance judgments and nonlocomotor body movements. *Ecological Psychology, 17,* 75-104.

Thompson, N. S. (1997). Communication and natural design. In Thompson, N.S. (series ed.). D. Owings & M. Beecher (vol. eds.), *Perspectives in ethology, Vol. 12: Communication*. New York: Plenum Press.

Tolman, E. C. (1926). A behavioristic theory of ideas. *Psychological Review, 33,* 352-369.

6

Kurt Lewin's Contribution to the Methodology of Psychology: From Past to Future Skipping the Present

Aaro Toomela

> To proceed beyond the limitations of a given level of knowledge the researcher, as a rule, has to break down methodological taboos which condemn as "unscientific" or "illogical" the very methods or concepts which later prove to be basic for the next major progress. [....] Like social taboos, a scientific taboo is kept up not so much by a rational argument as by common attitude among scientists: Any member of the scientific guild who does not strictly adhere to the taboo is looked upon as queer; he is suspected of not adhering to the scientific standards of critical thinking (Lewin, 1999, pp. 26-28).

Since the nineteen-forties, methodological thinking in psychology has gone through substantial changes. Contrary to the expectations of those who believe in progress and the cumulative nature of every science, these changes in psychology are related to a remarkable degree of oversimplification, a loss of productive thinking, and the dissemination of reductionist methodology.

Goodwin Watson, one of the founders and the first president of the Society for the Psychological Study of Social Issues, described eight significant differences between methodologies of pre-World-War II North American and German-Austrian psychologies (Watson, 1934). According to him, German psychology (1) was more interested in qualitative descriptions than in objective scores; (2) was more interested in psychological than in physical controls; (3) was predominantly concerned with wholes and relationships; (4) showed more concern about understanding a single case than the probabilities in a group; (5) saw individual trait differences as consequences of more basic type differences; (6) was more concerned with insight than with prediction; (7) was more systematic; instead of trying to incorporate all research results into a theory, German psychology acknowledged that some facts may be irrelevant or useless; (8) was more interested in thinking than in the accumulation of facts.

Watson predicted that these eight trends characterizing German-Austrian psychology would continue because a deeper understanding of mind is possible when the principles are followed. Analysis of present-day mainstream psychology, however, leads to the conclusion that Watson was wrong in his prediction; current mainstream psychology follows the traditions of pre-WWII North American psychology. The considerably more insightful methodological principles of German-Austrian psychology have moved into the periphery of psychological thought (Toomela, 2007a).

Kurt Lewin was one of the major representatives of the pre-WWII German-Austrian psychology. Not surprisingly, Lewin explicitly followed most of the methodological principles described by Watson. In this paper I suggest that the major contribution Lewin's works could provide for the future of psychology can be found in is his understanding of research methodology—the "field theory" he was developing was not so much a theory of the social world as much as "a method, namely a method of analyzing causal relations and building scientific constructs" (Lewin, 1997c, p. 201). In order to follow Lewin's contribution, however, we need to abandon the idea—unjustified as it is—that the last 50 or 60 years in mainstream psychology have necessarily advanced psychology beyond the level that characterized much of the Continental European pre-WWII psychology. In fact, I am suggesting, again (cf. Toomela, 2007a), that it might be justified to admit that the last 60 years in mainstream psychology have gone astray. In order to proceed in developing our understanding of the human mind, lessons from the past should be taken seriously. It does not mean that we need to go back in time; the goal is not to do psychology in the pre-WWII European way. Rather, future psychology can be built with the understanding that not everything that is new is better than the old and not everything that disappeared in the history of psychology disappeared for rational reasons (Toomela, 2007b). So, we may need to take the past seriously and skip the present in order to develop the future of our field of science

The following discussion of Lewin's possible contribution to the future development of methodological thinking in psychology is divided into two parts. In the first part, I briefly discuss Lewin's understanding of the methodological issues brought out by Watson (1934) and analyze the present-day mainstream psychology in more detail elsewhere (Toomela, 2007a). In the second part I discuss three additional methodological issues Lewin considered to be important, the principle of "contemporaneity," the necessity for definition of theoretical concepts, and the insufficiency of "phenotypical" observations without experimentation, without interference with the situation. The first two of these issues are related to shortcomings of current mainstream "quantitative" psychology; the last issue, in turn, is related to some fundamental problems in the modern "qualitative" research paradigm that turns out to be a much less powerful development in methodological thinking than the proponents of it believe.

Lewin and Eight Shortcomings of Pre-WWII North-American and Modern Mainstream Psychology

There are several methodological principles that characterized both the *Zeitgeist* of pre-WWII German-Austrian psychology and Kurt Lewin's personal understanding of important methodological principles. At the same time, all these principles are not taken into account in present-day mainstream psychology with no rational justification as to why they should not be followed (Toomela, 2007a).

First, German psychology of Lewin's time was more interested in qualitative descriptions than in objective scores. Lewin, on the one hand, was very keen to develop psychology into a mathematically exact science. On the other hand, he understood that (1) the mathematically exact is not necessarily quantitative—for example, topology, as a branch of mathematics does not deal with quantities but is still exact and principles of topology can be applied in psychology (Lewin, 1936). And (2) Mathematics is only applied in psychology. It follows that in some cases one may be faced with mathematical questions, which mathematics itself has not yet treated and it must not be assumed that psychology has to use the same dynamic concepts as physics. Only an investigation of psychological dynamics itself can decide which concepts are adequate for it (Lewin, 1935, 1936, 1997f). Modern psychology is concerned with the question of whether mathematical techniques used in psychology correspond to the phenomena that are studied only in the very un-influential periphery. Despite convincing theoretical analyses showing that most statistical data analyses may produce practically meaningless numbers (Essex & Smythe, 1999; Hoshmand, 2003; Martin, 2003; Michell, 2000, 2003a, 2003b, 2004), the production of such numbers continues.

Second, Lewin was clear about his attitudes toward the issue of psychological vs. physical control of the experimental situation. According to him, "To describe a situation 'objectively' in psychology actually means to describe the situation as a totality of those facts and of only those facts which make up the field of that individual. To substitute for that world of the individual the world of the teacher, of the physicist, or of anybody else is to be, not objective, but wrong" (Lewin, 1997e, p. 213, see also Lewin, 1935, 1997c, 1997f, 1997i for similar ideas). There are at least two reasons for this requirement. One is that a psychological field, i.e., a field in which behavior takes place is not equivalent to the "objective" physical or social fields because only some subjectively determined parts of the latter two constitute the psychological field (Lewin, 1997a, 1997c). Another reason is that similarities of behavior are not necessarily indications of similarities in the underlying state of the person. Thus, in order to understand behavior only through the external description of behavior without taking into account the psychological state of a person may be fundamentally misleading (Lewin, 1997i).

Third, Lewin was always concerned with wholes and relationships rather than with the isolated parts of the phenomena under study. The necessity for the wholistic approach followed from the principle that the change of one part of a whole implies a change of the other parts (e.g., Lewin, 1997f, 1997j). Another reason for a wholistic approach stems from the idea that the importance of an isolated element within a situation cannot be judged without a consideration of the situation as a whole (e.g., Lewin, 1997e).

Ignoring the whole leads to a distorted picture of the phenomenon under study. In the present-day context it is interesting to mention that Lewin was very critical about the practice of data collection that is almost invariably used in several branches of mainstream psychology now. He wrote,

> We are gradually giving up the idea that the answer to the questionnaires or interviews is an expression of facts. We are slowly learning to treat them as reactions to a situation, which are partly determined by the question, partly by the general situation of that individual. We have to learn to treat questionnaires, as we are accustomed to treat a projective technique. In short, we need most urgently a real theory of questionnairing and interviewing which offers more than a few technical rules (Lewin, 1997h, p. 284).

This kind of theory called for by Lewin has not developed as yet. Instead, answers to questionnaires are treated as context-independent "true" reflections (it is assumed that "error of measurement" can be extracted by sophisticated statistical data analysis techniques from the "true" scores) of underlying psychological characteristics.

One extension of the gestalt or wholistic approach was the call for an integrated theory of the whole field of psychology: "number of branches of psychology have reached a stage which makes their unification increasingly urgent. [....] Investigators are coming to feel that a mere piling up of facts can only lead to chaotic and unproductive situation. [....] Psychology needs concepts which can be applied not merely to the facts of a single field like child psychology, animal psychology, or psychopathology, but which are equally applicable to all of them" (Lewin, 1936, pp. 4-5). Indeed, the mind as a whole is studied from different perspectives that comprise different branches of psychology. The real significance of any of the findings and theories in one branch can be understood in the context of knowledge accumulated by all branches (see also Toomela, 2007c).

Fourth, Lewin's understanding of the role of an individual case in research and theory building also differed substantially from the present-day mainstream psychology. According to Lewin, the current practice of studying groups and practically ignoring individual cases and exceptions would be completely misleading: "Like any science, psychology is in a dilemma when it tries to develop 'general' concepts and laws. If one 'abstracts from individual differences,' there is no logical way back from these generalities to the individual case" (Lewin, 1997e, p. 212, see also, e.g., Lewin, 1935, 1997d). Current mainstream personality psychology, for instance, proposes theories, such as McCrae and Costa's Five-Factor-Theory of personality (McCrae & Costa, 1996, 1999), which exactly follow this line of thinking—the line of thinking which is not only illogical but also simply mathematically wrong (Molenaar, 2004, 2007; Molenaar & Valsiner, 2005).

Lewin was also more interested in insight than with probabilistic quantitative prediction (cf., e.g., Lewin, 1935, 1936). He was not explicit in being systematic and taking into consideration only those facts that are meaningful and ignoring the meaningless facts accumulated by a relatively atheoretical psychology; but his attitude in that respect was relatively obvious. So, for example, he did not consider to be meaningful "facts" constructed from individual differences, "facts" that were collected in studies of individuals isolated from the situations, or the facts derived from studies where individual and environment are treated as independent (such as answers to the question: which is more important, heredity or environment?) (cf. Lewin, 1935). He understood that only with the help of theories could one determine causal interrelationships.

Thus, the atheoretical inductive collections of facts that characterized North American pre-WWII psychology (Lewin, 1997j), may create facts that should be ignored in order to build a meaningful theory.

It can be conjectured that Lewin was also more interested in thinking than in the accumulation of facts. It does not mean, of course, that those scientists who dedicate their careers to the collection of facts do not think. Rather, the Lewinian kind of thinking is substantially more complex and potentially more productive in theory building than the thinking necessary for the study of relatively isolated decontextualized fragmented problems.

Finally, the only difference between Lewin's understanding of methodology and that described by Goodwin Watson as characterizing the German-Austrian psychology of his time seems to be related to the issues of typology. Lewin, who emphasized the necessity for understanding every single individual case seems not to pay attention to typology.

Taken together, methodological principles followed by Lewin were characteristic of pre-WWII era of German-Austrian way of thinking—and, correspondingly, much more sophisticated, productive, and meaningful than that utilized in modern mainstream psychology. There is a lot to learn from Lewin by studying how exactly he applied these principles in studies and theory building. Lewin's contribution to developing the future methodology of psychology, however, can be larger. Next I discuss three important methodological issues not discussed so far.

The Principle of "Contemporaneity," the Necessity for Definition of Theoretical Concepts, and the Insufficiency of "Phenotypical" Observations

The Principle of "Contemporaneity"

Present-day psychology often utilizes explanations for psychological phenomena that, for Lewin, would not be sufficiently scientific. Lewin understood that mind is qualitatively different from and yet continuous with the biological and physical world. Every mental phenomenon can take place only in an actual biological organism. The principle of "contemporaneity," as it was called by Lewin, follows logically from this understanding: "One of the basic statements of psychological field theory can be formulated as follows: Any behavior or any other change in a psychological field depends only upon the psychological field *at that time*" (Lewin, 1997c, p. 201, see also Lewin, 1935, 1936, 1997e, 1997f). There is one theoretical situation, when the behavior may depend on the earlier situation. It happens when there is exact understanding of how the current situation S^t depends on the earlier situation S^{t-n}, that is, the function $S^t = F(S^{t-n})$ is known. This is possible only when both situations, at time t and time $t-n$ are closed systems which are genidentic (Lewin, 1997c).

If we look into modern mainstream psychology, we find many theories which "explain" actual mental phenomena with the past, especially in evolutionary Social-Darwinist and genetic psychology. So, for example, about 20 percent-55 percent of the total variation in personality dimensions is attributed to genetic sources by different researchers (Jang, McCrae, Angleitner, Riemann, & Livesley, 1998; Pedersen, Plomin, Mc-Clearn, & Friberg, 1988). Similarly, many studies have been dedicated to the issue of the relative importance of genetic sources of variation in intelligence or IQ (see Mackintosh, 1998, for a review). It is assumed by such researchers that it is possible to isolate the effect of genetic sources from the effect of environmental sources.

In a Lewinian context we see that heritability numbers (whatever the exact number is) are meaningless; they have no explanatory power for at least two reasons. First, there is no direct effect of genes on personality or intelligence. Genes are the very "past" of the actual person's make-up. There are many (I am not sure whether it is established as yet how many exactly) steps from a gene to a protein, from a protein to an organ, from an organ to an organism, and from an organism to the behavior. What is beyond doubt, is that this path from a gene to a behavior does not constitute a closed system. On the contrary, we know that human biology is profoundly shaped by the social world and vice versa (Caccioppo, Berntson, & Sheridan, 2000). Thus, beyond the trivial and obvious fact that for a personality or intelligence to be possible, biological factors must be involved, there is nothing useful in the numbers of heritability. And instead of these meaningless numbers we need the theory about what exactly, in the actual "contemporary" biological make-up of a person is important in the phenomenon of personality or intelligence.

Second, for Lewin all behavior is the function of the mutually interdependent person and his environment. Person and the environment—the "life space" in Lewin's terms—constitute a *whole*. This fact is partly—and for that reason completely misleadingly—taken into account by some modern researchers in the field. So, in discussing how genes and psychological characteristics can be related, gene-environment "interaction" is defined by the leading scholar in the field, Plomin (Plomin & Crabbe, 2000) in this way: "Gene-environment interaction refers to genetic differences in sensitivity to experience" (p. 815). Consequently, for him, there is a unidirectional road from genes to environment; to call this "interaction" would be incorrect. Interaction should refer to a situation where genetic differences in sensitivity to experience are accompanied by experiential differences in biological processes, including gene expression, for example.

Even more, heritability estimates are based on the idea that by comparing genetically similar and dissimilar children in similar and dissimilar environments, it is possible to isolate the effects of environment from the effects of genetic factors. In studies of heritability, curiously, no clear theory of exactly how genes are related to behavior is provided. Even more, the theory of environment is extremely primitive in these accounts. It is assumed that children living in the same family share the same environment. But, as Lewin would also suggest, it is not the physical or biological environment *per se* that constitutes the environment for the person but rather the *psychological* environment. Externally, the same environment may have completely different meanings for different persons or even for the same person at different times. There is no proof that "shared environment" is actually shared. Also, without a theory of environment it is not possible to tell whether environments for children living apart are truly different. Physical, biological, and social environments can be characterized by an unlimited number of characteristics. Theory that explains what characteristics of the environment are important is absolutely necessary in order to claim that the environment of children has been different. Actually there are so many similarities in "nonshared" environments that it seems to be impossible to make any claims about the role of environment in these studies: all children in heritability studies have lived in the human social-cultural environment; usually, in case of adoption, not any person can adopt a child, the foster parents are carefully selected; in most cases children shared the country, the system of formal schooling, etc.

A similar problem characterizes evolutionary "explanations." Whatever characteristic of behavior, whether sexual, intellectual, or exploratory, is "explained" by the possible usefulness for adaptation in evolution is actually not explained at all. The past cannot explain the present. It becomes understandable now why Lewin (1997d) explicitly rejected such explanations and the necessity for research into finding heritability estimates:

> However, it does not help much to argue whether adolescence is a biological or psychological effect. It does not help either to try to describe, on a statistical basis, to what

degree this problem is biological or psychological in nature. Even if an answer could be found, it would be of as little value as, for instance, the determining of the degree to which heredity and environment affect intelligence. We still would not have gained any insight into the way in which bodily and social factors are working together and against each other, integrating the concrete behavior of the adolescent (p. 265).

All this said, it is important that "historical" explanation is actually necessary but insufficient for understanding mind: "As in psychology, in sociology both the historical and the systematic question 'why' is important, and neither question is finally to be solved without the other" (Lewin, 1997j, p. 24). Historical explanation becomes meaningless when proposed as the only explanation. In order to understand why participants in the actual "contemporary" situation are who they are, their history must be understood as well.

The Necessity for Definition of Theoretical Concepts

Many phenomena in modern mainstream psychology are not unambiguously defined. Rather, very often we find tens or even hundreds of different definitions for the same concept. Among them, emotion (Kleinginna & Kleinginna, 1981a), motivation, (Kleinginna & Kleinginna, 1981b), culture (Kroeber & Kluckhohn, 1952), intelligence (Jensen, 1998), and personality (Allport, 1937) to mention just some of the common concepts used in modern psychology. Knowing that there are many possible definitions for a concept, what would be more natural than to ask theoretically which of the definitions should be used in psychology and to justify why that particular definition is chosen. Instead, we find in modern mainstream psychology a situation where such concepts are commonly used without any definition or, in the "best" case, defined operationally.

Lewin would find this situation unacceptable for a science. According to him, "Psychology should be as much concerned with the question of what frustration 'is' psychologically, as with the effect of frustration. In fact, field theory considers it impossible to investigate the laws of frustration, hope, friendship, or autocracy without investigating at the same time what frustration, hope, friendship, or autocracy 'is' psychologically" (Lewin, 1997b, pp. 194-195). He criticized the vague approach where no definition is provided: "In short, the conceptual properties of the constructs, i.e., their logical interdependence as opposed to their empirical interdependence as discovered by experiments, are left entirely vague. An outstanding example is the construct *intelligence* which is very well defined operationally but so poorly defined conceptually that practically no logical derivation seems possible" (Lewin, 1997f, pp. 186-187).

The reason for the requirement of definition is related to the issue of measurement (Lewin, 1997b):

> To know what the conceptual dimension of a construct is is of great methodological importance. (1) Only those entities which have the same conceptual dimension can be compared as to their magnitude. (2) Everything which has the same conceptual dimension can be compared quantitatively; its magnitude can be measured, in principle, with the same yardstick (units of measurement). [....] Whenever the problem of psychological *measurement* arises we should ask: What is the conceptual type of the phenomenon we want to measure, and how is the measuring procedure related to this particular type? (p. 196).

So, without defining "conceptual dimensions" of concepts, neither logical derivation nor true measurement is possible. This issue is also brought up by some exceptional modern scholars: very often it is questionable whether psychological attributes themselves are quantitative at all. It is possible that quantitative structure is imposed on qualitative psychological phenomena. In such cases the quantification of data and the following utilization of quantitative data analysis methods is misleading and may end up with numbers that "are not just theory-free numbers, they are meaning-free numbers" (Essex & Smythe, 1999, p. 746).

Following a Lewinian way of thinking, in order to understand anything in science, we need a theory about what a thing or phenomenon under study "is"; we would need to define its conceptual dimensions, i.e. the dimensions that can be quantified, and only then we would be able to proceed with true measurement. Following that logic we would have to reject all concepts that are defined operationally without a theory—in fact we would have to reject the majority of concepts in the modern mainstream psychology as ambiguous—personality, intelligence, culture, emotion, motivation, individualism, collectivism, attitude, value, to name just a few. Just the thought that there are so many very different psychological phenomena that can be "measured" by the same "yardstick"—the Likert scale—should make us suspicious. Do we think that so many different phenomena share the same conceptual dimension that is measured by the scale? If so, what exactly are we measuring? In physics we need many different units for measurement—volt and ampere, meter and gram, second and joule, bar and calorie, watt and kelvin, mole and candela. Why is it that in psychology, in most cases, only two units are used, the Likert scale and the number of solved problems? Is the mind really so simple? I am afraid that we have no idea. Even worse, following Lewinian thinking we would also have to reject all derivations where such ambiguous concepts are used for "explaining" behavior or some mental phenomenon. Very little would be left from psychology after such "cleaning of the field." However, such a cleaning seems to be justified.

The Insufficiency of "Phenotypical" Observations

So far, the discussion of Lewinian ideas leads to a conclusion that modern mainstream psychology has lost fundamentally important methodological principles that can be found in Kurt Lewin's works in particular and also in the Continental European understanding of psychology in general (Kurt Koffka, Wolfgang Köhler, Lev Vygotsky, Alexander Luria, Heinz Werner are just a few outstanding names that come to mind when similar methodological ideas would be searched for in other scholars of pre-WWII Continental European psychology). Mostly this critique can be applied to so-called quantitative methodology.

There is an increasing trend in psychology to replace quantitative methods with qualitative methods (Rennie, Watson, & Monteiro, 2002). Several different qualitative research methods, such as grounded theory, discourse analysis, or phenomenology can be distinguished. What seems to be common to them is a more or less explicit rejection of the need for interference with the study situations. Rather, data are collected through the observation and recording of ongoing situations.

Lewin's research methodology, in modern terms, would be called qualitative rather than quantitative. However, Lewin (1997g) would reject modern qualitative research techniques as insufficient:

> As long as the scientist merely describes [...] he is open to the criticism that the categories used reflect merely his "subjective views" and do not correspond to the "real" properties of the phenomena under consideration. [....] The "reality" of that to which the concept refers is established by "doing something with" rather than "looking at," and this reality is independent of certain "subjective" elements of classification (p. 304).

In other words, any observation without experiment or theoretically justified interference with the research situation is open to the fallacy of "subjectivity." He also explains why experimentation is crucial (Lewin, 1999):

> Science tries to link certain observable (phenotypical) data with other observable data. It is crucial for all problems of interdependence, however, that [...] it is, as a rule, impracticable to link one set of phenotypical data *directly* to other phenotypical data. Instead, it is necessary to insert "intervening variables" (p. 32).

The same idea in a slightly different form has actually been discussed above—according to Lewin, externally the same behavior may originate from very different personal states of mind, and externally similar environments may have different meanings for different persons and for the same person at different times. It has been a common mistake not only in psychology but also in physics, to assume that things or phenomena should be categorized according to "phenotypical" similarities. Externally similar behaviors may belong to very different classes of behaviors because of the differences in underlying mechanisms and externally very different behaviors may belong to the same class (Lewin, 1935). Modern qualitative research seems not so much to build theories about the world but rather to create "multiple voices," to construct different possible stories or "discourses" about appearances. The problem is that the number of possible ways to link appearances into a superficially coherent story is practically unlimited. Experiment, theoretically guided interference with a situation, is a tool that constrains possible theories. Without such constraining of possible explanations, any fairy-tale would become an acceptable theory.

What Can We Learn from Lewin?

Lewin's ideas have direct implications for improving the methodological thinking of today—and tomorrow. First of all, it is necessary to understand that research methodology cannot come before a theory. Methods must be chosen in accordance with the questions a researcher wishes to answer. The results of research, of course, can change a theory so that new methods are called for. But in an established field of science such as psychology several principles can be proposed that should be taken into account in the process of the selection of research methods.

Following Lewin (among several other Continental European pre WWII psychologists) the first requirement for a theory is the need to understand a phenomenon as a whole. Without understanding *all the parts* of *the life space as a whole* the phenomenon under study cannot be understood. It follows that research methodology must avoid fragmentation. For example, methodology that ignores the fact that "objectively the same" environment can be psychologically diverse and vice versa, is inappropriate for building an acceptable theory.

Second, the aim of the studies is eventually building a theory in exact language where all concept, all parts and relationships of the whole theory, are made explicit and exact. There is no use to study relationships between constructs if the constructs are not exactly defined. In a theory the defined constructs should correspond to the parts of the life space. It is not possible to define constructs before studies. But equally it is not possible to get meaningful results from studies that define constructs only operationally. So, research methodology that is not aimed to understand *what* is studied in addition to *how* the studied construct is related to other constructs can only give theoretically useless data. Modern psychology is in a situation where the same name is used for hundreds of differently defined constructs. In this situation studies without explicitly defining the constructs and justifying the choice of the definition can produce only superficially meaningful results. Insight into the phenomena under study is not possible to gain in this way.

We see again that the interpretation of collected data in modern psychology is inappropriate in principle for understanding mind. Without the definition of constructs it is not possible to prove that a construct "measured" by some test, questionnaire or other research tool really measures the behavior of entities that share the same conceptual dimension. If the entities do not share the same conceptual dimension, magnitude comparisons become uninterpretable in principle. Furthermore, empirical psychological research must lead to exact mathematical language describing the mind and not vice versa. Psychology today actually follows the opposite—and theoretically meaningless—way, where mathematics tells us how to build psychology.

Next, it is important to take into account specific properties of the phenomena under study. Mind is an individual phenomenon that actively interprets the environment. Therefore, again, methodology that ignores the effect of the "psychological environment" of the individuals on the behavior and observed data collected in a study is inappropriate. Also, research methodology that ignores individuals as the real sources of interpretable data and treats data only at the group level is simply wrong for building the needed theory—theory that is about the ways *individual* mind operates. Among other implications it follows that all statistical data analysis procedures that create average group characteristics from individual data are inappropriate for understanding individual mind. Quantitative prediction can be useful for some practical applications but it is inappropriate for building understanding of psychological phenomena.

Fourth, another important characteristic of mind as a whole is that processes of a mind cannot be directly observed. There are hidden "intervening variables" between changes in the environment and behaviors that corresponds to them. Any study that relies only on phenotypical observation without interfering with the situation is doomed to produce results that are uninterpretable in terms of hidden processes.

Fifth, mind is built in a series of many steps. The behavior taking place at any given moment depends only on the structure of the life space at the very same moment. It follows, first, that all "explanations" of current behavior with the facts from past are not true explanations. And, second, research methodology must be developmental because only through developmental approach can we gain insight into what is really current and what is past in the behavior at the given time.

Finally, in a science it is possible to find many facts that are considered to be meaningful in one or another period of time. With the development of theories many facts become irrelevant. The questions asked in science follow from the theory of the time. The questions—and all answers to these questions—may turn out to be irrelevant when theories change. Also, if inappropriate research methodology is used, all facts gathered with such methods turn out to be irrelevant for theory building. The selection of facts to be taken into account must be theoretically driven. Following principles Lewin considered important for psychological research we may reach the conclusion that only a handful of facts from millions collected during the last half of a century in psychology can be meaningful.

Conclusions

Lewin was a representative of Continental European pre-WWII psychology. This psychology used sophisticated methodology, dedicated a lot of discussion to theoretical issues and rejected blind uses of scientific methods. Most of the fundamental principles of this psychology have disappeared from modern mainstream psychology with no rational reason. Mainstream psychology of today is not interested in (1) qualitative descriptions, (2) the psychological meaning of the situations for the participants of studies, (3) taking the idea of a whole seriously, (4) trying to explain all exceptions and explaining individual cases, (5) gaining insight in addition to quantitative probabilistic prediction, and (6) ignoring meaningless facts. Lewin also suggested that—and justified why—(7) true explanation of behavior relies on information about the actual present situation; past and future cannot be used as explanations because these two do not exist; (8) any meaningful measurement and logical derivation in science requires a theoretical definition of the concepts; and (9) observation without theoretically justified interference with the situation, without experiment is not productive. Lewin has a lot to tell us about the future of methodology in psychology.

References

Allport, G. W. (1937). *Personality. A psychological interpretation.* New York: Henry Holt and Company.

Caccioppo, J. T., Berntson, G. G., & Sheridan, J. F. (2000). Multilevel integrative analyses of human behavior: Social neuroscience and the complementing nature of social and biological approaches. *Psychological Bulletin, 126*(6), 829-843.

Essex, C., & Smythe, W. E. (1999). Between numbers and notions. A critique of psychological measurement. *Theory and Psychology, 9*(6), 739-767.

Hoshmand, L. T. (2003). Can lessons of history and logical analysis ensure progress in psychological science? *Theory and Psychology, 13*(1), 39-44.

Jang, K. L., McCrae, R. R., Angleitner, A., Riemann, R., & Livesley, W. J. (1998). Heritability of facet-level traits in a cross-cultural twin sample: Support for a hierarchical model of personality. *Journal of Personality and Social Psychology, 74*(6), 1556-1565.

Jensen, A. (1998). *The g factor. The science of mental ability.* Westport: Praeger.

Kleinginna, P. R., & Kleinginna, A. M. (1981a). A categorized list of emotion definitions, with suggestions for a consensual definition. *Motivation and Emotion, 5* (4), 345-379.

Kleinginna, P. R., & Kleinginna, A. M. (1981b). A categorized list of motivation definitions, with a suggestion for a consensual definition. *Motivation and Emotion, 5*(3), 263-291.

Kroeber, A. L., & Kluckhohn, C. (1952). Culture: a critical review of concepts and definitions. *Papers. Peabody Museum of Archaeology and Ethnology, Harvard University., 47*, i-223.

Lewin, K. (1935). *A dynamic theory of personality. Selected papers.* New York: McGraw-Hill.

Lewin, K. (1936). *Principles of topological psychology.* New York: McGraw-Hill.

Lewin, K. (1997a). Behavior and development as a function of the total situation. (Originally published in 1946.) In K. Lewin, *Resolving social conflicts and field theory in social science* (pp. 337-381). Washington, DC: American Psychological Association.

Lewin, K. (1997b). Constructs in field theory. (Originally published in 1944.) In K. Lewin, *Resolving social conflicts and field theory in social science* (pp. 191-199). Washington, DC: American Psychological Association.

Lewin, K. (1997c). Defining the "field at a given time." (Originally published in 1943.) In K. Lewin, *Resolving social conflicts and field theory in social science* (pp. 200-211). Washington, DC: American Psychological Association.

Lewin, K. (1997d). Field theory and experiment in social psychology. (Originally published in 1939). In K. Lewin, *Resolving social conflicts and field theory in social science* (pp. 262-278). Washington, DC: American Psychological Association.

Lewin, K. (1997e). Field theory and learning. (Originally published in 1942.) In K. Lewin, *Resolving social conflicts and field theory in social science* (pp. 212-230). Washington, DC: American Psychological Association.

Lewin, K. (1997f). Formalization and progress in psychology. (Originally published in 1940.) In K. Lewin, *Resolving social conflicts and field theory in social science* (pp. 169-190). Washington, DC: American Psychological Association.

Lewin, K. (1997g). Frontiers in group dynamics. (Originally published in 1947.) In K. Lewin, *Resolving social conflicts and field theory in social science* (pp. 301-336). Washington, DC: American Psychological Association.

Lewin, K. (1997h). Problems of research in social psychology. (Originally published in 1943-44.) In K. Lewin, *Resolving social conflicts and field theory in social science* (pp. 279-288). Washington, DC: American Psychological Association.

Lewin, K. (1997i). Regression, retrogression, and development. (Originally published in 1941.) In K. Lewin, *Resolving social conflicts and field theory in social science* (pp. 231-261). Washington, DC: American Psychological Association.

Lewin, K. (1997j). Some social-psychological differences between the United States and Germany. (Originally published in 1936.) In K. Lewin, *Resolving social conflicts and field theory in social science* (pp. 15-34). Washington, DC: American Psychological Association.

Lewin, K. (1999). Cassirer's philosophy of science and the social sciences. (Originally published in 1949.) In M. Gold (ed.), *The complete social scientist: A Kurt Lewin reader* (pp. 23-36). Washington, DC: American Psychological Association.

Mackintosh, N. J. (1998). *IQ and human intelligence.* Oxford: Oxford University Press.

Martin, J. (2003). Positivism, quantification and the phenomena of psychology. *Theory and Psychology, 13*(1), 33-38.

McCrae, R. R., & Costa, P. T. (1996). Toward a new generation of personality theories: Theoretical contexts for the Five-Factor Model. In J. S. Wiggins (ed.), *The Five-Factor Model of Personality* (pp. 51-87). New York: The Guilford Press.

McCrae, R. R., & Costa, P. T. (1999). A Five-Factor Theory of personality. In A. Lawrence, & O. P. J. Pervin (eds.), *Handbook of Personality: Theory and Research* (pp. 139-153). New York: The Guilford Press.

Michell, J. (2000). Normal science, pathological science and psychometrics. *Theory and Psychology, 10*(5), 639-667.

Michell, J. (2003a). Pragmatism, positivism and the quantitative imperative. *Theory and Psychology, 13*(1), 45-52.

Michell, J. (2003b). The quantitative imperative. Positivism, naive realism and the place of qualitative methods in psychology. *Theory and Psychology, 13*(1), 5-31.

Michell, J. (2004). Item response models, pathological science and the shape of error. *Theory and Psychology, 14*(1), 121-129.

Molenaar, P. C. M. (2004). Forum discussion of the Manifesto's Aggregation Act. *Measurement, 2*(4), 248-254.

Molenaar, P. C. M. (2007). Psychological methodology will change profoundly due to the necessity to focus on intra-individual variation: Commentary on Toomela. *Integrative Psychological and Behavioral Science, 41*(1), 35-40.

Molenaar, P. C. M., & Valsiner, J. (2005). How generalization works through the single case: A simple idiographic process analysis of an individual psychotherapy. *International Journal of Idiographic Science,* Article 1. Retrieved October 25, 2005 from http://www.valsiner.com/ articles/molenvals.htm.

Pedersen, N. L., Plomin, R., McClearn, G. E., & Friberg, L. (1988). Neuroticism, Extraversion and related traits in adult twins reared apart and reared together. *Journal of Personality and Social Psychology, 55*(6), 950-957.

Plomin, R., & Crabbe, J. (2000). DNA. *Psychological Bulletin, 126*(6), 806-828.

Rennie, D. L., Watson, K. D., & Monteiro, A. M. (2002). The rise of qualitative research in psychology. *Canadian Psychology, 43*(3), 179-189.

Toomela, A. (2007a). Culture of science: Strange history of the methodological thinking in psychology. *Integrative Psychological and Behavioral Science, 41*(1), 6-20.

Toomela, A. (2007b). History of methodology in psychology: Starting point, not the goal. *Integrative Psychological and Behavioral Science, 41*(1), 75-82.

Toomela, A. (2007c). Unifying psychology: absolutely necessary, not only useful. In A. V. B. Bastos, & N. M. D. Rocha (eds.), *Psicologia: Novas direcoes no dialogo com outros campos de saber* (pp. 449-464). Sao Paulo: Casa do Psicologo.

Watson, G. (1934). Psychology in Germany and Austria. *Psychological Bulletin, 31*(10), 755-776.

7

A Unified Topological Approach to *Umwelt*s and Life Spaces Part II: Constructing Life Spaces from an *Umwelt*

Lee Rudolph

1. Introduction: Can Topological Psychology Be Rehabilitated?

Kurt Lewin's book *Principles of Topological Psychology* (Lewin, 1936) is deeply flawed. Repeatedly, Lewin introduces high-powered, somewhat recondite mathematical terminology only to leave it high and dry, available as metaphor but inaccessible to characteristically mathematical reasoning and development—an inaccessibility vitiating Lewin's evident belief that his psychological conclusions are in some way supported by the power of mathematics. This point was made vigorously over 60 years ago:

> [T]hese definitions by themselves, torn from the body of the enmeshing mathematical theory, are unproductive of deducible conclusions. The host of theorems that form the actual machinery of topology should have been made to function and so to take over the work of rigorous deduction. Lewin in reality does not utilize *one single theorem* of topology. Always there is an interminable use of a few *definitions* ripped out of their proper context. This being the circumstance, it is futile to insist that any closely articulated system has been achieved (London, 1944, p. 287).

Yet Lewin's book remains suggestive; something feels right about the underlying intuition[1] that topology, which can roughly but not wrongly be called "qualitative geometry," may be the right mathematics for "qualitative psychology."

In the late 1960s, several mathematicians (notably René Thom and Ralph Abraham) read Lewin (cf. Abraham, 2006) and took up the project of bringing actual mathematical methods to bear on his subject matter.

The mathematics they applied—including the theories of dynamical systems, classification of singularities, and eventually chaos—was not only topological, it was also strongly analytic in the mathematical sense: it depended heavily on concurrent developments in the structure theory of differential manifolds and their mappings (a theory that by then was far more advanced than "the actual machinery of topology" and "host of theorems" that were available to Lewin's mathematical contemporaries); in particular, it made constant and essential use of the real-number system.

In his invitation to write a paper on Lewin's work for *From Past to Future*, Joshua Clegg suggested some common goals of the approaches to the "experiment" of Lewin and the other psychologists under discussion—among them, that experimental theory, method, and procedure were not to be artificially separated, but rather were all three to be grounded in the concrete, particular situations out of which structural and temporal wholes are organically generated. It is unclear to me whether work using an approach like that of Thom and Abraham has been (or may yet be) successful in furthering those goals. In any case, here I suggest a different approach. More specifically, I propose that there is a spectrum of "life spaces" of any person P, each constructed by some observer Q (who might be P) from P's *Umwelt* by (more or less) a single general method and distinguished among themselves in various ways including context, purpose, range of time, and time scale.[2]

There are important differences among, on the one hand, the mathematical models of "life spaces" that I propose to construct, and, on the other, both the class of mathematical models based on the real-number system, and premathematical models like those actually given by Lewin (1936). As far as I can determine from his examples, and the general way he talks about "regions," "paths," "Jordan curves," etc., Lewin—when endeavoring to construct concrete instantiations of the notion of "life space" he seems to have had in mind—in fact always (presumably unaware that there were alternatives) used "mathematical spaces" that were infinite, and indeed "infinitely structured," in the style of the real-number system and Cartesian coordinate spaces. Yet this model-making behavior contrasts markedly with Lewin's purported model-making goals, as stated explicitly in *Principles of Topological Psychology*, e.g., in the Glossary:

> *Space (region), structured finitely:* A space (region) which can be divided into distinguishable part regions, but which is not infinitely structured.

Space (region), structured infinitely: A space (region) whose part regions can be divided infinitely into further parts (Lewin, 1936, p. 215).

Life space ... can be represented by a finitely structured space (Lewin, 1936, p. 216).

From this point of view, my proposed models may after all constitute a rehabilitation of Lewin's work on his own expressed terms, being (like the model of *Umwelt* offered in the prequel of this essay, Rudolph, in press) both entirely finitistic and entirely "topological."

2. What Is a "Life Space," and What Should One Be?

Here is the full text of Lewin's glossary entry for "life space" (quoted elliptically above), followed by the full text of the next entry in his Glossary.

Life space: Totality of facts which determine the behavior (*B*) of an individual at a certain moment. The life space (*L*) represents the totality of possible events. The life space includes the person (*P*) and the environment (*E*). $B = f(L) = f(P,E)$. It can be represented by a finitely structured space.

Life space, foreign hull of: Facts which are not subject to psychological laws but which influence the state of the life space (Lewin, 1936, p. 216).

The use of functional notation "$f(L)$" contributes nothing to these glosses (and is abusive by mathematical standards; cf. London, 1944, p. 277). As I see it, what remains, taken together with the other two entries quoted earlier, comes down to something like the following.

Denote by P@T the "person" P "at a certain moment" T, by B(P@T) the "behavior" of P@T, by E(P@T) the "environment" of P@T, and by F(P@T) the "foreign hull" of P@T. The "life space," or more precisely "the state of the life space" at the "moment" T, is a finite set L(P@T) equipped with some sort of (necessarily finite) structure that represents both P@T and E(P@T). Further, L(P@T) is to "determine" B(P@T) via "psychological laws," whereas F(P@T) can merely "influence" L(P@T), and that exclusively via non-psychological "laws" (be they physiological, physical, or whatever).

For my purposes, I propose to make two simplifications of this formal account of what a "life space" is, or should be, before proceeding to a mathematical formalization.

In the first place, I plan to ignore all talk of "laws"; at such an early stage of formalization I believe such talk is likely to be incoherent and unhelpful. In this, I am consciously echoing Barker (1968, p. 1), as summarized and quoted by Heft (2001):

Figure 1

As R. Barker (1968) pointed out, psychology may be unique among the sciences in that it began explicitly as an experimental discipline and, unlike other natural sciences, never experienced a descriptive phase. And as an experimental discipline, psychology focused its efforts on attempting to discover "if x then y" causal laws of explanation.... In contrast, other sciences such as astronomy, botany, zoology and geology all began with active naturalistic description of its basic phenomena, and they continue to pursue this kind of work even in their mature, experimental phases. However, "the descriptive, natural history, ecological phase of investigation has had a minor place in psychology and has seriously limited the science" (R. Barker, 1968, p. 1).

Thus, I will be content to describe a time series of "life spaces" L(P@ T), where P remains "genidentical" [3] as the moment T varies, without attempting (here) to explain the dynamics by which a later "life space" in the series is derived from an earlier one.

In the second place, I will also jettison the notation B(P@T) and ignore all talk of "behavior." Operationally, distinguishing "the behavior ... of an individual" from mere change over time in the "state of the life space" of that individual might or might not be easy in various cases, but seems (to me) in general to presuppose an understanding (at least, a hypothetical understanding) of "psychological laws" such as I have already decided to ignore.

With those simplifications, a "life space" is now formally similar to an *Umwelt* as described by Rudolph (in press. There, I gave a stratification of the universe[4] from the point of view of an organism O "at a certain moment" T, as depicted in Fig. 1. In the terms of that figure, the "person" P@ T (given that the organism O *is* a "person" P) can formally be identified (tautologously, if perhaps tendentiously) with what is in the ATTENTION of P at T. The Lewinian "environment" E(P@T), being evidently a sort of "psychological environment," is contained in (or otherwise limited by) "what is in AWARENESS" for P@T, defined in Uexküllian terms[5] as what "is in touch with the nervous system" of P@T; more precisely, since Lewin distinguishes P from its "environment," E(P@T) is contained in (or otherwise limited by) the set-theoretical difference between "what is in AWARENESS" for P@T and "what is in ATTENTION." Finally, F(P@ T) is surely contained in the set-theoretical difference between "what is

Figure 2
After Lewin (1936), Figure 20

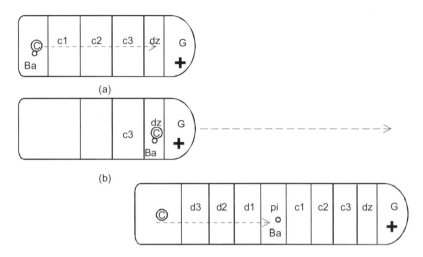

ACCESSIBLE" (physically) to P@T and "what is in AWARENESS" for P@
T; depending on how one understands Lewin's word "influence," F(P@
T) it might be further constrained to lie entirely within "what is AVAIL-
ABLE" to (the sensory organs of) P@T. Regardless, since I am ignoring
all "laws" and in particular all non-psychological "laws," F(P@T) has
no further role to play in my formalization of L(P@T) and so need not
be located precisely.

3. A Child with a Ball

Principles of Topological Psychology (Lewin, 1936) contains few
concrete examples of actual "life spaces." One of the most concrete is,
fortunately for my project, tied explicitly to motion pictures taken by
Lewin and still available (in Lück, 1988) for inspection and analysis.
Since *Principles of Topological Psychology* is out of print and hard to
find, I quote it *in extenso*. Throughout, "Figure 20" refers to the original
of Fig. 2.

3.1. What Lewin Described

The segment of Lewin's "moving-picture material" on which he
based the following example is, as nearly as I can tell, the last 53
seconds of 160 seconds recording some adventures of a child with a
ball (included in Lück, 1988, starting approximately 29 minutes from
the beginning).

We can offer an example from our moving-picture material. A two-year-old child C who still has trouble in walking up- or downstairs without support wants to place his ball on the landing. In order to do so he has to go up three steps. Topologically we could represent the initial stage of the situation as follows (cf. Figure 20a). Between the goal G and the child C there is a barrier which consists of the following zones: climbing the first step ($c1$), climbing the second step ($c2$), the third step ($c3$), and finally going beyond the edge of the landing which is still a danger zone (dz) from which the ball may roll back. Let us assume that the child has already picked up the ball (Ba). (The child C and ball may be represented as regions which have a partially common boundary.)

The child succeeds in bringing the ball up all three steps to the danger zone dz (Fig. 20b). Then he drops the ball and it rolls down again. Thereby the following situation comes into being (Fig. 20c). The goal is suddenly moved to a distance. There are now more regions between the child and his goal than in the original situation. In order to reach his goal the child must now go through the following regions: He must climb down the third step ($d3$), the second step ($d2$), the first step ($d1$), and pick up (pi) the ball. Then he must again climb up the first step ($c1$), the second step ($c2$), and the third step ($c3$) with the ball in his hands, and he must take the ball beyond the danger zone (dz) on the landing.

Without a doubt there occurs a significant change in spacial relations of C and G. Since all locomotions can be determined only relatively there is no reason for not speaking of locomotion in this case. The causes of this locomotion are essentially different from those of the active movement of the child between the first and second stages. Then it was the ball which separated itself from the child and carried out the locomotion to pi. At the same time however the spacial relationship of C and G underwent a marked change as a result of the locomotion of the ball. Since C did not bring about this change of position by active movement on his own part, and furthermore since he was not passively moved by another person, he might have the feeling that "the ground moved under his feet." Such an event may well be characterized as a locomotion of the surrounding field in relation to the person. Locomotions of this kind are often accompanied by other changes in the structure of the field (Lewin, 1936, pp. 113-115).

3.2. (Some of) What Lewin Didn't Describe

Of course Lewin was present, not only while the events filmed were taking place, but also before and after; nor (naturally) was his access to the scene, the child C, and so on, restricted to what could be recorded in a silent motion picture. Further, his aim, in using his "motion-picture material" to "offer an example," was presumably not so much to analyze the "material" in itself (or even in a larger context) but more to display for purposes of exposition what he presumably took to be an archetypal "life space" fragment. All that said, when once I had identified this fragment of Lück, 1988, as the "example from our moving-picture material" described by Lewin (1936, pp. 113-115), and had viewed it again (I had viewed it and some other fragments of Lück, 1988, before reading either Lewin, 1936, or von Uexküll, 1920/1926), I was struck by how little Lewin's account corresponded to what I saw!

My second viewing of the fragment came at a time when I was beginning to pull together (more or less) the ideas about mathematical modeling of *Umwelt* presented in the prequel of this essay (Rudolph, in press). During the latter part (September 2006 through April 2007) of that stage in my work on those ideas, I also was directing an undergraduate seminar, "Diving into Mathematical Research: Emotion Space." Consequently, on several occasions throughout those seven months I was able to enlist a number of extra pairs of eyes to view the fragment and some earlier fragments of Lewin's "moving-picture material" repeatedly, with the end in view of performing a microgenetic analysis along (what I hoped would be) topological lines. That analysis remains incomplete, but several points that arose during the ongoing process are directly relevant to my present concerns.

(1) What the "two-year-old child C ... wants" is far from manifest in the "moving-picture material."

As regards this point, obviously any viewer can and likely will make guesses as to the child's "goal"(s), "feelings," etc., at any moment, but equally obviously such guesses will be dependent on the viewer, and in particular on the information available to the viewer. For example, in the complete 160 seconds of footage devoted to the child and the ball by Lück (1988), several passages that precede the 57 seconds selected by Lewin for his example make it abundantly clear (to me and also to several undergraduate students) that the child's "goal" throughout has much less to do with the ball than with a woman, call her W, seated to the right of the terrace at the top of the steps. Once seen, those passages give meaning (or meanings) to observable actions of the child (notably at approximately 9, 39, 49, and 53 seconds from the beginning of the segment) that might seem insignificant to an unprepared viewer. One such meaning, for me, is that C has been given a task by W, and that C's "goal G" is related primarily to W, not to B.

(2) What is "in ATTENTION" for C is also—naturally—not manifest in this kind of "material," yet in at least some instances it seems possible to make a guess about that with considerable confidence.

For instance, at the four epochs just noted, C is almost surely attending to something in C's visual field that is "offstage left"; the prepared viewer can identify this "something" with W, but even the unprepared viewer is likely to hypothesize one or more offstage stimuli. The more daring viewer (prepared or unprepared) may even go so far as to hypothesize non-visual stimuli in the same general place; and indeed there is evidence (in the preceding part of the silent film) that W is speaking to C, as she obviously (on the evidence of facial movements) was when (as I guess) she first told C to throw the ball Ba (which she had just placed in C's hands) down the stairs, and thereafter set C the goal of retrieving Ba.

Other "things" that are almost surely "in ATTENTION" for C at different times are the "three steps" and "landing" of the stone staircase, and various body parts of C (notably hands and feet, at moments when great care is needed for successful "locomotion" and "manipulation"). Other "things" that require (in my opinion) a certain daring to declare "in ATTENTION" for C are the "zones" $c1, c2, c3$, and dz of the "barrier," precisely because these "things" are (on a fair reading of Lewin's account) not simply the "steps" and "landings" of the staircase as material objects, but rather some sort of "relation" among other "things" (C, Ba, the "goal," etc.).

(3) What is "in AWARENESS" for C is even less manifest, so all the more a matter of conjecture, yet still not beyond rational investigation.

In general, I think it is a reasonable assumption[6] that usually—but certainly not always—what is "in ATTENTION" for an organism O@T has been "in AWARENESS" for O@T' for T' in some (possibly very short) range before T, will be "in AWARENESS" for O@T'' for T'' in some (possibly very short) range after T, or both; on that assumption (tempered by judgments specific to particular situations), once a constructor of a person P's life space has assembled candidates for what is "in ATTENTION" for P over some range of moments T, that constructor also has some candidates for what is "in AWARENESS" for P over that range. More candidates will be supplied by the constructor's general beliefs about the structure of P's "receptors" and the functioning of P's "nervous system," along the lines suggested by van Uexküll (1920/1926, p. 134; quoted in endnote 5), as well as by specific evidence like that contained in Lewin's "motion-picture material."

It is not hard to imagine circumstances in which an observer could have considerable confidence in judgments about what is "in AWARENESS" for a study participant, based on measurements of a wide variety of physiological phenomena (at least in the case of laboratory investigations, though the increasing availability of microminiaturized electronic sensing devices may soon mean make similar measurements can be taken during relatively pure ethological studies as well). This doesn't apply very well to Lewin's "moving-picture material," however.

Although Lewin (1936) doesn't use the words "attention" and "awareness," I don't think it is unfair to say that he refers to such categories in some sense, for instance, in such passages as "The child *C* and ball may be represented as regions which have a partially common boundary" and "he might have the feeling that 'the ground moved under his feet.'"

3.3. Informal Axioms for Life Spaces

Thinking about the enumerated points in the previous section, I came to believe that, above all, a "life space" should be taken to be a construction of a particular observer, in a particular context, with a particular purpose, during a particular range of time; and, further, that a "life space" always has (indeed, defines) an associated "life time scale." Whatever the merits of those beliefs vis-à-vis Lewin's own conception of what a "life space" is and should be, in this paper I will adopt them as axioms. For a mathematical model, these axioms will need to be mathematically formalized; meanwhile, here is a premathematical formalization (not in one-to-one correspondence with the points above) of their content.

(A) A life space of P@T is a finite selection from and/or cross-section of "reality" (or "the universe," etc.), constructed by $Q@[T',T'']$, where Q may (but need not) be P, and T may precede the range of time $[T',T'']$, be included in $[T',T'']$, follow $[T',T'']$, or perhaps (for instance, in a model of time like the "garden of forking paths" of Borges, 1966; cf. Rudolph 2006a) be temporally incomparable to $[T',T'']$.

(B) $Q@[T',T'']$ may construct more than one life space of P@T, for instance, at different "levels of organization."

(C) Corresponding to a time-change from T to T', there may (but need not) be some change between a life space of P@T and "the same" (i.e., the "genidentical") life space of P@T'. Likewise, the "position" of P in a lifespace of P@T and in "the same" lifespace of P@T'may (but need not) change in correspondence with the change from T to T'.

(D) Analysis of the "locomotion" (or "trajectory") of P through the (changing) life spaces of P@T, P@T',…, $P@T^n$ may (but need not) lead to an identification of features of the life spaces that have some reasonable interpretation as "fields," "valences," etc.

(E) The structure of a life space (including the "position" and "locomotion" of P in that life space) is deduced (by $Q@[T',T'']$) from observed changes in P (if I were not eschewing talk of "behavior," I could say "from the behavior of P"). The purpose of the construction for $Q@[T',T'']$, or its use to $Q@[T',T'']$, is to understand or predict changes in P (i.e., differences between P@T and P@T').

That a life space (as so conceived) is "constructed," and that there can (indeed, must) be a multiplicity of such constructions, is a major distinction between life spaces and *Umwelt*s (as understood by Rudolph, in press). Note that the stated axioms are deliberately agnostic on the kind of data, and the mode(s) by which that data is collected, used in such constructions.

I next proceed to formalize the distinction between *Umwelt*s and life spaces by formalizing the (content of the) preceding axioms.

4. A Mathematical Model of "Life Spaces"

In the prequel of this essay (Rudolph, in press), I outlined a topological model of *Umwelt*, on which I will base my proposed model of life spaces. Ideally, the reader of this essay have that one available; for the non-ideal reader, I have included an Appendix (similar to but not identical with the Appendix of the prequel) in which mathematical prerequisites are briefly recalled.

Here is a summary of the syntax and semantics of the *Umwelt* model. The notation has been made slightly more precise (and so, unfortunately, somewhat more complicated) than in the prequel, by adding "(O)" in several places.

Syntactically, the model of the *Umwelt* of an organism O consists of two discrete series $\{Aw_i(O)\}_{i \in I(O)}$ and $\{at_j(O)\}_{j \in J(O)}$ (where i and j range through some ranges $I(O)$ and $J(O)$ of consecutive integers) and an assignment to each j in $J(O)$ of a value $i(j)$ in $I(O)$ such that for all j in $J(O)$ we have $i(j) \leq i(j+1)$. For each i in I, $Aw_i(O)$ is a finite topological space (say with topology $\mathbf{Top}_i(O)$), and for each j in J, $at_j(O)$ is a point of $Aw_{i(j)}(O)$. These spaces and points are assumed to satisfy the following axioms.

(Um0) The topological space $Aw_i(O)$ is a T0-space. (This purely technical condition, spelled out in the Appendix, assures that $\mathbf{Top}_i(O)$ has enough structure to distinguish topologically any two "things" in $Aw_i(O)$ that are distinguished existentially.)

(Um1) For any two successive integers i, $i+1$ in $I(O)$, either $Aw_i(O)$ is the subspace of $Aw_{i+1}(O)$ obtained by removing exactly one point from $Aw_{i+1}(O)$, or $Aw_{i+1}(O)$ is the subspace of $Aw_i(O)$ obtained by removing exactly one point from $Aw_i(O)$.

(Um2) For any integer j in $J(O)$, if j is even then $at_j(O)$ is a non-closed point of $Aw_{i(j)}(O)$, whereas if j is odd then $at_j(O)$ is a closed point of $Aw_{i(j)}(O)$.

(Um3) For any three successive integers $2k-1$, $2k$, $2k+1$ in $J(O)$, the non-closed point $at_{2k}(O)$ of $Aw_{i(2k)}(O)$ is also a point (possibly closed) of both $Aw_{i(2k-1)}(O)$ and $Aw_{i(2k+1)}(O)$, and the closed point $at_{2k\pm1}(O)$ belongs to the closure $Cl(at_{2k}(O))$ of the point $at_{2k}(O)$ in the topological space $Aw_{i(2k\pm1)}(O)$ (so, if $at_{2k}(O)$ is closed in $Aw_{i(2k\pm1)}(O)$ then $at_{2k\pm1}(O) = at_{2k}(O)$ in that space).

There is a simple way to represent a T0-space X graphically, by a so-called "Hasse diagram." To do this we first use the topology of X to define a so-called "partial order" on X, by declaring that a point a of X is "greater than" a point b of X (with b not equal to a) if, and only if, a belongs to the closure $Cl(b)$. Then we begin a diagram of X by representing each (abstract) point of X by a (graphic) point on a piece of paper (or a blackboard or …), subject to the condition that, if a is "greater than" b, then the graphic point representing a is "higher" (i.e., further from the bottom margin, or the chalk tray, or …) than the graphic point representing b; and we complete the diagram of X by adding graphic line segments between certain pairs a and b of points, subject to the condition that there should be such a line segment if, and only if, not only is a "greater than" b, but there is no c "intermediate" between a and b (in the sense that a is "greater than" c and c is "greater than" b). Of course a given space X will have many graphically distinct Hasse diagrams, but any two diagrams are equivalent in an appropriate mathematical sense, and any graphic diagram made of a finite number of graphic points with non-horizontal graphic line segments joining certain pairs of them is a Hasse diagram of some space.

An example is given by Barmak and Minian (2006, p. 4): for "the space $X = \{a, b, c, d\}$ whose proper open sets are $\{a,c,d\}$, $\{b,c,d\}$, $\{c,d\}$ and $\{d\}$," a Hasse diagram is as pictured in Fig. 3 (adapted from Barmak and Minian, 2006). The fact that in this X the only two closed points are a and b is reflected by the fact that in the Hasse diagram only a and b are "maximal" (i.e., have no other points "greater than" them).

A sequence of Hasse diagrams of a simple *Umwelt* model satisfying (Um0)-(Um4) is pictured in Fig. 4.

The series $I(O)$ and $J(O)$ of integers define two notions of (discrete) time for O; the first (reckoned by increasing i in $I(O)$) can be called "AWARENESS time," and the second (reckoned by increasing j in J) can be called "ATTENTION time." In terms of these "time"s, the series $\{Aw_i(O)\}_{i \in I(O)}$ and $\{at_j(O)\}_{j \in J(O)}$ are, tautologously, "time series."

Semantically, the topological space $Aw_i(O)$ represents what is in AWARENESS for O@T_i and the point $at_j(O)$ represents what is in ATTENTION for O@$T_{i(j)}$ during the part of the AWARENESS time epoch $T_{i(j)}$ reckoned by

Figure 3

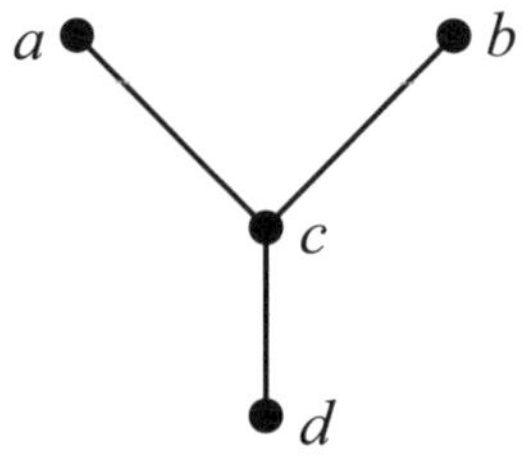

a b

c

d

Figure 4

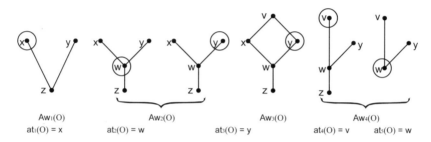

Aw₁(O)   Aw₂(O)   Aw₃(O)   Aw₄(O)

$at_1(O) = x$ $at_2(O) = w$ $at_3(O) = y$ $at_4(O) = v$ $at_5(O) = w$

one or more epochs of ATTENTION time. The intended meaning of the topology $\mathbf{Top}_i(O)$ is that it is a (minimal sufficient) way of indicating both how certain "things" that are in ATTENTION are "unambivalent" and others "ambivalent," and also how each "ambivalent" "thing" can "resolve its ambivalence" to other, "less ambivalent" "things." Specifically, a "closed point" is "unambivalent," a non-closed point is "ambivalent," and the "things" that belong to the closure of a non-closed point are all and only the "things" to which that non-closed point's ambivalence can "resolve." The model interprets "the state of ambivalence y can resolve to x for O@T$_i$" as "the point x of the topological space $\mathsf{Aw}_i(O)$ belongs to the closure of the point y of $\mathsf{Aw}_i(O)$." The formal axioms (Um1) through (Um3) together model a group of informal axioms for *Umwelts*, which can be abbreviated as follows (full statements appear in Rudolph, in press, section 2).

(1)   At any given AWARENESS time, some pairs of "things" in AWARENESS stand to each other in the relation of special to general, and other pairs do not.

(2)   This relationship between a given pair may come into, or go out of, existence as AWARENESS time changes.

(3)   On the other hand, if at a given time a pair of "things" (say x and y) in AWARENESS are related as general to special, and no other "thing" z is related to x as y is, it can be the case that either or both of the adjacent times in the sequence just x and not y is in AWARENESS.

(4)   A change in AWARENESS can be "O-driven" or "not-O-driven," and (independently of that) "continuous" or "catastrophic."

4.1. The Syntax of the "Life Spaces" Model

As noted by Rudolph (in press), for any given organism O neither O's AWARENESS time nor O's ATTENTION time is intended to reckon any sort of "physical time" (such as "thermodynamic time," defined by increasing entropy) directly. On the contrary, each *defines* a way to reckon time for O that is proper to O itself. On the other hand, Rudolph (in press) does assume, via axiom (Um3), that (for any given O) AWARENESS time is "weakly monotonic" with respect to ATTENTION time: the two never move in opposite directions, although AWARENESS time may stay unchanged while ATTENTION time moves forward. Here I make a further assumption, that there is a fixed standard of "physical time" such that, for any O, ATTENTION time and AWARENESS time are "strictly monotonic" with respect to that standard. More precisely, I assume the following.

(1)   To each physical state S of O there is a physical time $t(S)$, where the values of t are real numbers (they might be unrestricted, or they might necessarily lie in some predetermined subset of the real numbers, such as the integers).

(2)   Each epoch of AWARENESS time and each epoch of ATTENTION time for O corresponds to some interval $[a,b]$ of values of physical time t (it is not allowed that this interval be degenerate, i.e., that $a = b$, but it is allowed that b exceed a by an arbitrarily small amount). Moreover, each interval of ATTENTION time is contained entirely in some interval of AWARENESS time.

(3)   The intervals corresponding to two different epochs of AWARENESS time don't overlap except possibly at their endpoints, and they appear in the same order on the real t-axis as they do with respect to the given order on AWARENESS time; and similarly for ATTENTION time.

Also, I define a "clock" C to be a finite sequence of non-degenerate intervals $C_1, C_2, ..., C_n$ on the t-axis, each greater than the next, such that two of these intervals overlap (if at all) only at endpoints.

Let P and Q be persons (Q may be the same as P). Let $\{Aw_i(P)\}_{i \in I(P)}$, $\{at_j(P)\}_{j \in J(P)}$, $I(P)$, $J(P)$, the assignment of $i(j)$ in $I(P)$ to each j in $J(P)$, and **Top**$_i$(P) be the components of an *Umwelt* model for P as above.[7] Let $C = \{C_1, C_2, ..., C_n\}$ be a clock. Then, syntactically, a model of a life space of P constructed by Q using the clock **C** consists of two time series LS$_i$(P%Q@C) and P$_i$(P%Q@C) ($i = 1,...,n$), where LS$_i$(P%Q@C) is a finite topological space and P$_i$(P%Q@C) is a point of LS$_i$(P%Q@C), which satisfy the following axioms.

(LS1) For $i = 1,...,n$, LS$_i$(P%Q@C) is a quotient space X/R_i of a subspace X_i of the union of the spaces Aw$_k$(P) such that the time interval allotted to that space overlaps the union of the first i clock segments.

(LS2) The subspace X_i depends both on Q and on **C**. The equivalence relation R_i on X_i depends on Q.

(LS3) The subspace X_i contains all the points at$_{i(j)}$(P) with $1 \leq i(j) \leq i$, and the set of those points is a single R_i-equivalence class, which is the point P$_i$(P%Q@C) in LS$_i$(P%Q@C) = X_i/R_i.

4.2. The semantics of the "Life Spaces" Model

The intended semantics of this (deliberately) vague and very flexible model begins with the idea that the union of the spaces Aw$_k$(P) represents the entire "life history" of P, from the point of view of P's *Umwelt* (as modeled), through the last physical time epoch reckoned by the ith "tick" C$_i$ of the clock **C**. The finite structuring of the (semi-infinite) time interval ending with that epoch, given by the sequence of "ticks" of **C**, acts to reduce this "life history" in one manner—which might be called "filtering"—that is at least somewhat "objective" (insofar as **C** is objective). The capacities, biases, and judgments of Q act to reduce the "life history" in other manners, which are intended to be modeled by the mathematical operations of "passage to a subspace" and "passage to a quotient space": the subspace X_i is "what is of interest" to Q, for the purposes at hand; the equivalence relation R_i is "what is indistinguishable" to Q, given Q's capacities. Put slightly differently, the finite topological space LS$_i$(P%Q@C) represents a structured set of "things" (including, as always, relations among "things," etc., etc.) in that part of the "life history" of P visible during the first i "ticks" of the clock **C**, and the point P$_i$(P%Q@C) in that space represents the person P at the time of the ith "tick."

4.3. The Pragmatics of the "Life Spaces" Model

Mutatis mutandis, the following extended quotation from Rudolph (2006c) applies as well to FTS models as it does to the FSC (Finite Simplicial Complex) models described there.

So far I have sketched the syntax of FSCs, and described both a general semantics for FSCs and a more particular semantics in which the two primitive notions used to describe the syntax are interpreted as "focus of attention" and "collection of mutually interambivalent foci of attention." Given that semantics, all the rest of the mathematical theory of FSCs is automatically interpreted, whereupon one can begin to test the various propositions that comprise that theory—each of which is a statement about mathematical objects—against the various propositions that comprise the interpretation of that theory—each of which is a statement about psychology phrased in terms of attention and ambivalence. Further, as these various psychological propositions are considered and found more or less meaningful, credible, testable, useful..., then the mathematical propositions to which they correspond can be adopted or rejected as further axioms: after which modification of the mathematical theory, the process of interpretation and testing is taken up again. This reciprocal process is what I am calling the pragmatics of FSC models in qualitative psychology.

The Low-Dimensional Hypothesis (in strong and weak forms) and the Limited-Ambivalence Hypotheses given by Rudolph (2006c) as examples of possible pragmatics for FSC models both are easily transformed into hypotheses of FTS models. In addition, any number of mathematical ideas introduced by Lewin (1936) into his discussions of life spaces—for instance, the notion of "boundary of a region"—but not, by him, presented in a way that ties together the formal mathematical syntax with the empirical psychological semantics, can be assimilated into the pragmatics of FTS models.

4.4. The Child with the Ball

I unfortunately have neither space nor time to include in this essay what I would like to insert at exactly this point, namely, a pair of FTS "life space" models, one capturing in the new formalism what Lewin (1936) described graphically (in Figure 2) and verbally (in the material quoted in section 3.1), and the other doing the same for the verbal description in 3.2. Instead, I leave the elaboration of two such models—or (perhaps better) the task of imagining how it would be like to construct such models—to the reader. A later paper will take up the task again.

5. Conclusions

The rehabilitation of Kurt Lewin's "topological psychology" is both desirable and possible. Finite topological spaces provide a mathematical framework that captures Lewin's expressed intent that a "life space" should "be represented by a finitely structured space" (Lewin, 1936, p. 216). Within that framework, some at least of "[t]he host of theorems that form the actual machinery of topology" (in particular, the machinery of simple-homotopy theory) can and—I am confident—will be "made to function and so to take over the work of rigorous deduction" found lacking in Lewin (1936) by London (1944, p. 287).

Acknowledgments

The work described in Parts I and II of this essay grew out of earlier work funded by a National Science Foundation Interdisciplinary Grant in the Mathematical Sciences (DMS-0308894). I thank the Mathematical Institute of ETH–Zürich for support during the completion of this essay, and the National Science Foundation for partial support from NSF award IIS- 0713335 during final revisions. Jaan Valsiner, Josh Clegg, and the other participants in the Kitchen Seminar at Clark University have been invaluable resources and goads.

Appendix: Mathematical Tools

This appendix collects all (and, as far as possible, only) those mathematical tools needed for the model proposed. Following a standard convention for mathematical exposition, in this appendix I use italics to indicate the first, defining instance of newly introduced terminology (they are not used for emphasis).

A.1. Sets; Finite Sets

By a *set* I mean an arbitrary collection of "things." If x is (a symbol denoting) a "thing," and S is (a symbol denoting) a set, then $x \in S$ indicates that x *belongs to*—or is a *member* or *element* of—S, and $x \notin S$ that x does not belong to S. I adopt the so-called "Axiom of Extensionality," which says that a set S is determined entirely by what "things" belong to it. What a "thing" may be is another matter, possibly varying from context to context; whatever the context, I certainly want every set to be a "thing."[8]

So-called *set-building notation* exists in two variants. The schema for the first variant is $S = \{x \in V \mid P(x) \text{ is true}\}$, where x is a variable (i.e., place-holder), V denotes some fixed set, P denotes a "property," and for any "thing" x the notation $P(x)$ stands for the proposition that the "thing" x has the property P. The schema is read "S is the set of all members x of the set V such that $P(x)$ is true." Provided that sufficient care is taken in formalizing the notion of "property" and restricting the possible value of V, it turns out to be mathematically consistent (so far as anyone knows) to adopt the "Axiom of Comprehension," which states that the set $\{x \in V \mid P(x) \text{ is true}\}$ does exist (i.e., the notation does refer to a set, rather than being a non-referring formalism) and is uniquely determined; this set is called the *extension* of P in V. When the *universe of discourse* V is understood (or irrelevant to the discussion), the notation is often shortened to $\{x \mid P(x) \text{ is true}\}$ or even $\{x \mid P(x)\}$.

Of course, two formally distinct properties P and Q can very well have one and the same extension. For instance, many formally distinct properties are true of no thing at all, and each of these properties therefore has the *empty set* $\varnothing$ as its extension (in any universe of discourse whatsoever). Less trivially, $\{x \mid x \text{ is the morning star}\} = \{x \mid x \text{ is the evening star}\} = \{x \mid x \text{ is the planet Venus}\}$.

A *natural number* is one of the whole numbers 1, 2, 3, ... (Here the ellipsis "..." followed by a full stop means, as is usual in mathematics, that the series that begins before the ellipsis is understood to continue indefinitely.) A *counting number* is a natural number or 0. A *finite set* is a set that can be counted out by some counting number n. The schema for the second variant of set-building notation applies only to finite sets; it is $S = \{a, b, ..., z\}$, where a, b, etc., are (symbols denoting) things; here the ellipsis "...", being both preceded and followed by (symbols denoting) things, is understood to stand for a finite set of (symbols denoting) determinate things. Importantly, distinct symbols in such a notation are understood to denote distinct things; so, for instance, {the morning star, the evening star} is not a proper use of the notation (on the understanding that the morning star *is* the evening star). In this notation, the empty set $\varnothing$ is { }. An arbitrary finite set with $n \geq 1$ members can be denoted by $\{x(1), x(2), ..., x(n)\}$ so long as it is understood that for i not equal to j, the symbols $x(i)$ and $x(j)$ stand for two different things.

An important formal consideration is that, when the notation $\{a, b, ..., z\}$ is used, the particular order in which the things (denoted by the symbols) a, b, and so on, appear in the notation is irrelevant to the meaning of the notation. Thus, for instance, {the planet Venus, the planet Mars} denotes the same set as {the planet Mars, the planet Venus}; and all six of the notations $\{x(1), x(2), x(3)\}$, $\{x(1), x(3), x(2)\}$, $\{x(2), x(1), x(3)\}$, $\{x(2), x(3), x(1)\}$, $\{x(3), x(1), x(2)\}$, $\{x(3), x(2), x(1)\}$ denote the same set.

It is easy to formally transform an instance of the second variant of set-building notation into an instance of the first variant. For instance, {the morning star, the Washington Monument, the color green} denotes precisely the same set as $\{x \mid P(x) \text{ is true}\}$, where for any x the proposition $P(x)$ is the disjunction of the three simpler propositions "x is the morning star," "x is the Washington Monument," "x is the color green." (Logical disjunction formalizes the inclusive "or" of English, corresponding to Latin "*vel*" rather than to Latin "*aut*.")

A conceptual hurdle for many people, confronted for the first (or fiftieth) time with such a notation as $\{x \in V \mid P(x)$ is true$\}$, is that the notation—and indeed the notion of "set"—does not require P to denote a "meaningful" property. For finite sets, denoted according to the second schema, no similar conceptual difficulty should arise—at least to the extent that (1) a proposition that is true of precisely one individual is *ipso facto* "meaningful" (essentially, this formalizes the notion of proper nouns), and (2) an arbitrary finite disjunction of "meaningful" propositions is itself "meaningful."

A.2. Sets and Logic; Boolean Algebra

Several familiar and less familiar operations on sets correspond, under the Axiom of Comprehension, to logical operations on properties (or propositions). Full expositions of this correspondence, which closely related to so-called Boolean algebra, are widely available (for an interesting take on the subject, and other references, see McCawley, 1981); here I will simply summarize the situation and illustrate the operations with simple examples.

If S is any set, then the *singleton* of S, denoted (following the second set-building schema) by $\{S\}$, is the unique set containing S and only S as a member. Note that S is not the same as its singleton $\{S\}$; for instance, the singleton $\{\varnothing\}$ of the empty set $\varnothing$ is not itself $\varnothing$, for $\{\varnothing\}$ is not empty (like every singleton, it has precisely one member). The distinction between a set and its singleton corresponds (more or less) to the logical distinction between use and mention.

The *union* of sets S and T, written $S \cup T$, is $\{x \mid x \in S$ or $x \in T\}$, where (as usual) "or" is inclusive. Example: $\{x \mid x$ is round $\} \cup \{x \mid x$ is red $\} = \{x \mid x$ is round or red (or both)$\}$. More generally, the union of sets $S_1, ..., S_n$, written $S_1 \cup ... \cup S_n$, or $\cup_{i=1}^{n} S_i$, is $\{x \mid$ for at least one value of i from 1 to n, $x \in S_i\}$.

The *intersection* of sets S and T, written $S \cap T$, is $\{x \mid x \in S$ and $x \in T\}$. Example: $\{x \mid x$ is round $\} \cap \{x \mid x$ is red $\} = \{x \mid x$ is round and red$\}$. More generally, the intersection of sets $S_1, ..., S_n$, written $S_1 \cap ... \cap S_n$, or $\cap_{i=1}^{n} S_i$, is $\{x \mid$ for all values of i from 1 to n, $x \in S_i\}$.

If S and T are sets, and every thing that belongs to T also belongs to S, then T is called a *subset* of S; this relation is denoted $T \subset S$. Examples: $S \subset S, \varnothing \subset S$, and for every $x \in S$, $\{x\} \subset S$. Note that $T \subset S$ if and only if $T = S \cap T$; using the interpretations of sets as properties, and intersection as conjunction, we see that $T \subset S$ corresponds in Boolean algebra to the relation "if x has property P_T, then x has property P_S," which is called *implication* (or *material implication*, in distinction to so-called *logical implication*) of P_S by P_T, denoted $P_T \Rightarrow P_S$. Example: { $x \mid x$ is round and red} $\subset$ { $x \mid x$ is red } $\subset$ { $x \mid x$ is round or red)}.

Since $\varnothing \subset S$ for any S, any proposition with empty extension—which is to say, any categorically false proposition (e.g., "x is not equal to x")—implies every proposition. In a context where there is a "universal set" V (for instance, $V =$ ALL in the model described in this paper), every set is a subset of V, and it follows that any proposition with extension V—which is to say, any categorically true proposition (e.g., "x is equal to x")—is implied by every proposition.

If S and T are sets, then $\{x \mid x \in S$ and $x \notin T \}$ is called the *complement of T in S*, denoted $S–T$. Relative complementation formalizes the use of "but not" in natural language. Example: { $x \mid x$ is round} -{ $x \mid x$ is red } = { $x \mid x$ is round but not red)}.

A.3. Power Sets; Cartesian Products of Sets; Relations

If S is a set, then { $T \mid T$ is a set and $T \subset S$ } is called the *power set* of S, denoted $\wp(S)$. If S and T are sets (T might be the same set as S, under a different name), then the *Cartesian product* of S and T (in that order), denoted $S \times T$, is { $(x, y) \mid x \in S$ and $y \in T$ }, where for any "things" x and y, (x, y) denotes the *ordered pair* of which the first member is x and the second y. Example: if S is the set of four suits {♣, ♦, ♥, ♠} and T is the set of three "face card ranks" {J, Q, K}, then $S \times T$ consists of $12 = 4 \times 3$ ordered pairs, among them (♠, J) and (♣, Q). The ordered pair (K, ♦) belongs to $T \times S$ but not to $S \times T$. The ordered pair (♥, ♥) belongs to $S \times S$; it is not the same as either ♥ or {♥}.

If S and T are sets, then a *relation* between S and T (in that order) is a subset of $S \times T$. Just as in the case of sets (of which, of course, relations are a particular case), *relation-building* notation exists in two variants. The schema for the first variant is $\{(x,y) \in S \times T \mid P(x,y)$ is true$\}$, where x and y are variables, P denotes a "property relating x to y," and the notation $P(x,y)$ stands for the proposition x is related to y in the sense of P. The schema for the second variant of relation-building notation applies only to finite sets, and consists simply of listing the ordered pairs that comprise the relation.

The *diagonal* of a set S, denoted $\Delta(S)$, is $\{(x,x) \in S \times S \mid x \in S\}$. In the language of relations, the diagonal of S represents the relation of *equality* between elements of S.

A.4. Equivalence Relations, Partitions, and Quotient Sets

If S is a set, then an *equivalence relation on S* is a relation R between S and S with all three of the following properties. (1) R is *reflexive*: for all $x \in S$, $(x,x) \in R$ (equivalently, $\Delta(S) \subset R$). (2) R is *symmetric*: for all x and y in S, if $(x,y) \in R$ then $(y,x) \in R$. (3) R is *transitive*: for all x, y, and z in S, if $(x,y) \in R$ and $(y,z) \in R$ then $(x,z) \in R$. Examples: the diagonal relation $\Delta(S)$ is an equivalence relation ("equality" is the most stringent kind of "equivalence"). The *total* relation $S \times S$ is an equivalence relation ("no distinctions" is the least stringent kind of "equivalence"). If $S = \mathbf{Z}$ is the set of integers, the *parity* relation $\{(m,n) \in \mathbf{Z} \times \mathbf{Z} \mid n - m \text{ is even}\}$ is an equivalence relation. If S is a pile (set) of colored plastic beads, the *isochromatic* relation $\{(b,c) \in S \times S \mid b \text{ and } c \text{ have the same color}\}$ is an equivalence relation.

A *partition* of S is a family of subsets of S such that each member of S is a member of exactly one subset in the family. Let R be an equivalence relation on S. A subset C of S is an *R-equivalence class* if for every $x \in C$, a member y of S belongs to C if and only if (x,y) belongs to R. It is easy to prove that the set of R-equivalence classes, denoted S/R and called the *quotient set of S modulo R*, is a partition of S. Conversely, every partition gives rise to an equivalence relation: partitions and equivalence relations are two ways of talking about the same concept. A partition of S can be construed as arising from applying a (multiple-valued) predicate to S; as with set-building, not every partition will correspond to a "meaningful" predicate. Example: the isochromatic relation corresponds to the predicate "color."

A.5. Finite Topological Spaces

Lewin describes topology as follows.

> Topology, as the most general science of spatial relations, can be based on the relationship between "part" and "whole" or in other words on the concepts of "being-included-in." Closely related to these concepts is that of the "surrounding" of a "point" (Lewin, 1936, p. 87).

Another way to put this is that topology is a way to model "closer than" without having to model "close." What it is that all topological spaces have in common is exactly the (extensive) list of properties that can be deduced from that answer (suitably formalized) and nothing more. Of course, any particular topological space also has properties proper to it that cannot be so deduced. Some such properties are interesting in themselves; by further insisting that a given such property hold, one defines a class of special topological spaces, for instance *finite T0-spaces*, defined as follows.

A *finite topological space* is a finite set $X = \{x(1), x(2),\ldots, x(n)\}$ equipped with a (necessarily finite) set **Top** $= \{U(1), U(2),\ldots, U(n)\}$ of subsets $U(i)$ of X that satisfy three properties: (T1) the empty set and the set X both belong to **Top**; (T2) the union of any subset of **Top** belongs to **Top**; (T3) the intersection of any subset of **Top** belongs to **Top**. A subset Y of X equipped with the topology **Top** is called *open* if and only if Y belongs to **Top**, and a subset Z of X is called *closed* if and only if its complement X-Z is open. It is easy to show that analogues of the properties (T1)-(T3) of open sets are true for closed sets too: the empty set and the set X are both closed; the union of any set of closed sets is closed; and the intersection of any set of closed sets is closed.

Given any subset S of X, an *open neighborhood* of S in X is any open set U that contains S (for example, since by assumption X contains S, and by axiom (T1) X is open, it follows that X is an open neighborhood of S in X). The set of all open neighborhoods of a fixed set S is a subset of **Top**, so by axiom (T3) the intersection $U(S)$ of all these open neighborhoods of S is open, and by Boolean algebra $U(S)$ contains S, so $U(S)$ is an open neighborhood of S, called *the aperture of S*. The aperture of S is the *minimal* open neighborhood of S in the sense that it is contained in every open neighborhood of S. In particular, S is open if and only if S is its own aperture $U(S)$.

An element of X is called a *point* of X. Given any point x of X, an open neighborhood of the singleton set $\{x\}$ is also called an open neighborhood of x. We write $U(x)$ instead of $U(\{x\})$; the various sets $U(x)$, for x an element of X, are called the *minimal open sets* of X (or of **Top**). A point x of X is called an *open point* just in case $U(x) = \{x\}$.

An important fact about finite topological spaces is that the minimal open sets *generate* all the open sets, in the sense that every open set is a union of minimal open sets (this is not necessarily true in an infinite topological spaces, and is definitely false in some of the most familiar infinite topological spaces—like the real numbers, in which there are *no* non-empty minimal open sets, and in particular no open points).

It is perfectly possible for there to be points x and y of X such that $x \neq y$ and yet $U(x) = U(y)$. However, for many purposes, including the purposes of the prequel of this essay (Rudolph, in press), it is extremely convenient to consider only those finite topological spaces that satisfy, in addition to properties (T1)-(T3) above, property (T0): for all points x and y of X, if $x \neq y$ then $U(x) \neq U(y)$. In contexts where not all topological spaces satisfy (T0), those that do are distinguished by calling them (T0)-*spaces*.

Given any subset S of X, the intersection of the set of all closed sets containing S is a closed set $Cl(S)$ containing S, called the *closure* of S; it is the minimal closed set containing S, and S is closed if and only if S is its own closure $Cl(S)$. As with apertures, we write $Cl(x)$ for $Cl(\{x\})$. A point x of X is called a *closed point* just in case $Cl(x) = \{x\}$.

A6. Subspaces and Quotient Spaces

Let X be a topological space with topology **Top**.

Given a subset Y of X, a subset Z of Y is called *relatively open in Y* if there is some U in **Top** such that $Z = Y \cap U$. The set **Top**$|Y$ of all relatively open subsets of Y is easily proved to be a topology on Y, and Y equipped with the topology **Top**$|Y$ is called a *subspace* of X. Every subspace of a finite topological space is a finite topological space, and every subspace of a (T0)-space is a (T0)-space.

Given an equivalence relation R on X, the set **Top**$/R$ of all subsets W of X/R for which $\{x \in X \mid (x,x) \in R\}$ belongs to **Top** can be proved to be a topology on X/R, and X/R equipped with the topology **Top**$/R$ is called a *quotient space* of X. Every quotient space of a finite topological space is a finite topological space. It can happen that a quotient space of a (T0)-space (even a finite (T0)-space) is not a (T0)-space.

A7. Simple-Homotopy Theory and Finite (T0)-Spaces

Rudolph (2006c) suggested a way in which the *simple-homotopy theory* of finite simplicial complexes, founded by Whitehead (1939), could be used to model development, particularly development in psychology. Barmak & Minian (2006), in a considerable extension of work by McCord (1966) and others, have found a simple and elegant way to reformulate simple-homotopy theory in terms of finite topological spaces. Their key insight is that the fundamental operations preserving the simple-homotopy type of an FSC, *elementary expansion* and *elementary contraction*, correspond in the context of an FTS to the addition or removal of a single point that has an easily (but technically) defined topological property within the FTS, namely, the property of being a *weak* point. (See Barmak & Minian, 2006, for the definition and a discussion.) Any point that is not weak is *strong*.

It is easy to see that any FTS can be converted to any other FTS by adding and removing a series of points (in most cases, some weak and others strong), one at a time. An analysis similar to that for FSCs in Rudolph (2006c) justifies conceptualizing addition/removal of weak points as "gentle" changes in the FTS, and addition/removal of strong points as "catastrophic" changes (modeled by "simplicial surgeries" in Rudolph, 2006c).

Notes

1. This "intuition" is nowhere spelled out in Lewin (1936) but is reasonably explicit in Lewin (1982/1963/1951, *passim*); in any case, whether or not it was Lewin's intuition, it is mine.
2. For my purposes, I take the term *Umwelt* (literally, "surrounding world"; cf. van Uexküll, 1920/1926) to mean "an organism's environment *as structured for, by, and with* the organism." Various interpretations of the term are expanded upon by Sokol (in press).
3. An excellent, easily available overview of the concept of "genidentify," as introduced by Lewin (1922), appears online in Wikipedia: "Lewin defines the notion 'genidentity' as an *existential relationship* underlying the genesis of an object from one moment to the next. … Two objects are not identical because they have the same properties in common, but because one has developed from the other" (Anonymous, 2007).
4. Viz., "a construct consisting of (i) all the material things there are, (ii) all the relations among things of type (i), (iii) all the relations among all things of types (i) and (ii), and so on indefinitely (but not infinitely); in short, ALL" (Rudolph, in press); my use of the word "relation" is, I think, "consonant with the use of 'relation' by, for instance, Ryle (1949) and Laird (2007), though it may go beyond those authors' (more or less 'Radical Empiricist') intentions" (*ibid.*).
5. "By the structure of its receptors, every animal is cut off from a great number of physical and chemical influences coming from the outer world, and it is only through stimuli that the outer world gets in touch with the nervous system" (van Uexküll, 1920/1926, p. 134).
6. Reasonable or not, it is built into the model of *Umwelt* (Rudolph, in press) being adapted here.
7. In fact, the given method for constructing a life space model for P could be applied with very little modification to topological *Umwelt* models for P much more general than the finitistic models described by Rudolph (in press), for instance, to dynamical systems models in which AWARENESS time and ATTENTION time are continuous, the "AWARENESS spaces" $Aw_t(P)$ are differential manifolds, and ATTENTION $at_t(P)$ can be a subspace of $Aw_t(P)$ larger than a single point. Even in such a general case, however, the method produces a finitistic life space model.
8. Much of modern mathematics makes do with sets which are arbitrary collections of sets but of no other kind of "thing." All such sets in the so-called "cumulative hierarchy" come down, eventually, to (possibly extremely complicated!) constructions based on the *empty set* (which is—by Extensionality—the only set to which nothing at all belongs), described below. For modeling, however, it is very convenient to allow as members of sets certain "things" (often called *ur-elements*) that are not sets.

References

Abraham, R. (2006). Vibrations and Forms. http://www.ralph-abraham.org/articles/MS%23118.Vibrations/rmkplusfigs.pdf.

Anonymous (2007). "Genidentity," in Wikipedia. Accessed October 30, 2007, at http://en.wikipedia.org/wiki/Genidentity.

Barker, R. (1968). *Ecological Psychology*. Stanford: Stanford University Press.

Barmak, J. A., & Minian, E. G. (2006). Simple Homotopy Types and Finite Spaces. http://arxiv.org/abs/math.AT/0611158.

Borges, J. L. (1962). The garden of forking paths (D. A. Yates, trans.), in *Labyrinths* (D. A. Yates and James E. Irby, eds.). New York: New Directions.

Dacke, M., Nilsson, D.-E., Scholtz, C. H., Byrne, M., and Warrant, E. J. (2003). Animal behaviour: Insect orientation to polarized moonlight. *Nature*, 424:33.

Haugh, C.V., and Walker, M. M. (1998). Magnetic Discrimination Learning in Rainbow Trout (*Oncorhynchus mykiss*). *Journal of Navigation*, 51:35-45

Heft, H. (2001). *Ecological Psychology in Context: James Gibson, Roger Barker, and the Legacy of William James's Radical Empiricism*. Mahwah, NJ: Erlbaum.

Laird, J. D. (2007). *Feelings: the Perception of Self*. New York: Oxford.

Lewin, K. (1922). *Der Begriff der Genese in Physik, Biologie und Entwicklungsgeschichte*. Berlin: Julius Springer.

Lewin, K. (1936). *Principles of Topological Psychology* (F. Heider and G. M. Heider, trans.). New York: McGraw-Hill.

London, I. (1944). Psychologists' misuse of the auxiliary concepts of physics and mathematics. *Psychological Review*, 51, 266-291.

Lück, H. E. (1984). *Kurt Lewin: Feldtheorie und Theorie der Leistungsmotivation* (video lectures). Hagen: Fernuniversität Gesamthochschule Hagen, Zentrum für Fernstudienentwicklung.

McCawley, J. D. (1981). *Everything that linguists have always wanted to know about logic but were ashamed to ask*. Chicago: University of Chicago Press.

McCord, M. C. (1966). Singular homology groups and homotopy groups of finite topological spaces. *Duke Mathematical Journal* 33:465-474.

Porter, J., Craven, B., Khan, R.M., Chang, S., Kang, I., Judkewitz, B., Volpe, J., Settles, G., and Sobel, N. (2007). Mechanisms of scent-tracking in humans. *Nature Neuroscience*, 10:27-29

Rudolph, L. (2006a). The Fullness of Time. *Culture & Psychology* 12(4):157-186.

Rudolph, L. (2006b). Spaces of Ambivalence: Qualitative Mathematics in the Modeling of Complex, Fluid Phenomena. *Estudios de Psicología* 27:67-83.

Rudolph, L. (2006c). Mathematics, Models and Metaphors. *Culture & Psychology* 12(4):245-265.

Rudolph, L. (in press). A Unified Topological Approach to *Umwelts* and Life Spaces. Part I: *Umwelts* and Finite Topological Spaces. *Relating to Environments: A New Look at Umwelt* (ed. R.I. Sokol). Charlotte, NC: Information Age Publishers.

Ryle, G. (1949). *The Concept of Mind*. London: Hutchinson.

Sokol, R. I., editor (in press). *Relating to Environments: A New Look at Umwelt*. Charlotte, NC: Information Age Publishers.

Thorngate, W. (2006). The seductive danger of visual metaphors: It's about time, *Culture & Psychology* 12(4):215-219.

Uexküll, J. von (1920/1926). *Theoretical biology* (D.L. MacKinnon, trans.). New York: Harcourt, Brace & Company. (Original work published 1920, translation published 1926.)

Whitehead, J. H. C. (1939). Simplicial spaces, nuclei and *m*-groups. *Proc. London Math. Soc.* 45: 243-327.

8

Anti-Reductionistic Empiricism in Contemporary Psychological Research

Jeffrey S. Reber and Zachary B. Beckstead

At first blush, anti-reductionistic empiricism seems to be an obvious contradiction in terms. It has become almost axiomatic in both philosophy and psychology to assume that empiricism necessarily entails the reduction of human knowing to sensory experiences that are thought to be the building blocks of human cognition and behavior. Indeed, that most famous of empiricists, the British philosopher John Locke, made the reductionism in empiricism plainly evident in *An Essay Concerning Human Understanding* (1689/1984), when he wrote that external and internal sensory experience, "when we have taken a full survey of them, and their several modes, combinations, and relations, we shall find to contain all our whole stock of ideas; and that we have nothing in our minds which did not come in one of these two ways" (p. 42). This reduction to sensory experience has become a fundamental canon of modernist epistemology that is taken for granted by many laypeople and behavioral scientists alike, who will only "believe it when they see it," because they are convinced that empirical observation is requisite to truth (Quine, 1980). As Slife & Williams (1995) observe, psychologists too have embraced empirical reduction, so much so that for many, "our experience of the external world is the starting point for virtually every theory of conditioning or model of memory" (p. 68).

But nowhere is empirical reductionism more evident in psychology than in its preferred investigatory method—the scientific experiment. Psychology marks its birth as a bona fide discipline with the establishment of Wilhelm Wundt's scientific laboratory in Leipzig, Germany in 1879, and in the minds of many psychologists this date signifies a decisive break with philosophy and the hope of a burgeoning alliance with the natural sciences, whose experimental method psychologists have long emulated (Leahey, 2001). A defining feature of the experimental method psychologists adopted from the natural sciences is its emphasis on empirical reduction. Based on the assumptions of Newtonian physics and Cartesian mechanism, natural scientists developed the experimental method as a way to isolate and manipulate complex phenomena by breaking them down into their most basic elements and systematically observing how these components interact and produce predictable effects. To the extent that these observations are conducted in an objective, standardized, and repeatable manner the scientific community can more confidently conclude that their research approximates truth. Additionally, the replication of experiments across different spatial and temporal contexts gives the results of scientific research an air of universality and lawfulness. Finally, the widespread and impressive technological applications of science make a real difference in the quality of everyday life (Slife & Williams, 1995).

Given the epistemological and technological success of the empirical method in the natural sciences, it is not surprising that many psychologists, behavioral scientists, and people in general have elevated empiricism above other epistemologies and accept reductionism as a necessary and desirable component of any reasonable explanation[1]. The consequence for psychology is a pervasive acceptance of the belief that complex phenomena can and should be simplified through objective observation in controlled settings, like laboratories, so the phenomena can be explained, predicted, and controlled. This belief has led many psychologists to elevate experimental research above other possible approaches as the methodological gold standard for explaining psychological phenomena (Morris & Maisto, 1999).

In light of empiricism's epistemological dominance in psychology and its seemingly inseparable connection with reductionism it may seem curious or even absurd for us to write a paper on contemporary approaches to anti-reductionistic empiricism. One might well ask whether there really are any psychologists who conduct this kind of holistic empirical research and secondarily question why they do it. It may seem more reasonable to either practice reductionistic empirical research, like most everybody else, or to abandon empirical science altogether and adopt a non-empirical holistic or anti-reductionistic psychological method. There are a number of qualitative methods available that are less reductionistic than empiricism (e.g., hermeneutics, discourse analysis, grounded theory). It would appear more reasonable and straightforward for these psychologists who are committed to anti-reductionism to choose one of these alternative methods instead of trying to force empiricism to do something it doesn't appear to have been designed to do.

Yet, as we will show in our paper, this is precisely what a number of psychologists of the past and present have attempted to do. Like many of their more mainstream colleagues, these researchers strongly believe that empiricism is the best epistemology to approximate truth, but they are also dedicated holists who are convinced that a full account of psychological phenomena requires an examination of more than just individuals and their constituent parts. It also demands inclusion of the broader context of human experience and relationships. Thus, they maintain their commitment to these seemingly contradictory ideas of empiricism and holism and strive to develop a number of highly creative research studies that stretch beyond traditional experimental research paradigms to gain empirical insight into human relationships. Our purpose will be to explicate and examine two of the best known exemplars of contemporary anti-reductionistic empirical research—systems theory and field theory—identify the strengths and limitations of these two approaches, and highlight a few suggestions for each field of study that may facilitate more successful anti-reductionistic research in the future.

Systems Theory

Systems theory, or systems thinking, came into prominence in North America in the 1940s and 1950s with the work of Ludwig Von Bertalanffy (biology), Kenneth Boulding (economics), Robert Weiner (engineering), Edward Lorenz (meteorology), Ilya Prigogine (chemistry), and John von Neumann (mathematics). Though coming from divergent disciplinary backgrounds and often holding different and even contradictory theoretical and epistemological assumptions, these theorists shared a concern with understanding wholes or systems in their totality (Laszlo & Laszlo, 1997). That is, these theorists emphasized the interrelationship of natural and social phenomena in contrast to the traditional scientific view that saw the "world and all that it contains [as] an assembly of small and distinct parts, fit largely for analysis and study in isolation" (Laszlo & Laszlo, 1997, p. 9). Systems theory, then, emerged in the twentieth century as an alternative to reductionistic theories and methods in the natural and social sciences and called for a radical change in the way scientists understood and investigated natural and social phenomena. While the Newtonian and Cartesian explanatory framework and the experimental method that followed from it were useful in researching some phenomena (e.g., simple systems) the founders of systems theory argued that this reductionistic approach could not adequately capture the dynamic and complex relational phenomena of the physical and social world (Rapoport & Horvath, 1968). A more sophisticated empirical science was required.

Emergent, Dynamic, Open, and Embedded Systems

To understand the development of this more sophisticated holistic empiricism one must first examine the history and development of systems theory itself, which mirrors in many ways the complexity and dynamism of the phenomena it attempts to understand. As we have just mentioned, theorists from quite distinct fields of study, including cybernetics (Weiner), general systems theory (Bertalanffy), chaos theory (Lorenz), and game theory (Rapoport), among others, converged upon the common belief that science must deal with systems in their complexity and totality (for a more detailed history of these developments see Laszlo & Krippner, 1998 and Bausch, 2002). In their efforts, these theorists often used a variety of metaphors (e.g., computers and organisms) that entailed a number of divergent and sometimes incommensurate assumptions, from assumptions about causality (e.g., circular and formal cause) to ideas about how to investigate systems (e.g., computer simulation and naturalistic observation).

Despite their many differences, these systems theorists shared a host of family resemblances and core presuppositions. For example, these systems theorists agreed that a system was a complex whole with interconnected parts with emergent qualities. That is, systems theorists agreed that the properties of a system could not be deduced from studying the parts of the system in isolation. As such noted philosophers as Hegel and Whitehead had argued before, this is because the very identity of any thing, along with the properties and qualities attributed to it, is derived from the relation of that thing to other things and the whole. Water, for example, cannot be understood as water by studying hydrogen atoms and oxygen atoms individually. Water and its properties (e.g., wetness) only emerge when hydrogen and oxygen combine together into the whole of H_2O. It is for this reason that systems theorists contend that the properties of wholes are genuinely emergent—they are "marked by the appearance of novel characteristics exhibited on the level of the whole ensemble, but not by the components in isolation" (Laszlo & Laszlo, 1997, p. 8). A key feature of systems theory, then, is that systems manifest properties that are greater than the sum of their parts. Indeed, the saying, "the whole is greater than the sum of its parts" has become the credo around which all systems theorists unite.

Systems theorists also share the assumption that phenomena, natural and human, always exist as part of and in relation to a whole or system. For example, an individual is never found in isolation, but rather is always part of a family, society, institution or any other specific group. For the behavioral sciences, this implies that behavior is always undertaken and only understandable within a unique context. Systems theorists also posit that these contextual systems within which individuals live and act are themselves embedded within an ever-widening nexus of larger systems. This potentially infinite open-endedness of systems suggests a dynamism whereby systems can interact with other systems within increasingly larger and more complex systems. Thus, just as the qualities of a part stem from its relation to the system, the qualities and characteristics of open systems are derived from their relation to and dynamic interaction with other systems. This facilitates an exchange of information across systems that would be impossible within a closed system.

Finally, systems theorists share the belief that living systems may manifest a form of intentionality. That is, some systems (e.g., groups, couples) can have goals and purposes of their own, "a final objective toward which the system is striving" (Slife, 1993, p.101), which is not reducible to the goals of the individuals within the system. In other words, some systems demonstrate a systemic teleological thrust that is impossible to account for in classic Newtonian physics, which emphasizes antecedent causality. For some systems theorists this teleological principle has given rise to a view of systems as progressively evolving over time (Slife, 1993, p. 101). Ultimately, this notion of a systemic teleology, along with the assumptions of interconnectedness, emergence, embeddedness, and openness, plays a key role in orienting systems theorists toward a holistic perspective.

Systems Approach and Methodology

Given the rich theoretical complexity that systems theory developed in light of its commitment to holism a systemic method had to be designed that modeled and explained the complex systems "created by the multiple interaction of components (parts-mine) by...concentrating on the dynamics that define the characteristic functions, properties, and relationships that are internal or external to the system (Laszlo & Laszlo, 1997, p. 11). This holistic emphasis and systemic level of focus implies that researchers must approach a system in its totality and gain an understanding of the system as a whole before any analysis or study of the parts can be undertaken. Consequently, in the initial stages of research, the goal of the scientist is to identify the system and its inter-related components, and also the wider embedding context in which the system is nested (Laszlo & Laszlo, 1997, p. 11). After the system and its wider embedding context have been identified and analyzed, Laszlo and Laszlo (1997) posit that a systemic inquiry moves to a description of the sub-wholes (e.g., manager-employee dyad) within a system, an analysis of the parts within the sub-wholes and their relationships, and finally a return to the embedding context with an integration of the information learned from each previous step (1997, p. 12).

Interestingly, the work of early systems theory did not champion a specific method to be used in all disciplines. For Bertalanffy and others (see Buckley, 1968), systems theory provided a framework through which divergent disciplines such as economics and psychology could tailor their methods and tools to suit their objects of study. Indeed, systems theory provided researchers with a metatheoretical framework from which re-searchers could adapt its basic axioms to their particular field of inquiry. Nevertheless, the original intent of early systems theorists was to remain within the domain of science with its systematic, rigorous, and empirical epistemology and methodology (Bertalanffy, 1968; Buckley, 1968). In fact, even though the traditional experimental method could offer only a limited view of the system, it was still valued as a powerful empirical tool to verify systems theorist's truth claims. Furthermore, as researchers moved from systems to parts, systems theory sought to combine empiri-cal methods (e.g., naturalistic observation, experimental research) with theoretical modeling (including "qualitative" mathematical modeling), and computer simulation to fully explicate the dynamics and charac-teristics of any given system. In the minds of early systems theorists, there was room for both theoretical holism and traditional experimental methods. The goal, then, for any systems method was and is to render complex and holistic phenomena comprehensible through innovative theoretical tools and the employment of empirical methods. Clearly, systems theory walked the fine line between holism and reductionism by seeking to revolutionize scientific thinking through a more relational approach while, nevertheless, using empirical methods.

Systems Theory and Psychology

From the beginning, systems theorists envisioned applying their insights and methods not only to the "hard" natural sciences, but to the "soft" human sciences as well (Laszlo & Laszlo, 1997). Early theorists recognized that human systems such as cultures, societies, families, and couples represented far more complex systems than even the biological and computational systems used in developing systems theory. If systems thinking provided a powerful anti-reductionistic account of natural systems, its applicability to human systems was equally or more relevant (Laszlo & Laszlo, 1997). For those psychologists who felt beleaguered by the hegemony of the mechanistic and reductionistic theories of behaviorism, systems theory was like a breath of fresh air. It expanded the field of psychological research to include the broader context within which human behavior, thought, and feeling takes place and provided psychologists a systematic, but more comprehensive method by which to study the complexity of human life. Although far from a dominant force in psychology, systems theory's integration, at least at the level of theory, into the discipline of psychology can be identified in many areas in psychology, including cognitive (Sinnot, 1989; Van Orden, 2002; Schonbein, 2005), organizational (Mason, 2005; Cummings, 1980), developmental (Thelen, 2005), and personality and social psychology (Vallacher, Read, & Nowak, 2002), as well as family therapy (Broderick, 1993; Becvar & Becvar, 1983) and research (Walsh & Williams, 1997).

Psychology and Empiricism

The attractiveness of systems theory to psychology was due, in large part, to its success and status in the natural sciences. Systems theory offered psychologists an updated scientific model, one that was developing concomitantly with the revolutions in quantum physics. In spite of system theory's often successful incorporation into psychology, there are few theorists or schools in mainstream psychology that carry out its original goal of balancing an anti-reductionistic stance with empirical methods. In fact, since system theory's arrival to psychology, many psychologists who espouse some form of systems thinking have shifted from traditional empirical (e.g., quantitative) methods to qualitative methods. These psychologists found even the biological and computational metaphors problematic in that they did not apply to human sociality and experience in many ways (Midgely, 2001). However, there are still researchers within psychology who are attempting to follow the vision of a systems approach that combines an explicit rejection of reductionism with innovative empirical research.

Family Systems Theory

The family systems theory, as its name implies, borrows from systems theory the notion that the family is a complex whole with interconnected parts (i.e., family members). A change in any part (i.e., a family member's behavior, attitude, identity), therefore, has systematic effects and transforms the whole into a qualitatively different structure. For instance, as any parent would concur, after the birth of a child the family unit is never the same again! The addition of a child has obvious effects on the identity and behavior of each family member and their relationships to each other. Jealousy among siblings and tension between spouses, for example, can arise as a result of the needs of the new child and each family member's shifting identities and roles. A basic tenet of family systems theory, therefore, is that the behavior and attitudes of an individual family member cannot be understood without taking into account the behavior, and attitudes of the other family members. The focus for family systems theorists, then, is on understanding and treating the family as a whole and paying close attention to the dynamics, interrelationships and interactions between family members. Furthermore, family systems theory recognizes that a family is an open system and always embedded in and interacting with a wider nexus of familial, cultural, societal, and economic systems. Family systems theory, therefore, emphasizes the importance of context in understanding behavior and other phenomena. We will now turn to research examining the interactions of family systems and work systems as an example of anti-reductionistic empirical research.

A Brief Example

Recent organizational research has considered how family and work roles overlap and often cause conflicts for individuals in the areas of work and home (Grandey & Crapanzano, 1999; Adams, King, & King, 1996). As Hammer, Baur, & Grandey (2003) state, work–family conflict is a "form of inter-role conflict where engaging in one role interferes with engaging in another role…[with] the underlying assumption that high levels of interference from one role to the other makes meeting the demands of the second role more difficult" (p. 420). Work-family conflict can take the form of *work-to-family conflict* where obligations at work may make it more difficult for an individual to fulfill his or her family roles and *family-to-work conflict* where family demands may make it more difficult for an individual to complete his or her work roles. Employing a family systems theoretical framework, Hammer et al. (2003) extended this line of research to investigate the effects of work-family conflict on withdrawal behaviors (i.e., family interruptions at work, tardiness, and absenteeism) among both members of dual-earning couples (Hammer, Baur, & Grandey, 2003). In short, Hammer et al. considered how one spouse's withdrawal behavior at work was affected by the other spouse's work-family conflict in addition to their own work-family conflict.

In their study, Hammer et al. (2003) randomly selected employees at a large national bank who met the criteria of a dual-income earner (i.e., working at least 20 hours and living with a spouse for a minimum of three years), and gave them two identical surveys: one for them to complete and the other for their spouse to complete. Along with demographic information controlling for individual differences, these surveys measured work-family conflicts (e.g., "My family often dislikes how I'm preoccupied with work at home") and withdrawal behaviors (e.g., How many times have you been late to work?). Through regression analysis, Hammer et al. demonstrated that both work-to-family conflict and family-to-work conflict of the dual income earner did significantly affect the withdrawal behaviors of the spouse. In other words, the demands of family and work not only contributed to an individual's own withdrawal behavior but it was also positively correlated to their spouse's withdrawal behavior.

Strengths

There are many impressive features of this study as an example of a holistic and empirical systems method. Befitting a systemic approach, the couple, not the individuals involved, was the primary unit of analysis in this study. Hammer et al. (2003) identified the couple as the focus of their study and attempted to tailor their questions, and to a certain degree their methods, to elucidating the effect of each member's behavior on the other person's behavior. Although completed separately, both spouses were given identical surveys targeting their work-family conflict and withdrawal behaviors. Thus, the systems pattern of starting with the whole (couple), working down to an analysis of the individual parts (both spouses), and a synthesis of the whole-part relationship (regression analysis of the interaction between husband and wife) was followed in this study. Incorporating the larger context of a family system, even at the couple unit of analysis, broadens the focus of research that is typically dominated by individual and reductionistic analysis within the domain of empirical research. Moreover, we applaud these researchers' valiant attempt to understand behavior by situating it within the broader context of both family and work systems. This attention to context, especially the interplay of multiple contexts, is unfortunately rare in empirical research, yet Hammer et al. took on the difficult task of locating withdrawal behaviors in the dynamic interplay of the family and work systems empirically.

Weaknesses

In spite of their efforts for a more holistic form of empiricism, Hammer et al. (2003) fail to align a holistic theoretical orientation that posits the couple as the fundamental unit of analysis with holistic empirical methods. That is, Hammer et al. use a systems framework that emphasizes the contextual, dynamic, and relational properties of phenomena (in this case work-family conflict) while adopting empirical methods that reduce the contextual, dynamic and relational properties to contextless, static, and atomistic properties. The introduction of reductionism can be found initially when the researchers first administer their surveys to the couples. These surveys were given to and filled out separately by each spouse. In this way, the couple is never studied as a whole simultaneously, but instead each part of the whole is investigated in isolation through their responses to the surveys. Only after each couple's attitudes, dispositions, and behaviors have been quantified and measured do Hammer et al. attempt to integrate them into the whole. Thus, in contrast to the theoretical commitment of systems theory to studying the whole first and then the parts afterward, the actual practice of the research first measures the parts in isolation and then tries to derive the emergent properties of the whole. As with our previous example of water and hydrogen and oxygen atoms, such an atomistic approach would make any understanding of the whole and its emergent and unique properties difficult, if not impossible. In light of this, it would appear that any research that draws on systemic thought, in that it assumes a holistic theoretical foundation, but fails to maintain this holistic commitment in the application of its methods will inevitably result in a reductionistic empiricism.

Field Theory in Social Psychology

Much like systems theorists, social psychologists have long been interested in the social context of human behavior, and although, like other subdisciplines in psychology, social psychologists maintain an emphasis on the individual, they are also sensitive to the ways in which the individual is part of a larger social whole that must be taken into account when explaining the individual's feelings, thoughts, and behaviors (Myers, 2002). At the very least, social psychologists resist reducing the causes of a person's behavior to some set of internal, self-contained properties. In this effort, they have been especially effective at dismantling theories that postulate personality as an innate quality that is carried by people from context to context and remains essentially unchanged. Milgram's

(1963) now famous study of obedience, for example, illustrated quite effectively that a person's willingness to obey an authority had more to do with their proximity to that authority and the person being shocked, as well as the social status of the university where the study was conducted, than it did with an inherent trait or disposition. Thus, much like their systems theory counterparts, many social psychologists have adopted an anti-reductionistic or holistic conception of the individual as one nexus point among many within a web of relationships that must be studied in their totality if the activity of that individual is to be understood.

Field theory emerged in America in the late 1930s as the most influential anti-reductionistic approach to studying human beings within the subdiscipline of social psychology. Its chief proponent, Kurt Lewin, is considered by many to be the father of social psychology, due in large part to his pioneering work in field theory and in light of the wide-ranging impact that work has had on social psychological theorizing and research (Shaver, 1987; Stivers & Wheelan, 1986). One would be hard pressed to find a single textbook in the subdiscipline that does not make reference to Lewin's theoretical and empirical work. His equation for human behavior, $B = f(P,E)$, which postulates that behavior is a function of a person and the environment as it exists for that person, stands as a foundational tenet of social psychology theorizing (Brehm & Kassin, 1996). Lewin's field theory also played a significant role in the practical application of social psychological theory to "real world" issues and problems. Indeed, Lewin's oft quoted statement that "there is nothing so practical as a good theory" (Lewin, 1951, p. 169), illustrates his belief that theory and practice are inextricably connected and has become a foundational premise of applied social psychology, a rapidly growing field within the subdiscipline.

Essentials of Lewin's Field Theory

According to Lewin (1951), "the basic statements of a field theory are that (a) behavior has to be derived from a totality of coexisting facts, (b) these coexisting facts have the character of a 'dynamic field' in so far as the state of any part of this field depends on every other part of the field" (p. 25). A metaphor that helps illustrate Lewin's field theory is a conglomeration of bubbles pressed up against each other within a bounded space, such as the bubbles at the top of a root beer float. Any bubble that we might identify within the conglomeration has its particular size, shape, and location because of all the bubbles within the conglomeration (Lewin's first statement), which includes most obviously the bubble we're focused on and its own internal air pressure, as well as the bubbles directly adjacent to it that exert their pressure upon the bubble. Less obviously, but just as importantly, the bubbles that are farther removed are also relevant to the properties of the bubble under study and must be taken into account if the qualities of the bubble we are focused on are to be properly understood. The conglomeration of bubbles is fundamentally dynamic, such that if any bubble within the conglomeration were to pop, expand, or move there would be a change in every other bubble and the conglomeration as a whole (Lewin's second statement), even if the change might be imperceptible to the naked eye. For Lewin, the life space of any person must be similarly understood as a dynamic field made up of many coexisting elements, including the person, the physical environment, other people, past experiences, goals for the future, etc., all of which are relevant to the person's behavior and from which any change in any element will inevitably effect a change in every other element and the field as a whole.

It is important to note that Lewin's notion of coexisting elements depends on two interrelated principles: concreteness and contemporaneity. The principle of concreteness proposes that "effects can only be produced by what is 'concrete,' i.e., by something that has the position of an individual fact which exists at a certain moment" (Lewin, 1936, p. 33). Concreteness should not be confused with materiality. A psychological fact may be a concrete thing that has an obvious materiality to it, like a basketball, but it is inevitably more than that and can be other than that. The basketball exists as an element of the life space that is always and already in a particular sociocultural, historical context that transcends its material substrate. If a person has the goal of becoming a professional basketball player, if their father or mother played basketball in college, or if the person just missed a shot in the final game of a championship resulting in a loss, the basketball will exist in a particular way for the person that far surpasses its material makeup.

In addition to concrete facts that overflow their materiality there are concrete facts that have no perceptible material properties at all. The past and the future, for example, do not exist as material realities but as psychological facts in the form of present memories and goals. Lewin's principle of contemporaneity suggests that the temporal facts of the life space that are relevant to the behavior of a person exist as concrete elements of the here and now present, not in the past or in the future. He asserts that, "behavior depends neither on the past nor on the future but on the present field. (This present field has a certain time-depth. It includes the 'psychological past,' 'psychological present,' and 'psychological future' which constitute one of the dimensions of the life space existing at a given time)" (p. 27). In this sense then, the past and future only exist psychologically (i.e., as memory or anticipation), as simultaneous or coexisting regions of the life space at a given time. Along with these temporal regions of the life space, Lewin suggests social and cultural regions that are not material but are psychologically concrete and contemporaneous in the present context within which the person is situated.

As we have previously mentioned, behavior for Lewin is a function of the whole of the life space, which includes the person and the environment as it exists for the person. This is an important and essential point of field theory, because it means that "any type of behavior depends on the total field." (Lewin, 1951, p. 54). Consequently, to see a person and their behavior as separate from their environment is to misunderstand and inaccurately represent the causes of their actions. In like manner, to see a person as an organism that acts solely as its environment dictates is also inappropriate. Rather, as Lewin points out, field theory:

> demands that we no longer seek the 'cause' of events in the nature of a single isolated object, but in the relationship between an object and its surroundings. It is not thought then that the environment of the individual serves merely to facilitate or inhibit tendencies which are established once for all in the nature of the person. One can understand the forces that govern behavior only if one includes in the representation the whole psychological situation (Lewin, 1936, p. 12).

For Lewin, the idea of an inherent personality or core essence of a person that is separate and independent from his or her environment is not helpful in understanding a person's behavior. Even if there were some form of apriori personality present in the person when they arrived in this world, Lewin asserts that the person's behavior will never result from that personality alone, but always results from that personality situated in a particular environment or context, which is co-responsible for the behavior (Lewin, 1935). In this sense, it is impossible and undesirable to disentangle personality from a person's sociality or to reduce the whole of the life space down to any one of its constituent parts. On the other hand, it is equally necessary to acknowledge that the environment exists in a unique way for each individual given the particular material, sociocultural, historical, linguistic, embodied context into which they have been thrown and through which they have their life experiences. For Lewin, no two life spaces are exactly the same, and although there will inevitably be similarities across life spaces, there will always be differences as well.

Lewin (1951) illustrates this point by comparing the life space of a child to the life space of its parent. The life space of a child is more physically, temporally, and socially basic and limited than the life space of an adult, and as a result the child and its parent will perceive themselves and their environment quite differently. For the child, the physical dimension of the life space may for the most consist of a crib and a play-pen in one or two rooms, whereas the adult's physical dimension of the life space includes all the rooms in the house, the car, the neighborhood, a workplace, a city, county, state, and so on. A child's time perspective is limited as well. The psychological future may consist in anticipation of getting a cookie or fulfilling some immediate basic need. For an adult, however, the time perspective is expanded and more complex and will likely include abstract long-term goals, such as getting a college degree or a particular career. In like manner, the social relations of a child's life space are limited primarily to mother, father, and any siblings in the immediate family, whereas the adult's life space may include a number of extended family members, friends, acquaintances, ancestors, and so on. Certainly, the child and its parent playing together in the child's room inhabit the same environment in one sense, but psychologically, it exists in very different ways for both of them.

Field Theory and Group Dynamics

The basic statements and concepts of field theory are just as applicable and important in accounting for the behavior of groups as they are for understanding individual actions. As with the behavior of an individual, Lewin contends that group behavior is a function of a totality of coexisting facts, which include the group and the environment as it exists for that group. Group for Lewin is not merely the sum of its parts as a reductionist might see it (i.e. individual members and their life spaces), nor is it simply more than the sum of the parts as the gestalt psychologist would view it. Lewin sees both of these perspectives as hindrances to a full understanding of group dynamics. Rather as Lewin puts it, "The whole is not 'more' than the sum of its parts, but it has different properties. The statement should be: 'The whole is different from the sum of its parts.' In other words, there does not exist a superiority of value of the whole. Both whole and parts are equally real. On the other hand, the whole has definite properties of its own" (Lewin, 1951, p. 146).

Rather than emphasizing either an individual or group approach to a study of groups, Lewin asserts the importance of studying the parts (the individual members of the group and their lifespaces), the whole (the group entity and its particular lifespace), as well as their dynamic inter-play. Although he views the parts and the whole as inextricably related they are, nevertheless, different entities that may need to be studied, mea-sured, and understood in somewhat different ways. This aspect of Lewin's field theory seems to have been largely ignored by American psychology, which focuses almost completely on the parts (individuals), or the sum of the parts, and as a result, has gained only a partial understanding of group processes. American sociology, on the other hand, maintains an almost exclusive focus on the group and processes among groups and as a result has gained only a limited understanding of group dynamics as well. For a complete understanding of groups to be possible, from Lewin's perspective, the work of psychologists and sociologists needs to be brought together into a properly social psychology that attends to the individuals (the parts), the group (the whole), and the relationship of the individuals to each other as well as the relationship of the group to other groups within the larger group lifespace.

Another often neglected holistic insight of Lewin's field theory con-cerns the way in which the groups should be understood. For Lewin, "conceiving of a group as a dynamic whole should include a definition of group which is based on interdependence of the members (or better, the subparts of the group). It seems to me rather important to stress this point because many definitions of a group use similarity of group members rather than their dynamic interdependence as the constituent factor" (Lewin, 1951, p. 146). This is a critical point for Lewin because group behaviors and dynamics cannot be derived from the similarity of the group members. A focus on similarities leaves the researchers with correlated characteristics that are always at least one step removed from the dynamic itself and may be the result of an infinite number of causes that may have nothing to do with the group and its properties at all. To capture the dynamic of the group and to fully understand its qualities as a whole, researchers must endeavor to examine and understand the total-ity of coexisting facts within the group life space (i.e. the members and their interactions), which have the characteristic of interdependence. To restate it in terms of Lewin's equation for behavior: group behavior is a function of the group (which consists of interdependent members), and the environment as it exists for that group, and thus, it is only by examining the interdependence of a group's members as parts of the group lifespace that a full understanding of the group can be achieved.

Given Lewin's assertions that groups are different from the individual members that make them up and that any definition and study of groups should focus on the interdependence of group members, the question arises as to how one goes about studying a group and whether it is even possible to study the group entity. According to Lewin, such a study is indeed possible and necessary to a clear understanding of group processes. Lewin (1951) illustrates this by setting up the following group research scenario: "Suppose, for instance, that the life of a group containing five members were to be observed during a certain period. Let us assume that five observers are available" (Lewin, 1951, p. 153). He then shows how the traditional reductionistic, similarity based approach leads researchers to assign each observer to a different member of the group and only provides "five miniature 'biographies' of five individuals" (p. 153). From this data it would be very difficult, if not impossible to reconstruct anything about group life. For Lewin this individualistic approach is akin to trying to construct "meaningfully the behavior and personality of an individual from separate accounts of the history of his various muscles" (p. 153). One is reminded here of the dilemma posed by the parable of the five blind men of Hindustan, each of whom touches a different part of an elephant and tries to draw a conclusion about what elephants are based on their limited experience of only one part. Needless to say, this approach to group study fails because the observer will only attend to that which is important for the individual and will ignore or miss those interdependent activities which are important to the group as a whole.

As an alternative that is no more complex and no less empirical, Lewin suggests that it is possible to assign observers to record the different social interactions prevalent in the group. For example, he states, "it is possible to assign one of the five observers to direct observations of the subgrouping occurring in the group, another one to recording the kind and character of interactions" (Lewin, 1951,p. 154), and so forth. In this way, Lewin asserts that "...direct observations about properties of a group as a whole are possible" (p. 154). This does not mean that the individual biography approach is not useful. It may be very helpful in understanding certain aspects of the parts. In order to understand the group as a whole, however, Lewin contends that an empirical focus on the interdependent interactions of members will be more helpful.

Field Theory and Empiricism

Kurt Lewin's approach to group research illustrates his belief that the holistic commitments of field theory in no way demand a nonempirical method of study. On the contrary, field theory is explicitly empirical, but with a different emphasis than traditional empirical research. Instead of focusing on what is materially present and readily observable (e.g., the individual person or the group's members and their properties), as is typical of reductionistic empirical psychology, field theory directs the researchers' attention to the observable aspects of the relationships among the regions of the life space, which may or may not be materially present, but are all psychologically relevant and concrete. If the researcher is interested in the life space of an individual they can empirically examine observable features of the person's interactions with the physical, social, and temporal regions of that life space. In the case of the child's life space described earlier, for example, the researcher can examine how the child interacts with the physical elements of the life space (does the child exit the crib or play pen and in what manner does the child do so? How does the child manipulate a door handle, climb up on a chair, etc.?), together with the social elements of the life space (how do the child and its parent play together and communicate with each other?), and the temporal elements of the life space (how does the child's behavior, like finding a way past mom into the kitchen to get up on a stool to reach the cookie jar and get a cookie, resemble previous behaviors and predict future actions as well?).

Similarly, in the case of a group, a field theorist will examine the interactions among the regions of the group life space (i.e., group members), including their conversations, their posture and gestures as they interact, the amount of time they spend working together or apart, the subgroups that form, the roles that are adopted, and the products that result from their collaboration. For Lewin and other field theorists, all of these behaviors and interactions are observable and therefore can be studied empirically without negating the holistic theoretical framework that guides the study.

Field Theory in Action

Many social psychologists have modeled elements of Lewin's field theory in their own research and have attempted to maintain a fidelity to empiricism without compromising holism. Although there is no clearly specified theoretical descendant of field theory in contemporary social psychology today, one example of anti-reductionistic empirical research that follows in the tradition of Lewin's field theory can be found in social psychological investigations of behavioral confirmation. Also known as self-fulfilling prophecy, behavioral confirmation is a phenomenon whereby a person or group's beliefs about another person or group may lead them to treat that person or group in such a way that the person or group behaves in a manner consistent with the belief. One of the earliest and best known studies of behavioral confirmation was Snyder, Tanke, and Berscheid's (1977) study of self-fulfilling prophecy as it related to stereotypes about attraction. In this research, male participants were given a photograph and biographical information that led them to believe they would be having a phone conversation with a woman who was either attractive or unattractive. In fact, the females with whom the men conversed on the phone were not the women in the pictures, but were randomly selected for each condition from a pool of female volunteers. Consequently, the only real difference across the conversations was the males' belief that the female on the other end of the line was either attractive or unattractive.

In terms of Lewin's field theory, the males' belief, the researchers carrying out the study, and the supposed attractiveness of the females that supported the men's belief were all relevant and concrete facts of the conversational life space, even if the conditions were fabricated for the sake of conducting the research study. It is important to remember that the life space never consists of the environment as it really is in some impossibly objective sense, but always as it exists for the persons in it. In this case, it exists for the males in such a way that the female they were talking to was either attractive or not. And, just as was the case with the bubbles described earlier, if any change in any region of the lifespace takes place (e.g., the man sees a picture of an attractive woman with whom he will soon converse), then every other region of the life space will change in some way as well. Some changes may be more immediately present and perceptible, like those taking place in the conversation. For example, the "more attractive" women may encounter a male voice on the other end of the line that is warm, friendly, and a little flirtatious, whereas the "less attractive" may find a cold, distant, and short voice coming through the line. Other changes may be more remote. The cultural norms regarding how men should speak to an attractive or unattractive woman may come into play, for instance, or the men's past experiences with attractive and unattractive women may become more salient.

As each of the near and far regions of the life space are changed and come to work together to support the men's belief that the woman their speaking to is attractive or not, the behaviors of the men are sure to follow suit. This is exactly what the results of the study indicate happened. The men did treat the "more attractive" and "less attractive" women differently. That is, they did act on their belief as if it was true, and as a result, the women who were viewed as more attractive were treated with warmth, interest, and friendliness and the men who viewed their conversation partner as being less attractive were treated in a manner that was disinterested and cold. The women reciprocated the behavior of their conversation partner, such that if they were treated warmly they responded warmly and if they were treated disinterestedly they spoke in a more disinterested way. The males attributed the qualities of their partner's speech to their partner's attractiveness and did not see their own behavior toward them as playing any role in the outcome. In their minds the stereotypical beliefs about attractive and unattractive women were confirmed.

From the perspective of Lewin's field theory. this study, and other behavioral confirmation studies like it, is both holistic and empirical. The researchers empirically studied the males' and females' interpersonal relationship by observing the interactions between them and measuring the sociability, humor, and enthusiasm that took place. Then, they compared those observations and examined the differences between pairs in the attractive and unattractive conditions using statistical analyses, just as any psychologist applying the empirical method of science would do. In this sense, behavioral confirmation studies, like this one, illustrate the kind of anti-reductionistic empiricism Lewin hoped for. Observations are being made, compared, and examined in a manner that is consistent with empiricism, but they are focused on the dynamic interdependence of the regions of the life space that make up the whole of the conversation.

Although a genuinely anti-reductionistic empiricism seems to have been achieved at this point in the study, there are other levels of analysis and explanation where reductionism finds its way into the study and holism is compromised. For instance, as researchers move from describing the results of their research to explaining the process of behavioral confirmation they inevitably take the thick and rich complexity of the conversational life space as a whole and separate it out by each individual's part in it and stretch it out to make it fit sequentially on a time line (e.g., Snyder, 1992). In so doing, they reduce the experience and behaviors of the conversational pair to a step by step process, creating and only attending to each step at a time rather than the dynamic interactions that were observed initially. For example, in the first step of the sequence the researchers isolated and focused only on the males' acquisition of a belief about their female conversation partner. In the second step researchers only examined the males' behavior toward the females. At the third step they isolated and examined the females' behaviors, and at the final step they looked only to see whether the males' belief about their female counterpart was confirmed.

By reducing, isolating, and sequencing the men's and women's interactions in this way, the researchers created the condition of antecedence that is necessary for causal inferences to be made (Hume, 1748/1984) and proceeded to suggest a causal chain or sequence with each step bringing about the effect of the next one until the self-fulfilling prophecy was complete. Because the causal chain itself cannot be empirically observed, but can only be inferred from the antecedent relationship of the events, the researchers are left with an assertion of causation that is neither empirical nor holistic. At the level of explanation, then, it is the researchers' commitment to causation rather than empiricism that forces the reduction of the whole of the conversation to a series of cause/effect moments across a timeline. This reduction for the sake of causation is not a unique characteristic of behavioral confirmation research, but is symptomatic of all experimental research, including Field theoretical studies, that make causal claims. However, the consequence for Field theorists, like Lewin, is more significant because it compromises the holism they prize so highly.

As the explanation deepens, the reductionism continues and is further atomized within each step of the sequence created by the researchers. Step one, for example, which is based on the empirically observable event of the male subject looking over the female's picture and biographical information sheet is broken down into the males' internalized belief that the woman is or is not attractive. Because the males' belief cannot be observed empirically, it has to be assessed using some form of self-report measure. This is a two-fold reduction: First, the empirical event of examining the picture is reduced to an internalized unobservable belief, and second, the belief is reduced to a self-reported measure, which in studies of this type is usually a numerical score on a Likert-type scale of some sort.

In step two of the sequence, the holism of the conversational interaction between the men and women is further reduced by the researchers, who at this point are only interested in the males' behavior. Specifically, researchers only examined whether the males acted on their belief about the female as if it were true and numerically scored their observations on a Likert-type scale. Consequently, they only attended to and evaluated the males' side of the conversation[2]. Likewise, because the researchers were only interested in the females' behavior in step three of the sequence, they only examined the women's side of the conversation they had with the men and numerically reduced it to a set of ratings on a scale.

The final step, like step one, involved a post-conversation self-report measure of the man's belief that the female behaved in a manner that is consistent with his belief. As was the case in step one and with the independent raters' scores at steps two and three, the interaction between the men and women at step four, which was not experienced numerically, had to be transformed and reduced into some form of numerical measurement that could be subjected to statistical analyses and from which causal conclusions could be inferred. At each of these steps created by the researchers, the reduction of the conversational life space follows not from the demands of empiricism, but rather is prompted by other assumptions and concerns inherent in psychological science, including concerns with measurement, objectivity, causation, and statistical analysis, among others.

Conclusion

Systems and field theorists have each articulated holistic psychologies that are sensitive to relationships and context and have used empirical observation to study these holistic systems and fields in an anti-reductionistic way. Although this anti-reductionistic practice is not typical of empirical research in psychology, systems and field theorists seem to have found legitimately empirical means to observe relational aspects of the psychological phenomena they investigate, including observing conversations, subgrouping, and other forms of interaction among group members. Despite their success in combining holism and empirical observation other elements of the scientific method have led systems and field theory researchers to reduce the very holistic phenomena they strive to preserve. These reductionistic facets of the scientific method tend to emerge in the explanatory stage of their studies as researchers try to separate and isolate variables, infer a pattern of causation, and transform observations into numbers that can be used in statistical analyses. As each of these reductions are applied to the phenomenon of interest the researchers inevitably move farther away from the whole they are interested in and lose contact with the relationship among the parts within that whole.

In this sense, then, it is not empiricism that necessitates reduction, though it has been traditionally understood that way, but rather it is the explanatory assumptions inherent in the scientific method that require researchers, even those committed to holism, to break the whole down into its constituent parts. If systems theorists, field theorists, and other psychologists who share a commitment to holism are going to achieve the anti-reductionistic empiricism they prize so highly, the explanatory, reductionistic elements of their method will need to be addressed and resolved. One step toward that resolution may be found in the application of alternative, meaning based methods that use empirical observation but do not endorse the explanatory assumptions that demand reduction.

In terms well described by Wilhelm Dilthey (1900/1976) many years ago, meaning based approaches emphasize Verstehung (understanding) over Erklärung (explanation) and therefore favor the use of human science methods that emphasize meaning and interpretation over natural science methods that focus on explanation and objective measurement. These human science methods are typically, though not exclusively, qualitative in that they primarily use data in spoken and written language formats rather than numbers, and in that they interrogate the meaning of their textual data rather than infer some underlying causal pattern. Moreover, human science methods are explicitly holistic in that they not only recognize the interrelation of the parts of the whole they are studying but also acknowledge the researcher as a part of that whole, as well as the broader socio-cultural, historical, linguistic context within which the phenomenon, the researcher, and the study itself are situated. In this sense, practitioners of meaning based methods are holists through and through, recognizing that wholes are always embedded among and within other wholes and cannot be fully understood without taking that embeddedness into account.

For the systems and field theorist, the practice of a human science method that emphasizes meaning could still include empirical observations of group members' interactions, conversations, grouping, etc., but those observations would be recorded in the language appropriate to the observation. They would also be analyzed according to the type of observation and the context of acknowledged interpretation for the study as opposed to the supposedly objective explanation of the scientific method that inevitably reduces the whole. As parts of the whole they are studying, researchers would acknowledge their contribution to those observations in the form of assumptions and even biases that influence what they notice and record in the interactions they observe. They would also attend to the broader socio-cultural context within which the interactions and their observations of those interactions occur and would give voice to the importance of that context in their written accounts of their observations. Finally, they would share their accounts of their observations with each other, examining themes of meaning, evaluating similarities and contrasts, and making careful decisions about what seems particularly significant to an understanding of the phenomenon being investigated.

Although this overview of an empirical, meaning based, anti-reductionistic method is necessarily cursory, it suggests the possibility of alternative methods that could be adopted by systems and field theorists (and other psychologists who are committed to holism and empiricism) that would not force them into the reductionistic explanatory framework of the scientific method. As qualitative methods become more prevalent and valued in psychology they may be of great use to those psychologists who are as committed to holism as they are to empiricism and may help them stretch even further to creatively and thoughtfully study the complex and rich phenomena of human life. Given how thoughtful and creative systems and field theorists have been so far, we see great potential for anti-reductionistic empiricism in the future, so long as it is carefully framed within a framework of understanding and meaning that recognizes the necessity of holism at every level, including the level of the research process itself.

Notes

1. Consider, as just one example, how easily recognizable and nearly revered Ockham's Razor has become both in and out of science.
2. This is typically done by recording each participant's contribution to a conversation on a separate audio track so independent raters can listen to and evaluate only the side of the conversation being focused on at that point in the study (See Ridge & Reber, 2002 for a typical example of how this is done in behavioral confirmation research).

References

Adams, G., King, L., & King, D. (1996). Relationships of job and family involvement, family social support, and work-family conflict with job and life satisfaction. *Journal of Applied Psychology, 81,* 411-420.

Bausch, K. C., (2002). Roots and branches: A brief, picaresque, personal history of systems theory. *Systems Research and Behavioral Science, 19,* 417-418. Retrieved July 30, 2008 from Academic OneFile database.

Becvar, R. & Becvar, D. (1982). *Systems theory and family therapy: A primer.* Washington, D.C.: University Press of America.

Brehm, S. S., & Kassin, S. M. (1996). *Social psychology* (3rd ed.). Boston, MA: Houghton Mifflin Co.

Broderick, C. (1993). *Understanding family process: Basics of family systems theory.* Newbury Park, CA: Sage Publications.

Buckley, W. (1968). *Modern systems research for the behavioral scientist: A sourcebook.* Chicago, Il: Aldine Publishing Company.

Cummings, T. (1980). *Systems theory for organization development.* New York, NY: Chichester.

Dilthey, W. (1900/1976). The rise of hermeneutics (trans. T. Hall). In P. Connerton (Ed.), *Critical Sociology* (pp. 104-116). New York: Penguin Books.

Grandey, A., & Crapanzano, R. (1999). The conservation of resources model and work-family conflict strain. *Journal of Vocational Behavior, 54,* 350-370.

Hammer, L., Bauer, T., & Grandey, A., (2003). Work-family conflict and work-related withdrawal behaviors. *Journal of Business and Psychology, 17,* (3), 419-436.

Hume, D. (1748/1984). Locke, J. (1689/1984). From *An enquiry concerning human understanding,* as cited in I. Berlin's, *The age of enlightenment: Basic writings of Locke, Voltaire, Berkeley, Hume, Reid, Condillac, Hamann, and others.* New York: Meridian.

Laszlo, A., & Krippner, S. (1998). Systems theories: Their origins, foundations, and development. In Jordan, J. (Ed.), *Systems Theories and A Priori Aspects of Perception* (47-74). Amsterdam: Elsevier Science.

Laszlo, E., & Laszlo, A. (1997). The contributions of the systems sciences to the humanities. *Systems Research and Behavioral Science, 14* (1), 5-19.

Leahey, T. H. (2001). *A history of modern psychology* (3rd Ed.). Upper Saddle River, NJ: Prentice Hall.

Lewin, K. (1935). *Dynamic theory of personality: Selected papers.* New York, NY: McGraw-Hill Book Company, Inc.

Lewin, K. (1936). *Principles of topological psychology.* New York, NY: McGraw-Hill Book Company, Inc.

Lewin, K. (1951). *Field theory in social science: Selected theoretical papers.* New York, NY: Harper & Brothers Publishers.

Locke, J. (1689/1984). From *An essay concerning human understanding,* as cited in I. Berlin's, *The age of enlightenment: Basic writings of Locke, Voltaire, Berkeley, Hume, Reid, Condillac, Hamann, and others.* New York: Meridian.

Mason, G. (2005). Connectivity as a basis for a systems modeling ontology. *Systems Research and Behavioral Sciences, 22* (1), 69-80.

Midgely, G. (2001). Systemic intervention: Philosophy, methodology, and practice. New York, NY: Kluwer Academic/Plenum.

Milgram, S. (1963). Behavioral study of obedience. *Journal of Abnormal Psychology, 67,* 371-378.

Meyers, D. G. (2002). *Social Psychology* (8th edition). New York, NY: McGraw Hill.

Quine, W. V. (1980). Two dogmas of empiricism. In H. Morick (Ed.), *Challenges to empiricism* (46-70). Indianapolis, IN: Hackett Publishing.

Rapoport, A. & Horvath, W. (1968). Thoughts on organization theory. In Buckley, W. (Ed.), *Systems research for the behavioral scientist* (71-75). Chicago, Il: Aldine Publishing Company.

Ridge, R. D., & Reber, J. S. (2002). "I think she's attracted to me": The effect of men's beliefs on women's behavior in a job interview scenario. *Basic and Applied Social Psychology, 24*(1), 1-14.

Schonbein, W. (2005). Cognition and continuous dynamical systems. *Minds and Machines 15,* 57–71.

Shaver, K. G. (1987). *Principles of Social Psychology.* Boston, MA: Houghton Mifflin Co.

Sinnot, J., (1989). General Systems Theory: A rationale for the study of everyday memory. In Poon, L., Rubin, C., Wilson, B. (Eds.), *Everyday cognition in adulthood and late life.* (pp. 59-70). New York, NY: Cambridge University Press.

Slife, B. D. (1993). *Time and psychological Explanation.* Albany, NY: State University of New York Press.

Slife, B. D. & Williams, R. N. (1995). *What's behind the research: Discovering hidden assumptions in the behavioral sciences.* Thousand Oaks, CA: Sage Publications.

Snyder, M. (1992). Motivational foundations of behavioral confirmation. In M. P. Zanna (Ed.), *Advance in experimental social psychology* (Vol. 25, pp. 67-114). Orlando, FL: Academic.

Snyder, M., Tanke, E.D., & Berscheid, E. (1977). Social Perception and Interpersonal Behavior: On the self-fulfilling Nature of Social Stereotypes. *Journal of Experimental Social Psychology, 35,* 656-666.

Stivers, E., & Wheelan, S. (1986). *The Lewin legacy: Field theory in current practice.* New York, NY: Springer-Verlag.

Thelen, E. (2005). Dynamic systems theory and the complexity of change. *Psychoanalytic Dialogues. 15* (2), 255-283.

Van Orden, G. (2002). Non-linear dynamics and psycholinguistics. *Ecological Psychology. 14*(1-2). 1-4.

Walsh, W., & Williams, R. (Eds.). (1997). *Schools and family therapy: Using systems theory and family therapy in the resolution of school problems.* Springfield, Ill: Thomas Publisher.

9

Considering the Foundations for a Holistic Empirical Psychology

Joshua W. Clegg

The first question before us in this volume concerned the implications of methodological reductionism in the behavioral sciences. The work of the authors included here, and of the historical figures they have considered, suggests that reductionistic methods commit the fundamental empirical error of making inferences about one phenomenon on the basis of observations made of a different phenomenon—that is, that the irreducibly unique characteristics of a particular system or field of relations are inferred by reductive analogy from the characteristics of one or more of its constituent elements.

Concretely, this assertion means that it is a kind of basic stimulus error to assume that we can understand, for example, an individual's capacity to learn and apply knowledge from any combination of intelligence tests or that we can understand how friendships are formed and maintained from any set of aggregated counts of operationalized behavior (e.g., mean eye-contact durations, Likert-style "liking" ratings, etc.). That is not to say that these kinds of phenomena are irrelevant to understanding learning or friend-ship—as Lewin (1999/1949) argues, "in the social as in the physical field, the structural properties of a dynamic whole are different from the structural properties of their sub-parts. Both sets of properties have to be investigated" (p. 29)—it is merely to claim that no matter how much we know about the elements of some complex system, we will never properly understand the characteristics governing that system until we can observe it as a whole, operating system. This means, then, that a fundamentally reductionistic ap-proach to method will always produce unwarranted conclusions because it ignores the fact that relations are constitutive of all phenomena.

It is precisely because of this fundamental methodological problem that the second question addressed in this volume is of such importance—the question, that is, of whether empirical methods in general, and experimental methods in particular, can be pursued without a commitment to reductionism. The only possible answer to this question, of course, is an attempt to delineate the characteristics of such an approach and the authors in this book have at least begun that task. By way of summary, I will outline two primary elements of a holistic approach to empirical and experimental methods that I believe are reflected in this volume. The first is the assumption that theory, method, and procedure must be carried out as an indissoluble whole and the second is the assumption that holistic analysis must operate within particular integrated systems, fields, or units of relations.

The Communion of Theory, Method, and Procedure

A holistic approach to empirical methods requires, first, that the interconnection between theory, method, and procedure be preserved, or perhaps re-established. The steady narrowing of field in psychology, however, has brought with it a compartmentalization of these research enterprises, such that the development of one is carried out often entirely independent of the other. For all of the psychologists considered here, that separation was considered destructive of research. For them, a word like "method" did not simply apply to a set of procedures—it referred to a whole system of thought. It is only in the relatively recent past that psychologists have seen fit to sublimate and institutionalize particular de-contextualized procedures as universal and definitive answers to methodological questions.

Lewin (1999/1949) commented on this separation of the theoretical and methodological, though he was not entirely critical: "this laudable and necessary removal of philosophy from the authoritarian place of the boss or the judge over science has led to a tendency of eliminating all 'practical' relations between philosophy and the empirical sciences, including the perhaps possible and fruitful position of philosophy as a consultant to science" (p. 27). Though Lewin believed in an independent science, he foresaw the difficulties inherent in an increasingly anti-theoretical approach to psychology. In fact, he consistently asserted "the necessity for developing better concepts and higher levels of theory" (p. 28).

Like Lewin, Vygotsky (1987/1934) advocated a move away from scientific systems "bemired in prescientific concepts which shroud them in ad hoc semi-metaphysical systems and theories" (p. 54) but he still rejected the possibility of an atheoretical science: "he who considers facts, inevitably considers them in the light of one theory or another; fact and philosophy are directly interrelated" (p. 55). In fact, according to Vygotsky "the absence of a philosophy is itself a very definite philosophy" (p. 80).

The segregation of psychological method and general theory has only grown in the last half-century—as Jaan Valsiner phrases it, psychology has been "orphaned by its loss of connections with philosophy and biology" (Valsiner, 2003, p. 1)—and that segregation may provide some insight into why certain institutionalized procedures have gained ascendance over integrated theoretical and methodological systems of investigation. When procedures can be separated from their concrete theoretical and methodological contexts, it is not difficult, and in fact seems inevitable, that we produce a generalized and institutionalized procedural set (as is the case in contemporary mainstream psychology). Unfortunately, such sets further undermine the possibility of developing any truly theoretical method—under them certain procedures become rules of conduct, automatically disqualifying new, theoretically driven approaches such that "Psychologists' work becomes that of consumers' use of theories, not creation of news ones" (p. 6).

If the foregoing analysis implies anything about method construction it is not so much that we need more theory but that theory, method, and procedure cannot be separated without also sacrificing something of the phenomena investigated. Our topics of interest, the questions we ask about them, and the ways in which those questions are answered are all inseparably connected. I cannot, for example, ask questions about group processes and then dogmatically restrict myself to the study of individuals at isolated moments.

Unfortunately for psychology, when I artificially dissect theory, method, and procedure, the inherent relationships between these research activities are not eliminated but arbitrarily transferred across entirely dissimilar contexts. In such cases I am left, for example, with the peculiar circumstance of employing a procedure designed to compare aggregate characteristics (the mean) while investigating individual psychic processes. The net result, of course, is that I transform the phenomena under investigation according to the theoretical rules of my borrowed procedures even though those rules may bear no meaningful relation to the phenomena under investigation.

In sum, then, a holistic analysis requires integration across theory, method, and procedure; so much so that these should not be seen as clearly separable or distinguishable. Theories should not be purely abstract, pre-established doctrines, but should be concrete, contextualized, and inductive; methods should not be mere procedures but systems of thought and action organically tied to their explanatory systems. Procedures should not come from an acontextual, pre-packaged canon but should grow uniquely from the theoretical and methodological assumptions of those who carry them out.

Analysis into Units, Fields or Systems of Relations

A second principle feature of holistic empirical investigation that is highlighted in this volume is an analytic philosophy that restricts and localizes theory, method, and procedure to a particular, integrated whole—to a unit, field, or system of relations. This analytic imperative flows from the assumption that relations between elements are fundamental constituent elements of all phenomena, an assumption that requires us to replace the analysis of isolated elements with the analysis of meaningful units or fields of dynamic relations. As Vygotsky (1987/1934) argues, any method that

> Begins with the decomposition of the complex mental whole into its elements ... can be compared with a chemical analysis of water in which water is decomposed into hydrogen and oxygen. The essential feature of this form of analysis is that its products are of a different nature than the whole from which they were derived. The elements lack the characteristics inherent in the whole and they possess properties that it did not possess (p. 45).

For Vygotsky, the problem with the exclusive reliance on reductive analytical methodologies was that they restricted our knowledge to the elements of any given system and made impossible the investigation of the processes and structural relations of the system itself.

Instead of such reductive analytic procedures, Vygotsky (1987/1934) argued for an analysis by units rather than elements:

> We attempted to replace the method based on decomposition into elements with a method of analysis that involves partitioning the complex unity of verbal thinking into units. In contrast to elements, units are products of analysis that form the initial aspects, not of the whole but of its concrete aspects and characteristics. Unlike elements, units do not lose the characteristics inherent to the whole. The unit contains, in a simple, primitive form, the characteristics of the whole that is the object of analysis (p. 244).

For Vygotsky, these characteristics were unique to the whole, a whole which could not be further divided without losing those characteristics (Vygotsky, 1987/1934).

According to Vygotsky, unit analysis allowed for the investigation of complex systems because it reveals systemic relationships and not simply elemental features. For example, Vygotsky (1987/1934) asserted that in a unit analysis of human consciousness:

> There exists a dynamic meaningful system that constitutes a unity of affective and intellectual processes. Every idea contains some remnant of the individual's affective relationship to that aspect of reality which it represents. In this way, analysis into units makes it possible to see the relationship between the individual's needs or inclinations and his thinking (p. 50).

What reveals itself, then, in this type of analysis is a set of relations and not simply an elementary catalogue. It is an analysis where, as Lewin (1999/1949) phrases it, "structural properties are characterized by relations between parts rather than by the parts or elements themselves" (p. 30).

For the social sciences, this sort of analysis into units or fields of relations implies that it is meaningless to talk about individuals and their environments as separate from one another or as "influencing" one another. "Person" is indissoluble from "environment"—self from society, percipient from perceptual field, etc. From a holistic perspective, person and environment constitute an irreducible unit of analysis. This unit of relation, however, has often been explained on the basis of non-equivalent explanatory units—e.g., the nervous system, evolutionary or behavioral history, etc. Theoretically speaking, these other systems may constitute elements in the person-environment system but the characteristics of the person-environment system are unique and not reducible to those elements. We need theoretical models, then, that are not cobbled together from the laws and characteristics of other systems and we need methods that examine the person-environment system as a unique, irreducible whole.

More specifically, research employing this kind of unit or system analysis requires models of dynamic relations (rather than models of static entities) that are restricted to the unit under consideration and not generalized beyond it through any kind of reductive analogy. This sort of analysis also requires observational contexts that are global enough to include the complete unit under investigation, observational periods sufficient to observe the dynamics of the unit, observational protocols that document, record, or measure interactions rather than merely characteristics or entities, and a research situation that is functionally (or perhaps relationally or systemically) equivalent to the person-environment interaction that is being modeled. As a whole, this model of research produces procedures more organically tied to the psychological context under investigation instead of those highly artificial procedures contrived through multiple levels of abstractive (operationalized) transformation by analogy to other systems.

Because this model of research assumes that relations determine the nature of units or systems of meaning, the formal and functional properties that characterize one particular unit (or level of organization) are unique to that unit and may not be generalized to either sub or super units within any particular system of units (e.g., the properties of hydrogen and oxygen are not the same as those of water). Each unit, then, requires a particular theory of measurement or observation within the unit as well as a particular theory about the relationships between the unit and its related units. Methodologically, this means that mathematics can be used to model formal and functional relationships within and between units but not to make generalizations across units on the basis of aggregate frequentistic data. In fact, aggregated counts cannot meaningfully or logically connect the particular and the general because they contain no information about any particular case.

Kurt Lewin argued strongly for this conception of mathematics in the social sciences. He claimed that frequentist scientific philosophies were the result of a kind of backwards reliance on what he called Aristotelian modes of thought. For Lewin (1999/1931), the essential character of the Aristotelian view was the explanation of any given event (including human events) in terms of the internal characteristics of the object *"irrespective of its surroundings at any given time"* (p. 56). He contrasts this approach with what he calls Galilean modes of thought, modes which involve a "transition to concepts which can be defined only by reference to a certain sort of *situation"* (p. 56).

For Lewin, the reason the Aristotelian modes of thought dominate in psychology is because of our allegiance to frequentist models and our consequent aversion for the single case. According to Lewin (1999/1931), psychologists understand lawfulness to mean frequency—"repetition remains, as it did for Aristotle, to a large extent the basis for the assumption of the lawfulness or intelligibility of an event" (p. 46)—and this "extravagant valuation of repetition (i.e., considering frequency as the criterion and expression of lawfulness) dominates the formation of the concepts of psychology" (p. 47). The result of this inordinate passion for frequency, according to Lewin, is a distaste for the individual case. For the psychologist: "the individual event seems to him fortuitous, unimportant, scientifically indifferent" (p. 46). Such a conception is lamentable, given that the individual case is the only one available to concrete experience and intervention.

If Lewin's analysis of our discipline is correct, then many of the most cherished principles and procedures of scientific psychology are essentially the result of a specialized kind of superstition. Psychologists require of themselves a rigidly defined way of conceptualizing, observing, and numerizing phenomena that is "founded, at least in part, on the ambition to demonstrate the scientific status of psychology by using as much mathematics as possible and by pushing all calculations to the last possible decimal place" (Lewin 1999/1931, p. 48). Unfortunately, this reliance on frequentistic probability will never serve a holistic analysis by units or systems because such an analysis must always be of particular dynamic relations and not of averaged counts of elementary properties.

A final implication of a holistic analysis by units or fields is that, because person and environment are inseparable, the psychological unit of analysis necessarily includes the constructive agent. External interpretations and operationalizations are not equivalent with an agent's active creation of inter-subjective meaning. Any attempt to deny, ignore, or remove the consciousness of the constructive agent, then, will lead to a fundamentally erroneous reduction of the psychological unit of investigation:

> The denial of consciousness and the attempt to construct a psychological system without this concept, as a psychology without consciousness ... leads to the situation in which method has been deprived of the most necessary means and instruments for studying latent responses, such as internal movements, internal speech, somatic responses, etc., that are not observable with the naked eye. The study of only those reactions that are visible to the naked eye is totally powerless and untenable in explaining even the simplest problems of human behaviour (Vygotsky 1999/1925, p. 252).

In a holistic analysis, then, every psychological question includes the constructive agent as an inseparable part of the unit under consideration.

In a lament similar to Vygotsky's, Lewin (1999/1949) claimed that psychological science axiomatically disqualified terms like volition, emotion, or sentiment because they could not be "regarded as 'existing' in the sense in which the scientist uses the term" (p. 28). According to Lewin, this disqualification was not theoretically driven but was justified because "emotions were declared to be something 'intangible' to be pinned down by scientific analysis or experimental procedures" (p. 28).

These critiques by Lewin and Vygotsky reflect their frustrations with a set of institutional practices that appeared arbitrary, nonsensical, and thoroughly anti-intellectual. In fact, Lewin (1999/1949) attributed the methodological dogmas of institutionalized psychology more to superstitious orthodoxy than to careful theory:

> Like social taboos, a scientific taboo is kept up not so much by a rational argument as by a common attitude among scientists: Any member of the scientific guild who does not strictly adhere to the taboo is looked upon as queer; he is suspected of not adhering to the scientific standards of critical thinking (p. 28).

Lewin traced the source of this scientific taboo to a restriction of acceptable analytic units that "is based on arguments which grant existence only to units of certain size, or which concern methodologic-technical problems, or conceptual problems" (p. 29).

If, however, psychologists can free themselves of these arbitrary "methodologic-technical" requirements, then it is possible to conceive of an empirical paradigm where the active agent is central. In such a paradigm the research situation would have to be an interactive one, a situation where the "participant" is as responsible for producing meaning as the "researcher." This conception of research points to both participatory and emancipatory methods—methods where participants are active interpreters and transformers of both the research context and the socio-cultural one. This kind of research model, then, permits, may even require, the integration of social transformation with the modeling of dynamic psychological fields.

Conclusion

Considering this volume as a whole, the arguments for a holistic approach to empirical and experimental psychology are powerful. Reductionistic methods that ignore the constitutional quality of relations will never allow us to adequately conceptualize or observe psychological phenomena. It is imperative, then, that we re-envision the research activity in a more contextual, holistic way.

If we take seriously the notion of holistic empirical investigation, then we must begin holistically, re-establishing the indissoluble ties between theory, method and procedure and resisting the manualization of research procedures. We must also learn to develop theories of relations and not simply of elemental properties. Such theories must concern particular units, fields, or systems of relations and not be reduced to, or interpreted in the terms of, other systems. Methodologically, this kind of unit analysis requires a research situation that is functionally equivalent to the phenomena being modeled and thus also requires more contextualized and dynamic observational techniques and environments. Analytic procedures for this kind of unit analysis must also concern systems of relations, as in formal or interpretive models and not aggregations of characteristics, as in frequentist probability. Finally, for psychology a holistic analysis requires the integration of the active agent into theory, method, and procedure and so points towards both participatory and emancipatory methods.

References

Baldwin, J. (1930). Autobiography of James Mark Baldwin. In C. Murchison (ed.), *History of Psychology in Autobiography*, Vol. 1. Clark University Press, Worcester, MA.

Lewin, K. (1999). The conflict between Aristotelian and Galilean modes of thought in contemporary psychology. In M. Gold (ed.), *The Complete Social Scientist: A Kurt Lewin Reader* (pp. 37-66). Washington, D.C.: American Psychological Association. (Original work published 1931.)

Lewin, K. (1999). Cassirer's philosophy of science and the social sciences. In M. Gold (Ed.), *The Complete Social Scientist: A Kurt Lewin Reader* (pp. 23-36). Washington, D.C.: American Psychological Association. (Original work published 1949).

Valsiner, J. (2003). "Theory construction and theory use in psychology: Creating knowledge beyond social ideologies." The 10th Biennial Conference of International Society for Theoretical Psychology (ISTP). Istanbul. June 24, 2003.

Vygotsky, L. (1999). Consciousness as a problem in the psychology of behavior (N. Veresov, trans.). *European Studies in the History of Science and Ideas, 8*, 251-281. (Original work published 1925.)

Vygotsky, L. (1987). Thinking and Speech. In R.W. Rieber, and A.S. Carton (eds.), N. Minick (trans.), *The Collected Works of L.S. Vygotsky: Volume 1: Problems of General Psychology, Including the Volume Thinking and Speech.* New York: Plenum Press. (Original work published 1934.)

List of Contributors

Zachary B. Beckstead has an M.A. in psychology from the University of West Georgia and is currently in the Ph.D. program at Clark University. His research emphasizes the history and philosophy of psychology and a critical investigation into the epistemological and ethical foundations that underlie the discipline. His current research tackles the significant rituals and material objects used in the burial process that guide the bereaved in their journey. In addition, he is investigating the encounter between researcher and research-participant and "ruptures" in the psychological research setting that mark opportunities for research to move in unanticipated and exciting directions.

Eric P. Charles received his Ph.D. from the University of California, Davis, spent two years as an NIH post-doctoral fellow at Clark University, and is now an assistant professor of psychology at Pennsylvania State University, Altoona. His empirical work currently focuses on perceptual development, and his theoretical work focuses on foundational issues in ecological and evolutionary psychology. He is currently putting together an edited volume on Edwin Bissel Holt.

Joshua W. Clegg is a professor of psychology at John Jay College of Criminal Justice, CUNY. He earned his B.S. and M.S. degrees in psychology from Brigham Young University, where he was trained as a phenomenologist and theoretician, and his Ph.D. in psychology from Clark University, where he was trained as a social psychologist. His published work focuses on empirical research in social alienation and on theoretical work concerning research methodology and philosophy of science.

Alex Kozulin is research director of the International Center for the Enhancement of Learning Potential in Jerusalem. His recent books include: Kinard, J. and Kozulin, A., *Rigorous Mathematical Thinking: Conceptual*

Formation in the Mathematics Classroom (2008) and Kozulin, A., Gindis, B., Ageyev, V. and Miller, S. (eds.), *Vygotsky's Educational Theory in Cultural Context* (2003).

Jeffrey S. Reber is associate professor of psychology and associate dean of the College of Arts and Sciences at University of West Georgia. His Ph.D. is in general psychology with a dual emphasis in theoretical/philosophical psychology and applied social psychology. His scholarly publications emphasize critical thinking about psychology, the relationship between religion and psychology, and the meaning and possibility of altruism. His current program of research focuses on a social psychology that treats human relationships as fundamental.

Lee Rudolph is professor of mathematics at Clark University, where he is also an affiliate of the Social, Evolutionary, and Cultural Program of the Department of Psychology. His most recent book, *A Woman and a Man, Ice-Fishing* (2006) won the 2004 X. J. Kennedy Poetry Prize; its title poem first appeared in *The New Yorker*. He is a low-dimensional topologist who has recently been working on applications of topology to robotics as well as to social and cultural psychology.

Aaro Toomela is a professor of neuropsychology at the Tallinn University, Estonia. His current research interests concern, among other issues, research methodology, philosophy of science, school effectiveness, semiotically mediated processes, and prediction of recidivism.

Jaan Valsiner is a cultural psychologist with a consistently developmental axiomatic base that is brought to analyses of any psychological or social phenomena. He is the founding editor (1995) of the journal *Culture & Psychology*. He is currently professor of psychology at the Department of Psychology, Clark University, USA. He has published many books, the most pertinent of which are *The Guided Mind* (1998) and *Culture in Minds and Societies* (2007). He has edited (with Kevin Connolly) the *Handbook of Developmental Psychology* (2003) as well as the *Cambridge Handbook of Socio-Cultural Psychology* (2007, with Alberto Rosa). He is the editor-in-chief of the journal *Integrative Psychological and Behavioral Sciences* (Springer, from 2007) and the editor (from 2008) of History and Theory of Psychology, a Transaction Publishers book series. In 1995 he was awarded the Alexander von Humboldt Prize in Germany for his interdisciplinary work on human development, and Senior Fulbright Lecturing Award in Brazil 1995-1997. He has been a visiting professor in Brazil, Japan, Australia, Estonia, Germany, Italy, United Kingdom, and The Netherlands.

René van der Veer is professor of the history of education at Leiden University, The Netherlands. Among his current research interests are the history of attachment theory and the history of Soviet developmental psychology and education. His latest books are *Lev Vygotsky* (2007) and *The Transformation of Learning* (with Van Oers, Wardekker, and Elbers, 2008).

Index